LEGENDS

The AFL Indigenous Team of the Century, original oil painting by Jamie Cooper
© 2005, JCAP Australia.

First published in 2011
by Aboriginal Studies Press

All photographs courtesy of The Slattery Media Group unless otherwise noted.

Each of the players featured on the cover appear in the book, with their story. Their playing positions can be seen on p. 12.

Aboriginal Studies Press
is the publishing arm of the
Australian Institute of Aboriginal
and Torres Strait Islander Studies
GPO Box 553, Canberra, ACT 2601
Phone: (61 2) 6246 1183
Fax: (61 2) 6261 4288
Email: asp@aiatsis.gov.au
Web: www.aiatsis.gov.au/asp/about.html

National Library of Australia Cataloguing-In-Publication data:

Author: Gorman, Sean, 1969-

Title: Legends : the AFL Indigenous Team of the Century 1905– 2005 / Sean Gorman.

ISBN: 9780855757786 (pbk.)

Notes: Includes index.

Subjects: AFL Indigenous Team of the Century.Athletes, Aboriginal Australian—Australia—History. Australian football players—History. Australian football—History.
Dewey Number: 796.336

Printed in Australia by BlueStar Print Group

LEGENDS

The AFL Indigenous
Team of the Century

Sean Gorman

Aboriginal
Studies
Press

The AFL Indigenous Australian Team of the Century presentation lunch at the Crown Casino Palladium, 1 August 2005 in Melbourne, Australia. Back (L-R): Bill Dempsey, Michael O'Loughlin, Byron Pickett, Michael Graham, Chris Lewis, Jim Krakouer, Stephen Michael, Michael McLean, Peter Matera, Peter Burgoyne, Syd Jackson, Ted Kilmurray, Chris Johnson, Darryl White, Nicky Winmar and Glenn James. Front (L-R): Gavin Wanganeen, Maurice Rioli, Margaret Jackson (Qantas), Graham (Polly) Farmer, John Howard, Michael Long, Ron Evans, Barry Cable, Adam Goodes and Andrew McLeod.

CONTENTS

For my 'run with men'
Clay & Tom.

'I don't think we need to be treated differently but I think we need an awareness [of] where we've come from.'

Nathan Lovett-Murray, 2009

ACKNOWLEDGMENTS

This book has come about through the help and assistance of many people. While this is in no real order, I must start with the staff at the Australian Football League Players Association. To Cory McGrath especially, your efforts have been sensational. To Steve Alessio and Nadia Taib, your efforts in helping have been great. Much thanks.

To Tony Birch, Dean Lusher, Keir Reeves, Ciannon Cazaly, Barry Judd, Ron Joseph, Pippa Grange, Martin Flanagan, Daryl Adair, Che Cockatoo-Collins, Steve Hawke, John Harms, Paul Toohey, Patrick Dodson, Mick Dodson, Peter Docker, Jane Cunningham, Dave Whish-Wilson, Sara Wills, Antoinette Dillon, Andrea McNamara, Aiden Kelly, Niall Lucy, John Sincock, Les Everett, Phil Egan, John Lysikatos, Darren Moncrieff, Quentin Beresford, Tony Shaw (Wongutha), Sibby Rioli, Bob Speechley, Karina Gray, Mike Dolbey, Marie Michael, Paul Daffey, Damien Hale, Emma Riley, the crew at Mercers Cycles and Brian Ciccotosto, thanks for your help and advice when asked. Thanks also to Shaun Burgoyne, Chris Johnson, Michael O'Loughlin and Adam Goodes for your help.

To my Mum, Annette, who transcribed all the interviews, a big thanks.

To the Research Office at the University of Melbourne, thanks for supplying me with the money to undertake the research.

To Rhonda Black and the Aboriginal Studies Press staff at AIATSIS, thank you for seeing the merit in the project and working with me.

To my colleagues at the Centre for Aboriginal Studies, Curtin University, thanks.

To my family: Clay, Tom and Mon, your love and patience enables me to do what I do.

Finally, to the players who are in the Indigenous Team of the Century, thank you for allowing me to speak with you about the thing that has given us so much pleasure. You are Legends!

AUTHOR'S NOTE

This book began its life as an oral-history archive. Its purpose was to provide some insight into the lives of the men who have become well known throughout Australia for their association with the code of Australian Football. My motivation for writing this book was a simple one: it provided a great opportunity to document the lives of Indigenous men who have played elite football in Australia over time. My other motivation came from my observation that many non-Indigenous Australians have very little interaction with Indigenous Australians. One of the few areas where both come together to celebrate and participate as a community is through Australian football. This can be seen at just about any ground around the country, whether at the elite level or in urban, rural or remote areas. My aim then is to get people to ask a simple question: If we have a common love of football and we can create positive experiences through it, why can't this flow through to other areas? If Indigenous and non-Indigenous team-mates can work together playing football, why can't these types of relationships filter into other sectors in Australian society?

This book is not designed to be a definitive historical document, and it is not designed to be the 'last word' on the issues it discusses. It draws on a range of sources to tell each player's individual journey. This mainly consists of interviews I conducted with the players, while other sources have come from books, magazines and media reports. Statistical information for the book was gleaned from several sources. Primarily this was undertaken from the latest edition of *The Encyclopedia of AFL Footballers* by Russell Holmesby and Jim Main, the AFL's website, club websites, the AFLPA, various internet sources and previous correspondence from Col Hutchison. Where information was not available or contradictory this has been removed.

I have used all possible means to ensure that the information provided is correct and factual. I have also endeavoured to make sure that all of the players I interviewed for this project were satisfied with the final draft. In a few cases

I was not able to do this despite exhausting all available avenues. For the players who have passed away, I have written a brief piece about their playing life from the public record. I have also used several different descriptors for Indigenous Australians. The term 'blackfella' has been used as the generic term Indigenous Australians use to describe themselves and I have endeavoured to ensure that the correct skin/language names have been used in all cases.

Please be advised that this book contains images and photographs of Indigenous people who have passed away.

Introduction

Sport has been our greatest ally — Michael Long[1]

In early 2005, seven men and a voice came together in a room. They were there to discuss the selection of the Australian Football League's (AFL) Indigenous Team of the Century. The team would be announced in August of that year. In the room was media personality Ernie Dingo, former umpire Glenn James, Essendon coach Kevin Sheedy, AFL National Talent Manager Kevin Sheehan, senior journalists Mike Sheahan and Michelangelo Rucci and AFL statistician Col Hutchison. The voice belonged to lifelong footy fan and Yawuru statesman Pat Dodson. Dodson could not be there because he was in Western Australia filming *Liyarn Ngarn,* a documentary with the late English actor Pete Postlethwaite and Gunditjmara musician Archie Roach which was released in 2007. The documentary was about the 1992 murder in Perth of Indigenous man Louis St John Johnson, who was killed on his nineteenth birthday. He had been set upon by four non-Indigenous youths who bashed him, ran him over in their vehicle and left him for dead. Johnson was found several hours later by paramedics. They assumed he had been drinking and sniffing petrol. The paramedics took Johnson home and he died there some time later from massive internal bleeding after being advised to 'sleep it off'.

As the selectors pored over the list of players, the feeling in the room and down the line was a positive one. After several hours, the meeting wound up and the men in AFL House went their separate ways. They bid farewell to Dodson who had to get back to filming. In Western Australia, Dodson emerged from where he had conducted the teleconference to join Roach, Postlethwaite and the others involved in the filming, for a cup of tea. Everyone in the room was interested in the selection of the AFL's Indigenous Team of the Century. 'How did it go Pat?' someone asked. 'It went well,' said Dodson. 'But you know who I really think should play in the centre? Terra Nullius,' Dodson boomed. 'Why?' someone asked nervously. 'Because every time he gets the ball he just disappears. One minute he is here and the next he is gone!' There was a brief pause and then the room burst into laughter.

In 1992, I began a journey. Having finished a stint in the country where I had been working on farms and in shearing teams I re-entered high school as a mature age student on advice from a friend. I was 23. Doing my Year 12 again was a good way to get used to the rigours of study and at the end of it I needed to make a choice. I had to tick a box as to which university course I wanted to do. After twelve months I still had no real idea. At Murdoch University in 1993, for the first time, a degree was offered in Aboriginal and Torres Strait Islander Studies. I ticked the box and in that moment my first step was taken. I have been asked many times why I chose the degree I did. I still don't know why I ticked the box, but I can honestly say that through that simple action, and having worked with Indigenous Australians since then, my life has been enriched beyond any measure.

It seems like the blink of an eye, but eighteen years later I am still working and studying in the same field I began in. More importantly, I am still learning. The learning process has not been easy as many of the issues left me numb because of how profoundly disturbing they are. My initial shock and anger on learning about the issues that confront Indigenous Australians remains today. How could it not? I am still dismayed that the life expectancy of Indigenous Australians remains the worst of any developed country. I am still deeply saddened by the treatment of Indigenous peoples across all sectors in Australian society, and I am angered that many non-Indigenous Australians have very strong opinions about Indigenous Australians despite barely having ever spoken to a 'blackfella', or having read a single book on the issue.

The counter-balance to this is that I have always been a strong follower of the Indigenous game, Australian Football. The reasons for my love of 'the game' are many and varied but at the heart of it is something quite simple: it speaks to me. What I have come to appreciate is that many non-Indigenous Australians' only positive engagement with Indigenous peoples is by watching football on TV or being at the game. Blackfellas make up nearly twelve per cent of the playing stocks in the elite AFL, while the Indigenous population in Australia is only two per cent. Surely this says something about 'our game' and how it speaks to blackfellas. Surely it offers a key to bridging the gulf between 'us' and 'them'. I have seen with my own eyes how football clubs can help engage and heal communities. I have witnessed the redemptive power of football for both black and white Australians. It is through this social process that people come together and communicate, and that can create rapport. Rapport builds trust. Trust builds hope.

For me, football stories provide us with a starting point for other conversations. I consider this incredibly important because the role that sport has played in Australian history shows us something about Indigenous struggle in Australia. I firmly believe it is through stories about Indigenous Australians that people can begin to reconsider other areas where Indigenous people have enriched and contributed to Australian society.

A 'light-bulb' moment came when I was interviewing renowned AFL and Essendon champion, Michael Long, for this project. His quote, which appears at the top of this chapter, 'Sport has been our greatest ally' drove home to me that without sport perhaps Indigenous peoples' welfare and wellbeing might be worse than it is currently. For me, this is a powerful statement. It is powerful because Long himself had to stand firm amongst great public and media criticism in 1995. In this way, football enabled him to navigate complex issues and explain why he made the stance he did at the time. Football gave him the chance, and the voice, to speak out against prejudice.

In many respects, the Indigenous struggle on the football field is one that many Aboriginal and Torres Strait Islander Australians experience every day. The struggle could be epitomised by the indelible image of Nicky Winmar's defiant reply to a hostile Collingwood crowd in 1993. This, combined with Long's stance, has enabled Australia to look at racism at many levels, as a nation. But there have also been less notable struggles. For example, in the 1930s, Pastor Doug (later Sir Douglas) Nicholls was essentially turned away from Carlton as the trainers refused to touch him, presumably thinking he was dirty and not up to Victorian Football League (VFL) standards. Jim Krakouer was suspended for a total of twenty-five games, over a season's worth, due to retaliating to the racialised verbal and physical attention shown to him and his younger brother Phil in the 1980s. During their playing careers, West Coast Eagles players Chris Lewis and team-mates Phil Narkle and Troy Ugle received anonymous death threats and hate mail. The vitriol was so disturbing that the West Coast Eagles sought counselling support to help these players cope.

In many respects the struggle has come down to what the colour of a person's skin has represented. The history of Indigenous and non-Indigenous relations has a long and difficult past, and we are still grappling with it today. Academic Colin Tatz believes this is a matter of history and our perceptions of it:

Pastor Doug Nicholls was essentially turned away from Carlton as the trainers refused to touch him presumably thinking he was dirty and not up to VFL standards.

Sir Pastor Doug Nicholls. Courtesy Colin and Paul Tatz.

> The phrase from 'plantation to playing field' expresses the history of Black American sport...Aboriginal history has been the reverse. They went from relative freedom, albeit in an era of genocide, to the isolated and segregated settlements and missions which were created to save them.[2]

At AFL matches across the country today, large electronic screens broadcast a pledge to all patrons that racial vilification at the ground will not be tolerated and, if it occurs, will result in a substantial fine and ejection from the arena. However, it does not seem all that long ago that Indigenous players were able to be abused for the colour of their skin. Since 1990, when the VFL transitioned in to the AFL, the game has had many challenges, but racial vilification presented itself differently compared to the myriad financial and administrative issues that the new, expanded national competition faced. It seems that vilification was seen as an intrinsic part of the game and was used in the psychological struggle with opponents. The AFL's Rule 30, the racial and religious anti-vilification law, states:

No person subject to these Rules shall act towards or speak to any other person in a manner, or engage in any other conduct which threatens, disparages, vilifies or insults another on the basis of that person's race, religion, colour, descent or national or ethnic origin.[3]

For many people at the time, the ethos was 'what was said on the field stayed on the field.' It was a rationalisation to get an edge over an opponent, and if Aboriginal players could not take it they were 'weak'. Today this notion is preposterous, as racist behaviour has no place in sport or the broader society.

To try to get some measure of it, we could try to imagine what the sporting landscape would be in Australia if Indigenous Australians did not play Australian football. For example, Indigenous participation in international cricket is virtually non-existent. Jason Gillespie, a Kamilaroi man from New South Wales, is the only test cricketer to have played for Australia who identifies as Indigenous.

Because of Indigenous Australians' love of Australian football, Indigenous participation in football has become a highly celebrated aspect of the Australian game. It is because of players like Nicky Winmar, Barry Cable, Michael Long, Chris Lewis, Byron Pickett, Polly Farmer, the Krakouer brothers and many others, that football is a space where both the positive and negative historical issues of race relations in Australia one be investigated. In this way football ceases to be just a game but becomes a teacher, and through its lessons we may become, as Australians, a better team.

SPORT, HISTORY AND POLITICS

For many Indigenous Australians, sport, history and politics have become intertwined because of issues concerning wider societal struggles and the oppression they have experienced. Over time, many Indigenous athletes had to adapt to politics and policies in order to survive, as financial and social self-determination were not accessible. Academics like Anna Haebich and Colin Tatz have shown that in the late 1800s and early to mid-1900s, rations, curfews and reserve life created massive everyday hardship and poverty. As Tatz sees it, those who displayed ability in sport were able to supplement their seasonal incomes and rations with semi-professional foot races or boxing matches. This allowed them to become more socially mobile and gain a begrudging acceptance and status in the broader community.

This rich historical vein of sport, race and history, is not adequately appreciated by many non-Indigenous Australians, which is surprising given the status

5

in which they hold sport. This is in contrast to the USA, where many Americans are well aware of African-Americans (like baseballer Jackie Robinson) and their valuable social and historical input to the desegregation of baseball, boxing, basketball and American football, and the rise to prominence of African-Americans in these sports.

In this way, sport enables us to see the many overlapping themes of sport, politics, race and history. Tatz, for example, looks at key incidents, such as Cathy Freeman cloaking herself in the Aboriginal flag at the 1994 Commonwealth Games. This created a furore in the Australian media, as many commentators claimed that Freeman should have refrained because Aboriginal Australia is not recognised as a sovereign nation. As Tatz responded, 'Those who deplored her "un-Australian" behaviour have no understanding of Aboriginal history.'[4] What Tatz meant is that media commentators equally failed to acknowledge that no Indigenous Australian has ever formally signed an agreement that they have 'given up' their land to anyone. Put another way, the Mabo decision in 1992 proves in law that Indigenous peoples and societies were established in Australia prior to 1788, and so the notion of *terra nullius* is a fraud. Remember the Dodson joke?

This is a concept many non-Indigenous Australians do not or cannot acknowledge, and indifference becomes their way of handling that reality. Carlton premiership champion, Syd Jackson, sees things this way:

> I know a lot of my Aboriginal brothers and sisters became isolated, lonely and discriminated against because they had no attachment and lived lonely lives. I think the challenge we face is trying to get to the top level of work and acceptance because general society don't want to see them [Indigenous Australians].[5]

Discrimination has not just come from opponents requiring an 'edge', but from the sporting institutions themselves. As noted earlier, Doug Nicholls, Fitzroy Football Club's champion, and later Governor of South Australia, was not made to feel welcome at Carlton in the 1930s because it was thought he was dirty. In other words, he was dirty because it was an accepted 'truth' amongst non-Indigenous Australians that Aboriginal people chose to live in squalid conditions.

This is not to say that all Indigenous experiences of life and sport across Australia have been a homogenous struggle and one adversely affected by dysfunction and beset with disease. There are many stories that point to communities that are strong and healthy. The local heroes within those communities are not the ones who ended up playing in the 'big time', but those who chose to work among their family and their mob by making their communities stronger and facilitating opportunities for others.

To me, the strength of this project has been to hear what the players themselves think; how they reflect on their lives, their families, their communities, and their success. There are commonalities between the lives of many of the players, though by no means is there just one story. Most of the men chosen in the Indigenous Team of the Century come from financially impoverished places in regional or remote areas, meaning their move to the city was one away from community and support. For all, sport was the only game in town, and for the majority it was Australian Rules, whether played on a dusty playing field, bitumen road or a sports ground. Strong family connections link the men's stories; not all had happy childhoods, but most come from happy, stable families; families where boys were encouraged to play football, where their uncles and families provided the role models; in some, where mothers took the boys to footy practice. While they were encouraged to attend school, many struggled there.

A theme emerges of strong encouragement from family to take up the opportunities afforded them, to plan for their futures, and to contribute to the game and support other young men coming through the system. Above all, the men's respect for their football and their cultural forebears shines through; they are thrilled to have been chosen as part of the Indigenous Team of the Century (aware of the many others who were able, but who were not chosen), and to be able to stand on the dais with their footy heroes.

FOOTBALL AND HISTORY

For many years it was believed that the first Indigenous player was Joe Johnson, a 55-game defender who played in Fitzroy's 1904–05 premiership team in the VFL. However, this assumption has proven to be incorrect as Albert 'Pompey' Austin played for Geelong in 1872, debuting against Carlton after arriving from Framlingham mission.[6] In many ways it is not just Austin or Johnson who can be seen as the Indigenous pioneers of the game. Since the 1930s, the game has only seen a few Indigenous players in the VFL in each era: Doug Nicholls (Fitzroy: 1932–37), Norm McDonald (Essendon: 1947–53), Polly Farmer (Geelong: 1962–67) and Syd Jackson (Carlton: 1969–1976). In a sense, then, these players were all pioneers; each creating a space so that others might follow. Today there are cohorts of Indigenous players on all the AFL lists and these are increasing every year.

It was not until the early 1980s that the VFL/AFL saw an influx of Indigenous players, with the arrival of the Krakouers at North Melbourne and Maurice Rioli at Richmond in 1982. This added to the playing stocks of Phil Egan (Richmond), Robbie Muir (St Kilda) and Kevin Taylor (South Melbourne). More significantly, it was not until the advent of the West Coast Eagles in 1987 with the likes of Phil Narkle, Wally Matera and Chris Lewis that the 'racial' complexion of the AFL really started to change. With this came the stereotypical media reportage about 'Black Magic' and the explaining away of Indigenous players' skills as 'natural', without proper recognition of the hours of training and application that they had put in. This attention brought with it more hostility from supporters and culminated in the famous round four fixture between St Kilda and Collingwood in 1993, when Nicky Winmar raised his jumper, thereby revealing his black skin to a hostile Collingwood football crowd. At the time Winmar could not have conceived what the outcome of his action would be. Collingwood President Allan McAlister said at the time that Winmar and team-mate Gilbert McAdam would be respected 'as long as they conducted themselves like white people on and off the field'. In the broader community it sparked a debate about racism in football and society. The reason Winmar's stance has transcended sport, and the fact people talk about it still, is the power of its message: 'You cannot ignore me anymore'.

In 1995 Michael Long was in an incident when Collingwood ruckman Damian Monkhorst, who was being tackled by Long, implored that 'someone should get this black c**t off me'. Long refused to let the media spotlight on the incident drop, and he pursued the AFL on its lack of racism protocols. This led eventually to the introduction of the AFL's racial and religious anti-vilification laws: namely, Rule 30. Now, because of Michael Long, all those who play the game are protected from racial and religious abuse, and players undergo diversity education and cultural-awareness programs as part of being a professional sportsperson. Coincidently, Indigenous participation in the AFL in 2011 for both rookie and senior lists is approaching twelve per cent.

Rule 30 can be seen as a very important initiative, not only for Aboriginal players but also for players from multicultural backgrounds, for example, the Irish and African players, and Muslim footballers like Bhachar Houli who was at Essendon but now plays at Richmond. Without Rule 30, what might Houli's position have been given the anti-Islamic sentiments after the terrorist attacks of 9/11? It has taken these, and other moments of racism in the AFL, for us to reconsider the way we think about race and ethnicity, and the way racism relates to sport and society more broadly. But this can only be done if we view not just the game, but also the space on which it is played, differently. With increased sponsorships and professionalism, the MCG ceased to be simply an oval where sport is played; with the introduction of Rule 30, it became a workplace. In this way vilification is now seen differently as we view it through a different prism.

One of the biggest challenges for the AFL will be how they deal with the projected influx of Indigenous players into the game, especially those coming from remote areas like Austin Wonemaerri (Tiwi Islands), Liam Jurrah (Yuendumu) and Zephaniah Skinner (Noonkanbah). In the next five to ten years it is expected that Indigenous players will make up between 20 to 25 per cent of all player lists. There will be many positive outcomes from this if that happens. However, people like Koori elder and Shepparton's President of Rumbalara, Paul Briggs, feels that the AFL needs to do more. Speaking in the *Age* in November 2007, Briggs said: 'I still don't think the system is strong enough to handle [certain] cases. There needs to be a far more professional approach and strong case management of what these boys need. Once they take their footy jumper off and put their street clothes on it's just too hard for them.'

Many would say that the solution for Indigenous footballers to succeed beyond the playing field is simple: stay off alcohol and drugs, get an education and work hard. But our society also needs to ensure that when young Indigenous footballers fall by the wayside we don't just point to the colour of their skin and suggest it was because of their Aboriginality that the failure occurred. For us to understand Indigenous footballers we need to understand where they have come from, not just geographically, but socially, historically, economically, politically and culturally. To fail to acknowledge these primary aspects is to fundamentally miss the point of Indigenous peoples' experiences in Australian history. Perhaps we also need to ask ourselves another simple question: Why are there no Indigenous commentators, coaches, administrators, team managers, umpires or journalists working in mainstream AFL circles? Where are they?

CONCLUSION

The steps the AFL has taken to stamp out racism in football and raise awareness about Indigenous and multicultural issues should be commended by all members of the community. The results of the introduction of Rule 30 should be celebrated, while acknowledging that something needed to change. Since 1995 there have been a range of other positive outcomes, for example, programs and recognition of Indigenous participation in the AFL and the broader community. Indigenous culture and sporting achievement is recognised in games like

Dreamtime at the 'G the showcase game for the AFL's Indigenous round between Essendon and Richmond at the Melbourne Cricket Ground. The Marn Grook Trophy recognises the traditional Djabwurrung game and is also played out between Essendon and Sydney during the AFL home-and-away fixture.

The AFL also has the Sportsready program, which helps to identify and develop job skills and pathways for Indigenous footballers during and after their careers. The KickStart program is directed towards Indigenous youth between the ages of five and fifteen, promoting healthy lifestyles, school attendance, leadership and physical activity. This has led to the Indigenous Youth Series in South Africa and in 2006, the Flying Boomerangs, which identified AFL players like Nathan Krakouer (Port Adelaide and Gold Coast), Brad Dick (Collingwood), Joe Anderson (Carlton), Malcolm Lynch (Western Bulldogs) and Isaac Weetra (Melbourne). Others who were identified in recent years were Chris Yarran (Carlton) and Michael Walters (Fremantle). Then there is Rio Tinto's Footy Means Business program which helps identify and develop work opportunities for fifty young Indigenous men from all over Australia. In addition, the Department of Education, Employment and Workplace Relations' (DEEWR) Learn, Earn, Legend program, works with both Australian Rules and Rugby League organisations to promote educational and training outcomes; including funding the annual round nine Dreamtime at the 'G match, as well as the NRL Indigenous Allstars.

In the broader community, Western Australia's Clontarf Foundation, the brainchild of former AFL coach Gerard Neesham, is an institution which combines football and education to take 'at risk' Indigenous youth and turn their lives around. Similarly, Rumbalara in Shepparton has participated in both the Goulburn Valley and Murray football leagues since 1997, and has fostered many education and social initiatives to engender greater involvement between the local Koori and town communities.

On a personal level, working in this field for nearly twenty years has enabled me to sit down and talk with some of Australian football's most famous Indigenous players. What I have come to understand is that we should all be grateful that football is part of our lives as it enables us to see how far we have come as a community. Football, and our appreciation of it, can and does assist in developing a greater awareness about the contributions every player makes to the game. In some small way, we can watch television or go to a football game on any weekend during winter and come to a greater appreciation of what football means to us all. This can lead to greater engagements and appreciations at other levels, and the spirit of coexistence can take root. In a post-Apology Australia, and in a country that loves its sport, this seems a fitting path to take.

The Imalu Tigers pose for a photo during the Dreamtime at the 'G curtain raiser match between the Imalu Tigers v Brambuk Eels at the Melbourne Cricket Ground.

THE TEAM

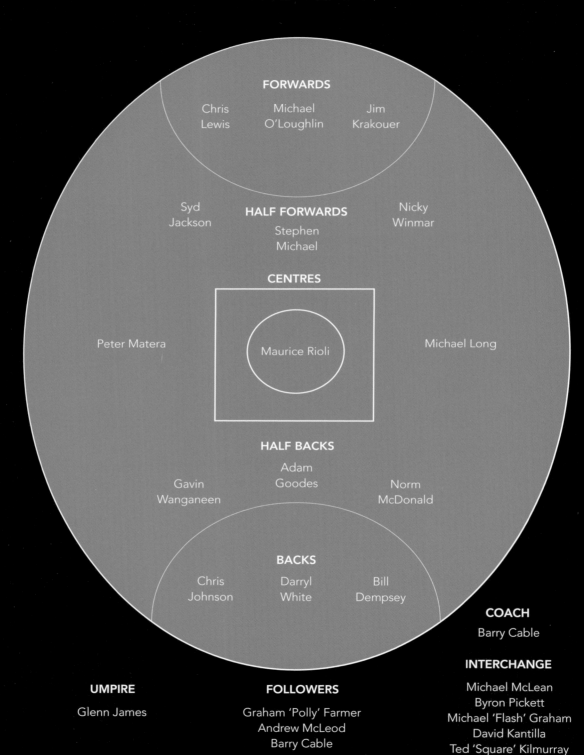

FORWARDS

Chris Lewis   Michael O'Loughlin   Jim Krakouer

Syd Jackson

HALF FORWARDS

Stephen Michael

Nicky Winmar

CENTRES

Peter Matera

Maurice Rioli

Michael Long

HALF BACKS

Adam Goodes

Gavin Wanganeen

Norm McDonald

BACKS

Chris Johnson   Darryl White   Bill Dempsey

COACH

Barry Cable

INTERCHANGE

Michael McLean
Byron Pickett
Michael 'Flash' Graham
David Kantilla
Ted 'Square' Kilmurray
Peter Burgoyne

UMPIRE

Glenn James

FOLLOWERS

Graham 'Polly' Farmer
Andrew McLeod
Barry Cable

THE PLAYERS

Image courtesy Colin and Paul Tatz.

GRAHAM 'POLLY' FARMER

RECORD

1953–1971

Games: 356: East Perth 176; Geelong 101; West Perth 79

Goals: Total goals not available: Geelong 65; West Perth 55

State: Western Australia 31, Victoria 5

Premierships: East Perth 1956, 1958, 1959; Geelong 1963; West Perth 1969, 1971

Sandover medal: 1956, 1958, 1959

Simpson medal: 1956, 1959, 1969

Tassie medal: 1956

Captain: Geelong 1965, 1967

Club Best and Fairest: East Perth 1954, 1955, 1956, 1957, 1959, 1960, 1961; Geelong 1963, 1964; West Perth 1969

All-Australian: 1956, 1958, 1961

Geelong Team of the Century (starting ruck)

AFL Team of the Century (starting ruck)

AFL Hall of Fame Legend

‘Every time I went out onto the football field I set my mind to be the best on the ground and win the game. And so that is how I prepared myself. I knew how to prepare myself so that the difference between good days and bad days was infrequent.’

Graham 'Polly' Farmer

On the day of the AFL's Indigenous Team of the Century ceremony in August 2005, Polly Farmer met with his old friend Ted Kilmurray. They had arrived at the same time at the Crown Casino foyer. Both men had flown over with their wives, as they were to be inducted into the very prestigious club. Farmer had not been feeling the best in the lead-up to the ceremony. He had contemplated not coming over for the event, but decided against it. There were just too many people he wanted to catch up with and the late Bob Davis, his old mate and the man credited with recruiting him to the Geelong Football Club, had suggested it would be good for him to make an appearance. As the Farmers and Kilmurrays made their way into the casino they noticed Davis on the other side of the stairs. As the men, known to one another as 'Polly' and 'Square', made their way over to Davis many of the people who walked past them would have no idea just how far these men had come, as virtual brothers, from Sister Kate's Children's Home in Perth.

After perfunctory greetings, Davis pointed to the direction they need to go. They made their way upstairs and walked along the plush corridors. In front of them was a foyer where many well-dressed people were enjoying a drink before the function. Davis, who was leading the group, stopped at another doorway and suggested to the group they go in. They stepped into a formal reception room which, unlike the foyer, was virtually empty. One of the people in the room was Ron Evans, the AFL's Chairman. Evans engaged the group and they spoke casually for a few minutes. It began to dawn on the Farmers and Kilmurrays that they were in the wrong room and they actually should have been out on the foyer. Before they had time to make their way out two large, fit men dressed in suits entered the room, obscuring a smaller bald man who was following. It was the Prime Minister of Australia, John Howard. Howard walked straight up to Farmer and shook his hand warmly and the two spoke for some time. Farmer then went around his group and introduced them all to Australia's Prime Minister.

The journey that had led Farmer and Kilmurray to this point had come from two things: football and the men's ability to play it. Now in their early seventies, their individual stories had for various reasons seen them removed from their families and placed at Sister Kate's. In the context of sport and history this was going to be a big day to celebrate the amazing lives of the men who had brought so much to the game. On this day it would be Polly Farmer who would lead the charge, just as he had led the ruck divisions and the hopes of thousands of fans throughout his playing career, creating a legacy that is still talked about today.

Readers who open Steve Hawke's book, *Polly Farmer: A Biography*, will see a photograph of a young Polly taken when he was at Greenbushes during the Second World War. What is apparent is that Polly Farmer does not look overtly Indigenous, with his Anglo features and blond hair. Born in Fremantle in 1935 in the height of the Depression, it would be precisely how Polly Farmer looked that would determine his life's trajectory. Being of a mixed Indigenous descent, with his mother lacking the means to support him, young Polly grew up in the care of Sister Kate's Children's Home. He recalls:

> Sister Kate, she was an Anglican nun and she came out here and she started a home in Parkeville which was a home for young orphans from England. She did such a good job that she felt she wanted to do something for the people of Western Australia and she saw that the young part-Aboriginal [people] didn't belong either with the Aboriginal race or with the European. They were left on their own a little bit and she felt that she would like to help a little bit [for them] to become part of the way of life that was taking place in Australia.[7]

Despite how these institutions are seen today, and not knowing the specific nature of his placement, Farmer is very grateful for the time he spent at Sister Kate's:[8]

> I came to be at Sister Kate's because I was born without a father and my mother couldn't look after me so she put me into the home. I was well educated, taught right and wrong and given a Christian

upbringing. It was good for me because I was really just a baby when I went there so I did not know any different. I knew my mother because she used to come out to the home and saw us. But I didn't really know much about my mother.[9]

During the war years, the children at Sister Kate's headed south to Greenbushes, near Bridgetown, because the original home at Queens Park was close to a munitions factory and the risk to the children was deemed too great by the authorities. Returning to Queens Park after the war, there was a supportive environment which was quite progressive for the time. This was probably because of the staff (young single women), the accommodation (cottages) and the lack of overzealousness when it came to religious instruction and work which allowed Sister Kate's to feel like home.[10]

The children at Sister Kate's had to do chores but were not overburdened with heavy workloads like those experienced at the Moore River Native Settlement and made famous by the film *Rabbit-Proof Fence*.[11] This left a great deal of time to play games. For Farmer this meant cricket in the summer and football in the winter. It was football that captured the imagination of young Farmer and he was passionate about it:

> Football was in the neighbourhood. Football was played in the local competition, which at that stage was Kenwick. I was probably thirteen or fourteen. Then later I got an apprenticeship as a motor mechanic and I used to travel into the city for my job and then back so I could play with Kenwick. Then I went to Maddington.[12]

This is not to say it was all plain sailing for Farmer as he, like many of his Sister Kate's family, faced the very real chance that when they reached the age of sixteen they would be sent into the country to work on farms for several years, severing any chance to make the most of any opportunities in the city. The Native Welfare Department had been sending young Indigenous men and women to work as labourers and domestics for years. As Farmer points out, 'The only thing I did not want to be was farming.'[13] With his apprenticeship at Winterbottom's car dealership in 1951, he was one of the few young Indigenous men to be employed in this type of work rather than working on the land. Playing in the South Suburban League in Perth was the platform that would springboard Farmer into the big leagues:

I had a year training with Perth first but because Square [Kilmurray] had already gone to East Perth and there was a chap who was interested in us, George Sweetapple, who was one of their Presidents, I thought 'I'd like to go to East Perth.' It may have been a coincidence that George Sweetapple was Vice-President of the club but someone must have told him about the South Suburban League and there were some good footballers out there and he used to come and watch us play.[14]

Despite his seemingly amiable nature, Farmer was very serious about his football and he was also intensely loyal to Kilmurray. In 1953, Farmer made his league debut with East Perth, following Kilmurray, who had begun the year earlier. Mick Cronin was the coach and he helped develop the young players. Cronin could obviously see potential in Farmer who, despite his light frame, could read the play amazingly well and who had an expert skill that he would become known for, his handball:

I was the understudy for Ray Perry [no. 1 ruck at East Perth]. I was very skinny but the only advantage I had is that I handballed a fair bit. I did it for my own benefit because I had the ability to get hold of the ball. I could not duck and dive but I could get it and handball and I learned to take advantage of it.[15]

In 1954, when Ray Perry retired from the game, the name 'Farmer' started to become synonymous with quality football and he won his first league Best and Fairest with East Perth at the age of nineteen, a feat that he would emulate seven times more with the Royals. State games followed and in 1956 Jack Sheedy was lured down to East Perth from East Fremantle. This would have a great influence on Farmer as Sheedy led by example and instilled into his charges a degree of grit Farmer had never known:

Jack asserted authority on the field with his personal displays...Not only was Jack assertive in his playing ability but also with his physical presence. He used to frighten other players from other sides.[16]

This type of presence instilled a degree of confidence in the players and in 1956 Farmer played as the starting ruck for Western Australia in the Australian Football Championships, and then went on to win a Sandover medal. This further developed Farmer's belief in himself; something he needed if he was to move on to the next level, and beyond. His determination to be the best developed to such an extent that Farmer felt he could not be beaten by anyone:

> Every time I went out onto the football field I set my mind to be the best on the ground and win the game. And so that is how I prepared myself. I knew how to prepare myself so that the difference between good days and bad days was infrequent.[17]

This kind of attitude saw Polly Farmer become one of the country's elite footballers. By 1960, he had won three Sandover medals and three Simpson medals, a Tassie medal, state and All-Australian selection and, as East Perth's leading ruck, he experienced three Western Australian Football League (WAFL) premierships and a host of club awards. During his career he also experienced racial vilification but he is at pains to say that this did not really bother him greatly:

> I never took any notice of it. I think anything that was said out on the field was to put people off, but it didn't break my concentration and when I was called names I'd look at myself and say to myself well I can't see it. It never worried me. I still was called 'You boong, you nigger.' That was understandable because you do anything to try and put people off their game. I didn't go out of my way to chase people and thump them because they called me a boong.[18]

His achievements and standing in the WAFL began to draw the attention of recruiting scouts from the VFL, in the form of Richmond, St Kilda and Geelong. Despite his achievements, Farmer's choice of club and his motivations were modest as he simply did not want to go to the VFL and play with a powerhouse side:

> I wanted to get with a club that had struggled and were looking to achieve some sort of success, and I wanted really to be part of the success story...I had a lot of confidence in my own ability. All the clubs that I've been to were struggling when I went to join them...I suppose it was just pride, wanting to be part of a battling side that had a chance and offering them something.[19]

In the end Farmer signed the clearance form to go to Geelong as he felt the country lifestyle was an added bonus to playing football. As he points out, 'If it came down to be just a business transaction I'm sure we should have gone to St Kilda, because package-wise it was overall substantially greater'.[20]

In 1962, at the age of 27, Polly Farmer's VFL career began. As with many inter-state recruits, the media hype surrounding Farmer was the biggest that the VFL had seen to that point.[21] This saw unprecedented numbers of spectators turn out at games to see just what all the fuss was about. It did not take too long to see that the big reputation and the big investment were warranted. In the first of the practice matches, Farmer gave a great account of himself in the deft physical art of ruck-play. This, when combined with his deadly handball, made him a very potent player. As Geelong had a very good roving combination in Billy Goggin and Colin Rice, the Cats were set for a stellar season and the buzz around town and in the media was immense. Unlike many recruits who had been lured to the VFL, Farmer's status had serious substance; he was an experienced campaigner of nearly a decade at the senior football level. Farmer would need to call on all of that experience in the very first game of the 1962 season as the Cats were set to take on Carlton at Princes Park. This saw Polly pit his skills against Carlton champions Graham Donaldson and John Nicholls.

As luck would have it, Farmer injured the anterior cruciate ligament on his left knee in the opening moments of the game. Despite being in a great deal of pain, he played on for the entire game, which saw Geelong come from behind to win decisively. After the game he sought advice and treatment and made the decision to keep playing. After four games he took time off over several weeks and came through the reserves, but in a return game against North Melbourne he fell awkwardly and had to undergo surgery. With his 1962 season over, he set about strengthening his leg with a punishing weights and cycling regime, ready for the 1963 season. In his time away he had time to contemplate his football career and the reality that he may never play again. When the 1963 season began, the physical pressure was compounded, with heavy grounds and wet weather:

> The hardest part was getting used to the conditions, the cold and rain, the grounds [also] because they were built on a muddy soil. So when it rained it became very squelchy and muddy. The players [in the VFL] had to learn to be more courageous than here [WA]. Here you could duck and hope not to be caught, but over there you had to take your chances on getting the ball and getting run over if you couldn't move the ball on. I had to make my adjustments when I got there [Victoria]. I had to learn that if I planted my feet on the ground they stayed there and I held my body up. I had to learn to balance better.[22]

Farmer returned as best he could for the 1963 season. He had modified his style, got stronger and had experienced VFL football. But the question remained as to whether his leg would stand up to the strain. Many felt that Farmer's absence in the Geelong finals campaign had cost them the 1962 premiership. In 1963, Geelong memberships had risen from only a few seasons before, in the expectation of something bigger. In the first five games, Geelong's form was solid. Farmer performed so well that he was chosen to represent Victoria against South Australia and 1963 would be remembered as the year that Geelong got serious, making the finals. This was borne out with solid wins against Essendon, a side they had not beaten in several seasons, and a very physical game, resulting in a victory against a tough Hawthorn at home at Glenferrie. Farmer was pivotal in the wins as he brought those players around him into the play.

The grand final of 1963 was played in the first week of October because of washed-out games in the middle of the season, pushing the VFL season back by a week. On a very warm Saturday, a massive crowd of 101,452 witnessed a classic game between two traditional rivals. As he had displayed all season, Farmer's ruck-work and handball would be vital to Geelong securing victory, which they did by 49 points. According to many, Farmer was the best player afield and it reflected his stellar season.

Despite Farmer not winning another premiership with Geelong after this, he did go on to captain the club in 1965–67. As the club let go players that were not required, Farmer felt that some of the old camaraderie and mateship had started to dwindle. Petty club jealousies saw key figures like Bob Davis and Leo O'Brien leave. Becoming frustrated at the way that he and those close to him were being treated, Farmer returned to Perth. As Farmer explains:

> It was a question of rebuilding and I was in that stage where the team wasn't good enough and the people on the committee did not have vision to say, 'Well we've got to rebuild this team by getting and turn- ing players over.' Geelong were a battling side and my chances of being successful there were nil because there was no plan for success by rebuilding the team.[23]

When word spread that Farmer was looking to return west there was discussion in some Perth clubs about securing his services, though some clubs' board members felt that his asking fee was too high given his well-publicised injuries and his age. Eventually Farmer wound up at West Perth where he became a playing coach for the 1968 season. Despite his age, Farmer was still very agile and fit but, in order to give West Perth a physical advantage, the Cardinals' gym was upgraded and beach running was introduced into the pre-season campaigns. Farmer's fundamental rules of playing team football and keeping the ball moving at all costs were drummed into the players.

West Perth managed to reach the preliminary final in 1968, where they lost to Farmer's old club, East Perth. In the following year, West Perth played off against arch-rival East Perth in the WAFL grand final, a game they would win by 73 points. In 1971, another WAFL premiership would be added to the tally with a replay against East Perth. This was Farmer's last senior game of football and it brought the curtain down on one of the truly amazing football careers in Australia.

Reflecting on his life achievements, Polly Farmer can be satisfied that his contribution to the game has been immense. He reshaped the way the game was played and was in many ways he was a man before his time. He has been awarded many football plaudits and also received an MBE in 1971, the first Australian Rules footballer to do so. In 1996, the Western Australian Transport Minister announced that a bypass through Perth city would be called the Graham Farmer Freeway in his honour. Even though he has achieved much there has also been a level of sacrifice to get the best out of himself as a footballer and a person:

> Apart from my commitment to my family, footy was the only thing I was interested in. So in my desire to succeed I did all the things I had to, to do that. I was involved in it because of the love of wanting to play. What I found with most people who are successful in life, with studying and going to university, the first thing they give up is their sport. But we did not have that opportunity because that is all we had, so it became our number one priority, where as for others it was just part of the passing parade.[24]

Polly Farmer has proven to be the epitome of a champion but he is also acutely aware of the historical issues that have impacted upon Indigenous Australians:

> One of the great problems with all ways of life is you have a pecking order and the pecking in Australia has always seen that the Aboriginal race has been at the absolute bottom. Every one else who comes to Australia is above the Aboriginal.[25]

It is with these thoughts that Graham Farmer's achievements can be seen in a particular context. That context is typically Australian; an Australian story of struggle and adversity and how, with absolute dedication, commitment and an opportunity, that adversity can be overcome. With limited chances and absolute belief in his talent and skill as a footballer Farmer was able to do what many could not.

RECORD

1953–1965

Games: 257
Goals: 431
State: Western Australia 3
Premierships: East Perth 1956, 1958, 1959
Sandover medal: 1958
Club Best and Fairest: East Perth 1958

'Football opened a lot of doors for me. When I got the [Sandover] medal it opened a lot more. You'd go some place and you'd mention your name and then they'd start talking footy, it makes it a lot easier. '

Ted 'Square' Kilmurray

In late November 1960, Ted Kilmurray pulled his rig into a Golden Fleece roadhouse on the outskirts of Kalgoorlie. It was 6 pm and he needed to fuel up both his truck and himself as he readied for the drive to Perth. In another seven hours he would be in Perth and back home. It had been a big week on the road delivering supply orders to all sorts of government agencies and departments throughout the state. It was hard work but he loved the road and meeting people.

Having filled the truck with diesel he went to the toilet, washed his hands and face, combed his hair and stepped into the dining room of the roadhouse. He was the only one there. He sat down, looked at the menu and decided on steak and vegies. He had heard from one of his truck-driving mates that that one of the hotels in town did a steak sandwich that you would pay a week's wage for. Kilmurray entertained the idea for a moment but then decided against it, knowing that venturing into a hotel could sometimes bring unwanted attention, even hostility. Hotels in the 1960s were not places for Aboriginal people; there were rules against it. Besides, Kilmurray had a good job and the last thing he needed was a meeting with his manager to explain why his eye was bruised and his lip was split.

The waitress walked over to Kilmurray's table, 'Can I take your order please?' Kilmurray popped his head over the menu and started to speak, 'I reckon I will....' The waitress gasped, 'Oh no...No. It can't be! You're Ted Kilmurray. You're the 1958 Sandover medallist!' The waitress squealed and rushed back into the kitchen. She reappeared quickly with an older man in tow, dressed in a white shirt buttoned up to his neck and a black apron. He was wiping his hands excitedly with a tea-towel. 'See Dad, it's him...it's him!' The man smiled and extended his hand, 'Mr Kilmurray, this is indeed an honour, sir. I have been an East Perth man all my life and can I say that you and Polly Farmer are the best players the Royals have had for years, hands down.' The man looked at his daughter holding a small pad and biro and snatched them out of her hands. 'Please…can I have your autograph?' Kilmurray obliged. Looking at the autograph the cook smiled, 'And tonight…Mr Kilmurray, dinner is on the house.' 'Steak and vegies then,' said Kilmurray. Within minutes Kilmurray's dinner arrived, he ate, had a cup of tea, paid his fuel bill and bid the cook and his daughter good night. As he drove through the night on his way home, Kilmurray smiled the smile of man who was well satisfied that his standing as a footballer had served him well. It had given him a job and enabled him to meet people he would not normally meet, and they would always treat him with respect.

Despite meeting many people during his life, Kilmurray knew that without football it could have been very different. From the outset his life was determined by his Aboriginality. Kilmurray explains:

> I was born at Wiluna [Western Australia]. Our family was born at Wiluna. My mother was working on a station out there called Wonga Wol which is probably 100 miles [160 km] out from Wiluna. I'm the second youngest in a family of five. My older sisters remember where we came from. I don't remember much about it because I was a baby about six months old. I can't remember being brought down to Sister Kate's at Queens Park. All of my family ended up at Moore River and then after two months we went to Sister Kate's in about 1935.[26]

For Kilmurray, Sister Kate's, in what was at the time Perth's outer eastern suburb of Queens Park, was a great experience:

> It was fabulous, fabulous. It was the best thing that ever happened to us really. I just think that we were so lucky to be taken down there to have somewhere to live and learn something you know. When you see how some of the people are now. I can remember going through what they called the nursery. They had about eight or nine houses and you started off at the nursery, as you got older you went up to another place. I actually never left the nursery because the woman in charge there sort of didn't want me to go to another house.[27]

The woman Kilmurray is speaking about is May Holt, known to the children at Sister Kate's as Nanny:

> May Holt. She was the one. I stayed at her place. I never left it. I was the little golden-haired boy. It was just like one big family.[28]

Kilmurray's recollections of his childhood at Sister Kate's are all positive:

> You'd get a few that'd say it wasn't good, but it was the best thing that happened to me. We used to call Sister Kate 'Granny'. They never called her Sister Kate, it was always Granny. Granny got my mother down [from Moore River] and it meant the whole family was down there. I hadn't started school but she was the cook there [Sister Kate's] and she was cooking meals for like forty or fifty kids. It was a full-time job. We used to have to help peel the spuds, or wash the turnips and clean up after. We had the church which all the kids liked going to. They never used to push it [religion] on you, most of the kids wanted to go.[29]

Fortunately, Kilmurray's experiences in institutions like Sister Kate's went well. Like his good friend and fellow 'home-kid,' Polly Farmer, it seems that the time spent there was productive, as the children were properly cared for and shown real affection and love. This was helped by the fact that many of the children were encouraged to play sport, despite the fact that they experienced significant disruptions when the Second World War was underway:

> The reason why we were shifted to Greenbushes was when the war was on Sister Kate's home was not far from a munitions factory. Nanny Holt and another lady called Nurse Thomas took all us kids down to Greenbushes and we were there for seven years. We were lucky that all the kids wanted to play sport. At Greenbushes we had so much freedom and the school benefited because when sports days were on, the school used to dominate. One fella was a senior southwest champion. Polly was a champion and when they would have a big sports meeting he was equally as good as the bigger boys, and the teachers and the headmasters all encouraged it because it was such a good thing. We used to compete against each other to see who could be the best left-foot kick or right-foot kick or anything else to do with football. There was a lot of other kids that could have easily made league [football] because they showed potential when they were

kids. It wasn't only football it was cricket also. We had some good cricketers amongst us too.[30]

In 1947, they moved back to Perth from Greenbushes and there were several changes in Kilmurray's life. The main one was that Kilmurray would not return to the happy and familiar surrounds of Sister Kate's in Queens Park. The second was that as he was entering his teenage years there was a greater expectation that Indigenous children would begin the process of transitioning from school into the workforce. Both of these issues would manifest themselves in 1948, some 10 km away in the semi-rural suburb of Kenwick and Sister Kate's Memorial Farm (SKMF). Sister Kate died in 1946, and a property on the banks of the Canning River was purchased by the Aborigines Department. The intention of the SKMF was to train boys to work in agriculture. At the time, it was expected that young Indigenous men and women would go on to become farm labourers for the men, and domestic servants for the women, rather than have the potential of white-collar careers.

The constants in Kilmurray's life at this time were his Sister Kate's family and his football. As the farm was located in Kenwick, Kenwick Football Club was the obvious route for football for Kilmurray and Farmer and it was here that they started to make a name for themselves in the community. Kilmurray explains:

> We more or less put Kenwick on the map for sport, because we had kids like Polly and we had a good side. I'd say there was about ten of our kids that made up the side. It was good because we were playing against men so we learnt to look after ourselves. We were only a B-grade side Kenwick but we were a good B-grade side and the local people [who] were not connected to the home used to look after us. We used to travel with them to go to the football. Then Kenwick wanted to go to A-grade, but Maddington which is the next town [suburb] down wouldn't let us; they wanted all of us kids to play for Maddington. We didn't want to break up our side so we went there. So we'd play on the Saturday in the amateurs [for Kenwick] and on Sunday we'd go and play for Maddington in the A-Grade and we won two premierships with Maddington between 1950 and 1953.[31]

By 1952, Kilmurray started to feel the tension between the institutional expectation that he move to the country for work and what he wanted to do with his life. His preference was to stay in Perth, maintain his lifestyle and keep playing football. As the competing forces in Kilmurray's life began to ramp up, things started to play out in a very public way in the Perth media. As Kilmurray was only seventeen he was still under the legal guardianship of Ruth Lefroy who had taken over as principal of the SKMF. Lefroy, from an established and well-known farming family, felt it was the boy's duty to go into the rural hinterland to help out on the land. Kilmurray faced the very real prospect of being sent to Bencubbin, some 280 km from Perth, effectively stalling any football ambitions until he turned twenty-one. The *Sunday Times* asked their readers to write in and express how they felt about the issue. The following week the resounding sentiment within the Perth community was to allow Kilmurray to stay and pursue a job and football career in the metropolitan area.[32] Kilmurray reflects on the time:

> I was lucky I suppose. The boys from Kenwick went out and worked on farms in the country. Polly and I were lucky enough to be able to stick around [in Perth]. They wanted to send me up into the bush [but] somebody got onto the story and they took it to the *Sunday Times* and there was an article: 'Why should this boy go?' I was young and I suppose for a month there were write-ups in the *Sunday Times* about 'the boy being sent to the bush and he didn't want to go.' I didn't want to go. I couldn't see much future in going to the bush so in the end I was able to stay and that's when I came under notice from East Perth.[33]

The man who took a shine to the football ability of Kilmurray was George Sweetapple, the Vice-President of East Perth Football Club, and a businessman who could see the real potential that Kilmurray could bring to the Royals. While both Farmer and Kilmurray were playing great football for Maddington, in Kilmurray the Royals could see an exceptionally skilful and ready-made player, whereas Farmer was still quite gangly and easily knocked off-balance. In the first five games of the 1952 season for Maddington, Kilmurray was playing at full-forward and gathering kicks at will, averaging seven goals a game. Making the grand final that year against Cannington, Maddington ran out as premiers and Kilmurray was set to springboard into a league role for East Perth.

In the 1953 pre-season, Kilmurray impressed the East Perth selectors, in particular coach Mick Cronin. Cronin was known as a very fair player on the field and a gentleman off it. As a club, East Perth were known as a team of battlers with their last premiership being years earlier, in 1936. Kilmurray loved East Perth and likened it to a home away from home:

They were great because everyone was a volunteer, no one got paid. [The] President didn't get paid, nor did the secretary or the managers; it was all a love job. Poll and I and another 'home-kid' called Jack Hunt who also played with East Perth, we got a flat out at Scarborough and people at the East Perth footy club didn't think we used to eat well enough. So they used to invite us home for roasts on Thursday night. We never went short, we lived well.[34]

This sense of community seemed to translate into good football for Kilmurray and he quickly became a popular team man. But it was the transformation of East Perth from a side of battlers to finals contenders that was the measure of success with the Club:

It was like a big family at East Perth. But East Perth was changing from an older side to a team of young ones. We had Johnnie Watts, Malcolm Brown, Syd Jackson, Malcolm Atwell; they were all state footballers and they were just coming on.[35]

Kilmurray became known as an inventive player and an expert exponent of the flick pass, a style of handball using the open hand rather than the clenched fist; something designed to get rid of the ball quickly in congested play. The only issue for many, especially umpires, was that if done incorrectly it looked too much like a throw and the player was penalised:

I instigated the flick pass but it got out of hand, not from me but other people who were doing it wrong. I did it for about three years and then I just didn't because other blokes were doing and it looked like a throw.[36]

Eventually the flick pass was outlawed from the game altogether, but the other style of football that Kilmurray could lay some claim to, one that has remained, is the 'snap', a deceptive skill that requires timing, balance and an ability to read the play. As a full-forward Kilmurray would meet the ball at speed as it came into the East Perth forward line. If the ball hit a pack of players and fell loose he would gather it. Alternatively, if he marked it at full pace he would keep running away from the goal and snap the ball back over his right shoulder with his left boot. This often resulted in a goal. It was a way of keeping the ball moving at a time when football was not played in this fashion.

From the mid-1950s to the early 1960s, East Perth established itself as a powerhouse team. From 1956 to 1961, East Perth would play in six straight grand finals, winning half of them, 1956, 1958 and 1959. In 1955, despite some irregular form, Kilmurray, along with Farmer, was picked to play his first state game against Victoria at the MCG. The memories are bitter-sweet still:

> It's a trip I wanted to forget because I went over as full-forward for WA and I played on a bloke called Herb Henderson who was Victoria's top full-back. He was from Footscray and I never touched the ball that day. But Herb Henderson came to the hotel we were staying at the next morning, he picked me up and showed me all over Melbourne and then we went home for a roast tea at night and then he brought me back to the pub.[37]

Perhaps Kilmurray's biggest personal year was 1958 where East Perth won the premiership by beating East Fremantle in a two-point nail-biter. Kilmurray then went on to win a Sandover medal by five votes from East Fremantle's Alan Preen. He reflects:

> I still think my best year was '60 when I was runner up to Poll for the medal. I won in 1960 the *Daily News* award which in those days was pretty good. It was for a hundred pounds [two hundred dollars].[38]

During his time as a player Kilmurray is the first to admit he did not react much to racial taunting:

> I can't say that I copped it any more than anybody else, but I never took much notice of it. I can recall an incident against West Perth and I'd just about had enough of being called names. So in the middle of the ground I stopped and I just said, 'Alright, I've had enough! Do you want to make anything of it?' Polly used to get it and Syd Jackson used to cop it also.[39]

Like many footballers of the time, perhaps the bigger concern for Kilmurray was whether to head to Melbourne or stay in Western Australia. Kilmurray chose to be happy with his lot, without chasing any personal glory or acclaim:

> I was asked a couple of times to go over east but I wasn't interested. I won a Sandover medal and that was the highest award you could get here [WA]. I think I would have got more recognition if I probably had gone over [to Victoria] but I wasn't interested in going over really. I was happy here and I was starting to make a bit of money.[40]

Square Kilmurray's recollections of his football life and the opportunities it has afforded him are something he truly appreciates. His ability to play football and be part of successful junior sides with many of his Sister Kate's brothers, especially Farmer, has given him a sense of personal achievement. This has translated into other areas of his family life and work. Perhaps his biggest realisation is the role football played in enabling those opportunities to become real:

> Football opened a lot of doors for me. When I got the [Sandover] medal it opened a lot more. You'd go some place and you'd mention your name and then they'd start talking footy, it makes it a lot easier. I still think though that the biggest thing is education. We were lucky at Sister Kate's as right from the time we went to kindergarten we then went [on] to state school. Then we went to high school. I wasn't a bright student but I got through. When I go to schools to talk I emphasise that education is going to go further than sporting ability because not all are going to make a top sports person.[41]

BILL DEMSPEY

RECORD

1960–1976

Games: 343
Goals: Total goals not available
State: Western Australia 14
Premierships: West Perth 1969, 1971, 1975; Buffaloes 3, years not known
Simpson medal: 1969
Captain: West Perth 1973, 1974, 1975, 1976
Club Best and Fairest: West Perth 1966
West Perth Team of the Century (back pocket)
MBE 1976

'When I first came to Perth I started off working as a removalist and I didn't like it. In Darwin I went to year ten and when I got here [Perth] I knew I had to further my education, so I went to night school…That's one of the reasons I went to night school, to stop me thinking about Darwin. '

Bill Dempsey

On 17 June 1967, Victoria was set to take on Western Australia in a state match at the Melbourne Cricket Ground (MCG). It was the middle of winter, the air had a distinct chill and it had been raining. As the parochial Melbourne crowd of 44,133 opened their flasks of tea and munched on homemade sausage rolls and sandwiches, many would be unaware that they were about to see history in the making. In years to come, the names of Long, Davey, McLeod, Stokes, Jurrah and Rioli would all be big Top End names that would grace football's biggest stage. On this miserable day, however, Bill Dempsey would be the first Indigenous player from the Top End to walk onto the hallowed turf and stake a claim for Territory football. As the Western Australian players ran out onto the ground they felt the nip on their bare shoulders and legs. Dempsey sucked in the chilly air. 'So this is the MCG,' he said to himself.

The Victorians were on the opposite flank, warming up. Dempsey peered over and could make out some familiar figures, the main one being Polly Farmer, adorned in the Big V. This did not sit right with Dempsey. As he made his way over to the centre circle, where he was named as the starting ruck-rover for WA along with ruckman Keith Slater and rover Billy Walker, he wanted to unsettle the great Polly Farmer. As Farmer ambled over to the centre circle Demspey stared. 'Bit rich you being in the Big V, hey Poll?' Dempsey dead-panned. Farmer looked over to the wiry Dempsey and said slowly, 'Bill...just get on with the game.' The siren sounded, umpire O'Connell bounced the ball and the crowd erupted, blissfully unaware that 1967 was the start of a legacy that would not be fully realised for many years to come.

For many followers of the Australian code of football at the time, Bill Dempsey would be something of an unknown. Coming from Darwin as a young seventeen-year-old, Dempsey would establish himself as one of the most versatile footballers to have played the game, especially in Western Australia. His style seemed to verge on the casual, and Dempsey played in a similar way to the modern-day Brisbane champion, and fellow Indigenous Team of the Century inductee, Darryl White. Dempsey's rangy build, loose gait and easy carriage belied a player who could seemingly do anything on a football field and one who would later be judged one of the finest post-war ruckmen in the land.

Born in 1942, Bill Dempsey's early childhood life began in the Retta Dixon Home for Children in Darwin, following his father's death after illness:

> I went to the mission when I was three nearly going four due to circumstances prevailing at the time and the government policy. The reason why I went there was because me father died of meningitis. He went to the War as a soldier and fought in New Guinea. And when he came back he contracted meningitis. I had a little sister then too and they both died within a couple of months of each other and the authorities then deemed that I should be placed in an institution which was in Darwin. If the authorities hadn't grabbed me I probably would have grown up in Alice Springs.[42]

Despite having been removed at such a young age Dempsey is very aware of his identity and his family history:

> My father is an Alice Springs man and on my mother's side they come from Arnhem Land. So Dad is Arrernte and Mum is from the Ngalakan people. So I've got a combination. My grandfather was an Irishman, hence the name Dempsey. He lived in Alice Spring for a long, long time and he tried to marry a full-blood woman but the authorities and the police wouldn't let him. They had three kids anyway, one of them was my Dad, William.[43]

It was at the mission that Dempsey became involved with other children who were in a similar situation. Institutional life was not easy but he found that through sport he could partially alleviate any negative feelings or sense of isolation:

> [Growing] up in a mission, there were about 200 kids and they were all sporty. We played rugby and basketball but football was our love.

I loved basketball. We just played all sports [but] we never played cricket. For some unknown reason when I grew up cricket in the territory was a whiteman's game. We played everything else but never cricket. We played a game called rounders, it's like baseball, you've got the three bases and we used to play with a broomstick and a tennis ball.[44]

Through the education he received at the mission, Dempsey became very aware what his prospects were in life, and the direction he was being pushed into, given his identity:

Some government people came to the mission once. I was always a bit of a stickybeak and I heard the government officials saying to the missionaries that the kids needed to look good. You feed them and clothe them and send them to school but don't encourage them to go on after grade seven because they're only going to grow up to be stockman and working on the road and the girls are going to be doing work for other people. So don't waste your time encouraging them to be educated.[45]

As Dempsey grew older and his sporting ability developed, it became apparent that owing to his family connections with the Buffaloes Football Club in Darwin, he would have little choice in playing for any other team:

Most of the boys in the mission that I grew up with were pretty lucky because there was a local side called the Buffaloes. The Buffaloes were put together by the local Aboriginal people because other teams wouldn't give them a game so they formed their own team. One of the captains at the time was my uncle. His name was Steve Abala, captain of Buffaloes. When I was eight-years-old he just said to my mother, 'This lad's a Buffalo boy Dorothy. I don't care what you say.' So that's how I came to play for Buffaloes.[46]

The Buffaloes were a strong part of Dempsey's upbringing in the Top End, enabling him to be with his family, and to develop into a young man and a strong footballer:

I was born to play for Buffaloes. You know that was my destiny and I accepted it. All I wanted to do as a kid [was] play for Buffaloes. The Buffaloes looked after us kids, they used to pick us up and take us [to games]. The Buffaloes were supported by the Labor Party, so there was that combination, the Labor Party, Buffaloes and us kids from the mission. It was terrific. We had a big group of Buffalo people who played and officiated and they influenced us and looked after us and became mentors. We looked up to them and we were proud of the Double Blues.[47]

Dempsey's best friend throughout his childhood years was Jimmy Anderson. They had grown up at the mission and spent many hours together playing football. According to Dempsey, Anderson was considered the best young recruit in Darwin and in 1959 he was offered a chance to head to Perth to try out with the West Perth Cardinals. As Dempsey recalls it, he was also asked to go down to Perth with Anderson, to act as a steadying influence for his friend:

How I got recruited was there was a man that came from West Perth. He captained them and coached them and he was in the Native Affairs Department. His name was Jack Larcombe. He got transferred to Darwin and he coached a team up there called Wanderers and he was looking for players to go to West Perth, while coaching. There was a guy that I played with in the mission, Jimmy Anderson, he was two years older than me. He was like the king of the home. He was the boss. He and I played in the ruck for the Buffaloes. Jack Larcombe wrote to West Perth and said, 'There's a young Aboriginal boy up here his name is Jimmy Anderson.' He was 19. They brought him to Perth and he only lasted three weeks. He went back to Darwin because it was cold and he was by himself. So they [West Perth] said to Larcombe, 'What should we do?' He said, 'Well you know he's got a mate and they [are] like brothers.' Larcombe suggested I should go with him and be his anchor. So we got here and the same thing happened after about three or four weeks, Jimmy says, 'Bugger this, I'm going.' I said, 'You can't do that.' Jimmy said, 'If you come back to Darwin I'll belt you.' City life didn't suit him. I stayed as I was starting to find my feet and I had some friends.[48]

In 1960, aged 17, Bill Dempsey was trying to adjust to life in Perth and the demands of league football at West Perth. In his own words he was 'petrified'. He had thought about heading back home to Darwin on many occasions but felt compelled to pursue his football dreams and future:

I'd never seen crowds like that. It was a eye-opener with the finals series and seeing that many people together and there was some damn good footballers out on the track it was awesome for me as a 17-year-old kid.[49]

Of his first coach at West Perth, Arthur Oliver, Dempsey has this to say:

I found him to be a thorough gentlemen and he encouraged me in lots of ways and I learnt a bit off him. I started to play regular in '61. They tried me all over the place, full-back, down the middle, as a forward. I actually came down as a centre half-forward but I only played three games there in all my career.[50]

Dempsey's second coach was Clive Lewington, and he was pivotal in helping the young recruit deal with the on-field transition he had to make:

Lewington was another thorough gentlemen. He earned a lot of respect from the players and you wanted to go out and win for him. They started to move me down to the back-line which I didn't like, but an old friend of mine, [Froggy Snape] in Darwin said, 'Be versatile and play where they put you.'[51]

When Dempsey began playing football in Perth, there was only a handful of Indigenous players in the WAFL and racism on the field was rife. This posed several personal obstacles which he needed to negotiate:

[When] I went to West Perth I was the only Aboriginal player in the side. There was eight teams and fifty on each training list. That makes it about 400 players in all. Out of that 400 there were five Aboriginals playing footy. Polly Farmer, Ted Kilmurray, a bloke called Les Davies and me good old mate, Irwin Lewis and me. [Racism] it was very bad, but there was a bloke here Roy Porter who played for West Perth. He took me under his wing and he said to me, 'You're going to cop at lot of shit. You are going to have to take it but you get even when the opportunity comes and when you whack them you make sure they stay whacked, but don't hit them straight away.' Playing in 343 games I was never reported, never once. So that's how I got over racism.[52]

While working hard to establish himself as regular league player for the Cardinals, in his private life too Dempsey worked hard. He realised that in order to make the most of his situation he would need to go back to school as a means to improve his education, but it was also a strategy to deal with his loneliness:

When I first came to Perth I started off working as a removalist and I didn't like it. In Darwin I went to Year 10 and when I got here [Perth] I knew I had to further my education, so I went to night school. I used to work during the day, go to training and then go to night school; for five years I did that. I studied English, maths and accountancy because I always wanted to be an accountant. So after a while I went into the building industry and one thing led to another. Moving to Perth I missed Buffaloes. I missed Darwin itself because it was such a laid-back happy-go-lucky way of living. That's one of the reasons I went to night school, to stop me thinking about Darwin.[53]

By the mid-1960s, playing as a ruck-cum-back pocket, Dempsey had established himself as one of the best players in the WAFL. This translated into regular league and state selections as well as media awards. Dempsey won virtually every media award available which allowed him to pass on the benefits of his football skills to his family. In 1966, he won a new car and decided to drive home to Darwin to play in the off-season with his beloved Buffaloes:

I never had a new car in me life. So I decided to head up to Darwin and show off a bit. I was only there two days and me Mum kept it and I never saw it again. I flew back.[54]

Around this time a number of VFL clubs were poised to get his signature: Footscray, South Melbourne and Richmond all wanted Dempsey to play for them, but he declined all three. For Dempsey, family always came first:

All I wanted was a contract to say it's 'x' amount of dollars because I needed to support my family. I said, 'If you give me something like that good, because my family can't eat glory, I need money.' If I broke my leg and got hurt or whatever I still had to have an income. So they said, 'No, you're not that good, who do you think you are — Polly Farmer?' I said, 'No, I'm younger and better looking.' West Perth knew that these Victorian sides were chasing me and they put it to me that if I wanted to start up a scaffold company they'd support me, so I got what I wanted.[55]

West Perth were a good solid team but they found it difficult to move up to the next level and achieve strong finals success and premiership glory. In 1968, this was set to change as West Perth lured Polly Farmer to be captain–coach of the Cardinals. This was a massive coup; Farmer was a legend as well as someone who bought with him a standard of professionalism not seen at WAFL level before. Dempsey saw that the chance to play alongside Farmer would herald one of the most formidable rucking combinations in the country:

> They were exciting times. Polly bought a new concept into the way we played football and the way we trained. He was a great leader and had great knowledge of the game, he was fearless and he expected to win every game. We all toughened up under him and were training five nights a week and then played on Saturday. A lot of the players were in awe of him because of who he was. We had our thing worked out and it was good playing alongside him. He was a great planner and expected the best out of the players.[56]

It took two seasons but eventually West Perth made the grand final against their cross-town nemesis, East Perth, who had beaten them in three previous encounters in the 1969 season. This was a great personal achievement for Dempsey as his mother, Dorothy, flew down from Darwin, her first time in a plane. It was also the first time she had seen Dempsey play:

> It was the best grand final I played in. There was a big contingent from Darwin, about 200 people came down. In Darwin my Mum never used to watch me play footy because I didn't play for the team her brothers played for, Wanderers; I played for Buffaloes. That is the first time she saw me play footy in that 1969 grand final. I could see me Mum behind the goalposts and after the game I waved to her and she waved back.[57]

At the end of a very physical game, West Perth had beaten the Royals by 11 goals and Dempsey had won the Simpson medal for best player afield. West Perth would go on to win another premiership in 1971 under Farmer, his last season, and Dempsey would also play a pivotal role. Dempsey would play another five seasons with mixed results. Despite Dempsey being the captain, playing solidly and polling well in the Sandover in 1974, West Perth finished last. In the following season, spurred on by the embarrassment of having finishing last, West Perth won another premiership.

In 1976, after playing seventeen seasons and accruing 343 games of senior football in Western Australia, Dempsey had played his last. He was awarded an MBE in the same year for his services to football and halfway through the home-and-away fixture, came to realise that his body simply could not go on:

I couldn't jump and that was the only thing keeping me going in the ruck. As a young fella I had leaps that could match it with the bigger fellas. But in the end I couldn't get off the ground so I thought it was time to let go.[58]

Today Bill Dempsey works for the Western Australian Department of Housing and Works. Here he assists Indigenous communities in the Kimberley region to identify building projects and enable programs that see local communities build, repair, upgrade and maintain houses in their communities:

My main job is to help them get funding to fix up their own houses. We put together a works plan. We buy all the materials with the funding money but the workers come from the community and not from outside. The whole idea is about self-determination and pride. It makes them part of the solution.[59]

Dempsey is not involved in football these days but he does reflect on what football has given him:

When I came to Perth in 1960, I was a ward of the state. I had to get permission from the Department of Aboriginal Affairs to leave Darwin to come to Western Australia and play. This pissed me off naturally. There's only three boys from the mission that went to high school. I was one of them. I thought I'm not going to be a bloody stockman, I'm not going to work on the roads and all that sort of business, I'm going to bloody try and do something for myself and my family, and that spurred me on. A lot of our mob weren't stayers, they were like Jimmy Anderson. It was very hard in those days. To solve any of these problems today you've got to be educated and if they don't you're behind the eight ball.[60]

SYD JACKSON

RECORD

1963–1976

Games: 240: East Perth 104; Carlton 136

Goals: 243: East Perth 78; Carlton 165

State: Western Australia 1

Premierships: Carlton 1970, 1972

Club Best and Fairest: East Perth 1966

Life membership: South Bunbury Football Club, East Perth Football Club, Carlton Football Club

South Bunbury Team of the Century (centre)

East Perth Team of the Century (centre)

Carlton Hall of Fame: 2006

'My first recollection of Aussie rules football and playing footy was all in the mission. There was no rules; it was just in the mission grounds and you just had to fight to get a kick and there was only one or two footballs anyway, with about fifteen kids trying to get a kick. So I guess that's the way we started. There was no realisation as to how important football was, but it was a situation of three or four of us learning to have a kick and we were able to play against other schools. For us to get out of the mission and play different sports was important. '

Syd Jackson

For me if it wasn't for my football, I know my life as part of Australia's Stolen Generation could have been starkly different...I worked for what I got and there was a lot that I lost in terms of my family, culture, my language and important things like that. I had a lot of help from people who supported me and I worked hard to reward them by not failing.[61]

In 1968, Syd Jackson was set to go on the trip of a lifetime. He had been recruited by Carlton but was not able to play because of a clearance wrangle from his WAFL club, East Perth. Instead, he was hoping to show his skill on an international stage with a football trip later known as the Touring Galahs. It was organised by Ron Barassi and Harry Beitzel to showcase Australian Football and was set to take in Ireland, England and North America. Not only was it a chance for the VFL's elite to display the Australian code of football to the world but an end-of-season trip of epic proportions. There was only one thing Jackson needed, a passport.

Jackson went down to a passport agency in Melbourne's CBD. Here he filled out several forms in triplicate with the only section remaining blank being his birth details. Jackson handed the forms back to the clerk who looked over the papers. 'Mr Jackson,' the clerk commented warily, 'you need to furnish us with documentation of your birth before we can issue you with a bona fide passport.' Jackson shrugged. He did not feel particularly concerned because he knew there was some flexibility with his birth date and year, despite the records 'officially' showing it as 1 July 1944. Why should now be any different Jackson thought. 'Just ring the Office of Births and Marriages in Perth,' Jackson said as his mind wandered to the impending adventure to the northern hemisphere.

The attendant went inside his office, made the call and emerged some minutes later with a pained look on his face. 'Mr Jackson it appears there is no record of your birth in the Perth office. They have checked the electoral role and the birth records and you are not on there. Technically, you don't exist.' The words of the clerk rang in Jackson's ears. Jackson himself enquired, to see if this was the case. A few weeks later a letter about Jackson's identity was supplied by Mr

Frank Gare, Western Australia's last Commissioner of Native Welfare. In it the letter it said, 'Records for the period 1940 to 1951 state that no reference to the birth of Sydney Jackson can be found.'

If anyone does not understand the impact of the removal of Indigenous children from their families resulting from the Stolen Generations they should take notice of Jackson's life. Taken away by a formal arrest warrant when he was three, he was separated from his family for twenty years and would meet his parents only twice before they died.[62] He was one of the lucky ones.

Jackson has absolutely no doubt that his mother, Jinna, and his father, Scottie, loved him, shown by his mother deliberately evading the police and the departmental gaze in their concerted attempts to track and capture 'half-caste' children like Jackson and his sisters. As both of his sisters had been removed and detained at the Moore River Native Settlement (made famous in the *Rabbit-Proof Fence* film), Jinna did everything in her power to ensure that Syd did not end up there, or in any other state-run institution. But the arm of the Native Affairs Department was long and powerful and eventually Jackson and Jinna were tracked down at Tarmoola station just near Leonora. Initially Syd was to be transferred 'under escort' to Sister Kate's but he ended up at Moore River Native Settlement with his sisters. After a short time, he was removed from his siblings and taken to Carrolup Native Boys School near Katanning, and then finally to Roelands Native Mission situated just between Collie and Bunbury in the southwest of Western Australia.[63]

It would be years later that the pieces to the puzzle could start to be put into place, as Jackson explains:

> For a long time I thought I was a Noongar because as a kid I was brought up in the southwest in a place called the Roelands Native Mission. Years later when I caught up with my sisters and other members of the family I learnt that I was born in Leonora which I learnt that I was part of the Wongi people out of Leonora and Kalgoorlie. My actual clan group is the Wongi people. I had very mixed feelings about that because you know you're living in Noongar country and you're bought up as a Noongar, then being told that you're from that area (the goldfields) it took some time to sink in over the years and to accept the fact that I'm from up there.[64]

But it was in the heart of Noongar country that Syd Jackson would come to learn some hard life lessons about what it meant to be an Aboriginal person in a white society. Despite the picture-postcard setting of Roelands Mission, the lifestyle of the inmates [Jackson's words] was geared around religious discipline and hard work. Long days started at 5 am and saw the children involved in all manner of chores designed to 'train' them for the rigours of farm life. Milking cows, herding sheep, mucking-out pig pens and feeding livestock while maintaining the orchards and vegetable gardens, as well as fencing, painting, cleaning and general maintenance. This was punctuated with school, where discipline was strictly enforced.

Jackson does not remember his life on the land fondly, 'In the missions we were used as slave labour to work the farms that kept the white mission owners in the lifestyle to which they were accustomed.'[65] It was in the realm of sport that Jackson could begin to seek some release from the grind of the everyday and experience life outside the institution:

> My first recollection of Aussie Rules football and playing footy was all in the mission. There was no rules; it was just in the mission grounds and you just had to fight to get a kick and there was only one or two footballs anyway, with about fifteen kids trying to get a kick. So I guess that's the way we started. There was no realisation as to how important football was, but it was a situation of three or four of us learning to have a kick and we were able to play against other schools. For us to get out of the mission and play different sports was important. I think we beat most schools at running, high jumping, long jump and all those types of things. The local mayor and the local football club, called South Bunbury, heard about us and recruited three or four of us from the mission, that's how we actually started in the juniors. We played reasonably well and we used to be picked up every Sunday to go and play in the juniors and that progressed into the senior ranks at South Bunbury footy club.[66]

It was here that the old football adage took root for Jackson that success comes when preparation meets opportunity. By the late 1950s, the Roelands kids began attending Bunbury High School. Football and cricket were prominent, and provided the chance to show the school community what the Roelands boys could do.

As conversations around town began to filter out about the Roelands kids and their football skills, Dr Ern Manea, a prominent Bunbury physician, the

Mayor of the town and President of the South Bunbury Football Club, liked what he heard. He asked about the boys from Roelands. As fate would have it, these enquiries would determine the pathway for Jackson. In his first year with the South Bunbury colts, Jackson experienced a premiership, a type of success that whetted his appetite for more. It also whetted Manea's. His involvement with Roelands increased and he was able to use his considerable influence to place the older Roelands boys into employment and apprenticeships, as well as use his links to South Bunbury to help them.

The Maneas organised a carpentry apprenticeship for Jackson and because of accommodation shortages in Bunbury, Jackson boarded with them at their house. This caused some resentment among Manea's friends and colleagues but he would have none of it. As far as Manea was concerned, Jackson was part of the family. This stable family life produced dividends for Jackson, which were reflected in his football, where he won the South West Football League's Best and Fairest award, and the Hayward medal, becoming the youngest player to do so. Jackson also came into contact with football royalty through Ron Barassi who was raising money for charity and stayed with the Maneas when he came to Bunbury, sharing a bedroom no less.

In the early 1960s, interest from metropolitan football clubs increased. Jackson explains:

> After winning the two Hayward medals, East Perth approached Dr Manea. East Perth came down to play a combined South West League side for a charity match. They [East Perth] saw me play but it took some time because there was support from South Bunbury footy club to look after me as they didn't want me to be exploited. They made sure that I was looked after. I really wanted to go to South Fremantle because they were the red and white colours of South Bunbury. There was a high-ranking official with South Bunbury that said we don't want any blackfellas playing there. So I said I'll go over there where Polly Farmer and Ted Kilmurray were playing. The conditions of the contract suited me better. I'm glad I went there.[67]

This is not to say it was easy for Jackson leaving Bunbury and heading to Perth:

> In my own head it was pretty difficult to leave because I had a lot of team-mates there. I was put on a bit of a pedestal there as far as I was the best player in the South West League at the time and you were under pressure to go and prove yourself up there [Perth].[68]

At the age of 19, in 1963, Jackson commenced his debut season for East Perth. It was a stellar effort by anyone's standards and despite receiving a two-week suspension and therefore ineligible, he tied in the polling for the WAFL's Best and Fairest, the Sandover medal. For five WAFL seasons Jackson played 'mercurial, often match-winning' football.[69] This saw Jackson make two grand finals with the Royals as well as being awarded a state guernsey in 1967. Like many before him, these successes allowed Jackson to build a significant profile and this attracted the recruitment scouts from the east.

WAFL recruitment laws saw Jackson's transition into the VFL stymied and he sat out the 1968 season. He became the Carlton runner for that year, giving him the chance to experience and acclimatise to the crowds and the excitement of the VFL. It was post-season that the Touring Galahs proposal arose, and the absence of a passport needed to be resolved. Jackson called Dr Manea and, as luck would have it, Prime Minister John Gorton was in Bunbury on official business. Manea approached PM Gorton, complaining that it was the year following the 1967 Referendum which had offered the promise of ameliorating Indigenous suffering and subjugation. Manea insisted that Jackson's predicament was an issue of basic human rights. So strong was Manea's argument to Prime Minister Gorton that he arranged a passport for Jackson the following day. Once in Melbourne, Jackson needed to acclimatise on many levels:

> I was out of sorts because it took me probably two years to fully settle here and the winters were winters then. I had to work and find a job in those days. You had to be seen as not being idle during the year. You had to work as part of the contract. It was difficult because the discipline of the football here is a step up again. As far as your training and your fitness and your punctuality, your whole appearance, you were under more scrutiny. The press was always around and the fact that I was touted to be one of the best that came out of Western Australia, I was under a lot of pressure to perform. Also there was heaps of it [racism] when I played. I was the only focus out there and I copped most of that, so you can imagine some of the things that were said you know. 'You black bastard.' 'Go back to the desert!' 'Midnight.' All those sorts of things actually fired me up, not in the sense I retaliated, but by playing a lot better and focusing, that's the way I dealt with it.[70]

Ironically, despite the hardships it was actually through playing football that Jackson was able to deal with alienation and discrimination. 'I got so comfortable playing football that I was more comfortable in the middle of the MCG than sitting in my lounge at home because I knew what I could do.'[71]

Jackson also used humour and his very different take on Australian history compared to his team-mates. In 1970, Barassi was trying to get more effort from Jackson's on-field performance. He plucked Captain Cook out of the ether and implored Jackson to employ more endeavour in his football just as Cook had. 'Endeavour, do you remember that Jackson?' Syd looked at Barassi and calmly replied, 'How can I forget that? That was the boat Cook came here on and he was the bloke who took all our land.'[72]

Despite having a semi-rocky relationship with Barassi and only commencing his VFL career in 1969, Jackson's status would be cemented with just one game, the 1970 grand final. This is the game that is seen by many as the one that changed the face of football. Played in front of a capacity MCG crowd in excess of 121,696 people, it is now considered a classic:

> While Barassi and I had a sometimes stormy relationship and he was
> quite willing to slam me in the media when he felt I wasn't playing well
> enough, his coaching on that day was inspirational. Seven goals down
> at half-time meant there was no point in his usual withering tirades.
> Instead he stayed positive and gave us a simple plan and a belief that if
> we stuck to it we could turn it around. He was right and it has got me
> many a free meal since then.[73]

Only now can Jackson can sit back and acknowledge his contribution to the game and the many hurdles he had to overcome. Jackson has never forgotten where he came from, nor has he forgotten what has been done to both him and his family. But he has also used his negative experiences to create something positive, by ensuring he did not disappoint those who had helped him along the way. This is a creed he still follows today and sees him heavily involved in many ways with the Indigenous community in Australia:

> I've got a mixture of things I do now. I'm doing a lot of government
> consultancy work with cross-cultural work and Native Title. I'm
> getting Indigenous people employed within Parks Victoria, DMC
> Department of Environment and Sustainability. I've been doing that
> for the last fifteen years. I also work with Sarina Rosso in engaging
> people in getting them job-ready. I do a lot of corporate work and
> help out with the Carlton footy club now and then with some of the
> Indigenous players. I set up the Indigenous Sports Foundation, the first

Indigenous football camp which the AFL Players' Association runs to bring all Indigenous players together and talk about football and life in Melbourne. I also do work for the organisation, Woolkubunning Kiaka Association, and this is very important to me.[74]

These roles and responsibilities are not something that he takes lightly and he still remembers many of his 'brothers and sisters' who have not made it. 'Today, people look at me walking around in my suit and doing my work and wouldn't get close to understanding the grief I carry around in my head every day.'[75] Jackson understands the importance of history and the way we need to remember what happened:

Displacement was the biggest situation which a lot of our people faced. The biggest challenge for them was the prospect of never reconnecting and never knowing where they came from or who their parents were. That leads to the challenge of them surviving. I know a lot of my Aboriginal brothers and sisters became isolated, lonely and discriminated against because they had no attachment and lived lonely lives. Discrimination leads to a lot of depression and they see that there's no life for them in this great country of theirs. I think the challenge we face is trying to get to the top level of work and acceptance because general society don't want to see them [Indigenous Australians]. I think the challenge is employment, education and trying to get into those areas that will get them through to some sort of normality.[76]

Syd Jackson's life is a great one at many levels, but it is football that has kept him alive and able to deal with adversity and alienation. Given the short life spans of so many of the children that went through the mission system, it says something about Jackson that has lived to tell the tale.

BARRY CABLE

RECORD

1964–1977

Games: 383: Perth 225; North Melbourne 115; East Perth 43

Goals: 505: Perth 324; North Melbourne 133; East Perth 46

State: Western Australia 22, Victoria 1

Premierships: Perth 1966, 1967, 1968; North Melbourne 1975, 1977; East Perth 1978

Sandover medal: 1964, 1968, 1973

Simpson medal: 1966, 1967, 1968, 1969, 1977

Tassie medal: 1966

Captain: Perth 1972–3

Coach: Perth 1972–3; North Melbourne 1981–4; East Perth Captain–Coach 1978; All-Australian 1979

Club Best and Fairest: Perth 1965, 1966, 1967, 1968, 1969; North Melbourne 1970 East Perth 1971, 1973

All-Australian: 1966, 1969

North Melbourne Team of the Century (starting rover)

AFL Hall of Fame Inductee

Australian Sports Hall of Fame

Western Australian Hall of Champions

MBE 1997

'I had a contract with the Perth Football Club that would allow me to go to Victoria for one year to see what it was like. So I selected 1970. I was turning 28 that year, and I went to North and it was all the things I thought it would be playing Victorian footy. I'd heard so much about it being a tighter game, muddier conditions and bigger crowds. We only won two or three games for the year and the tough thing being the gun recruit and being in the bottom team [was] they just hammered you all day.'

Barry Cable

I never look at a situation and think I can't find a way out.
I look at those things as temporary.[77]

By the end of the 1979 WAFL football season, Barry Cable had retired from football a satisfied man. He had many personal awards to his name and a 406-game playing record at both the state and club levels. He had been part of premierships both in the WAFL and VFL and was considered by his peers to be one of the game's greats. Perhaps the most satisfying thing was that his career had contributed to the healthy status of football in Western Australia. This was shown in the 1979 Australian football carnival in Perth which neatly coincided with Western Australia's 150th anniversary. There could have been no more fitting finish, with the Sandgropers running out winners over the Victorians by fifteen points. For Cable, there was a buzz in the Western Australian air.

Eighteen days later, as Cable sat having breakfast at home he felt good. He had kept fit by religiously adhering to a rigorous training campaign which saw him go for a 10 km run or a 30 km ride each morning, followed up by a workout in his home gym. As he sipped his tea, Cable's thoughts were not on football but the work he needed to do on his Orange Grove property a few suburbs away. As summer was approaching he needed to clear firebreaks and tidy up a few things. The work would take him all day.

As Cable and his wife Helen drove out to the block, Helen turned to her husband, 'What time do you think you will be done Barry?' Helen asked. 'Better make it four,' came Cable's reply. At 8:30 am Cable kissed Helen goodbye and started about his day. He unlocked his shed, pumped some diesel from the 44-gallon drum into the tractor, put on his workboots then climbed into the seat of the tractor, fired it up and headed out into the paddock. As Cable drove along slowly, he worked out what he needed to do. Process is everything for Cable, to make sure you do not waste time or energy getting the job done. It was his first rule in football and had been the same since he was a boy. Having a process had never let him down.

Suddenly, without any warning, the tractor tilted sharply. It was as if it were being pushed over by some invisible force. As the heavy machine started to roll onto him Cable had no time to think; he simply tried to jump out of the way as best he could. Suddenly Cable found himself on the ground and immediately felt the gut-wrenching pressure of the tractor pressing down heavily and painfully on to his right leg. The weight of the machine had him pinned. Cable quickly faced the sickening and agonising realisation that the tractor, while going nowhere, was still in gear, and that the massive back tyre was grinding into his leg. As Cable lay there, his calls for help were met by the drone of the tractor engine, and nothing else. It was at that moment Cable knew he needed to take control. The years of hard discipline playing football and cycling had trained him for this one moment. As the macabre spectacle played itself out, Barry Cable, football champion, father and husband needed to draw on every ounce of his physical and mental strength. As the adrenalin kicked in, Cable realised that this would be his longest quarter, and the stakes were much higher than a premiership. This was life and death.

Barry Cable's life began in the large wheat-belt town of Narrogin some 230 km southeast of Perth. Cable was raised by his mother when his elderly father passed away:

> I'm identified as a Noongar and I'm from Narrogin. I lost my father
> when I was 6 so I was bought up with my mother. He fell over as far as
> I know, broke his hip. He was an old man and he died of pneumonia
> but my mother was a young lady.[78]

For Cable, the town of Narrogin holds many fond memories. They revolve mostly around sport and the range of sports he was able to play. But football was the main choice because of the greater social interaction it gave him:

> Narrogin was a terrific town. I played cricket during the summer, I
> cycled a lot; I was a mad cyclist. I did basketball in the summer as well
> and I also quite a bit of cross-country running. I [also] used to play a
> bit of tennis. At the end of the day cycling is a very individual sport
> and whilst I enjoyed it you just never had that interaction with other
> people like you would in football.[79]

Cable's earliest football memory is playing on the road, something which later led to his affiliation with the Imperials Football Club:

> I used to kick on the road a lot. I kicked the top off me toe that many times it's unbelievable. Football was like the number one sport. In my day every town had a little footy team because you know there was so much shearing and farming going on and blokes working doing fencing and all that sort of stuff. So the population was a lot bigger in those areas. In those days they didn't have juniors like you have today. You more or less played either A-grade, B-grade. Because I came along through that era I just happened to get into the reserves at Imperials. I was just fortunate that I was good enough to hang in there and progress playing against grown men, like shearers.[80]

Cable's football ability stood out as much as his blond hair on the football oval. As a consequence he was identified as a potential prospect for the WAFL. However, Cable's first opportunity to head to Perth left him with mixed emotions:

> I was asked to go down to East Fremantle [Football Club] first and we broke down in the car coming from Narrogin. I got there late and they'd picked their teams and they didn't even give me a start. So you can imagine I wasn't terribly pleased. [Then] a gentleman by the name of Sixer Sykes, called Sixer because he was six foot [1.82 cm], had played for Perth footy club and he was the first man to go down to Narrogin to open up the new Coventry Motors. He was the manager, and he saw me playing a few games. I was only sixteen at the time and I was never really interested going back there [Perth] again. Sixer came and spoke to me and said, 'Well, what about coming down and having a run with the Perth footy club?' So I said, 'Yeah I'd love to.' So I went down.[81]

Cable's fate was sealed and with his mother's support the transition from Narrogin to Perth was good:

> I was basically living with my mother and she felt that if you've got something you should pursue it. I was pretty well half-way through my butcher's apprenticeship so it was then a matter of trying to figure out what to do. My brother said he would buy a house in Perth for

my mother and us to live in and that's all that really mattered to me at that time.[82]

With his girlfriend, Helen, moving into the new family home a few months later, Cable was set to take on the demands of being a league footballer with the Perth Demons. Cable played his first league game for Perth in 1962 where he came in as a wing. Cable, along with the Demons' other wing, the pacy Harold Little, would find himself coming up against some very good players, many of who were state representatives at the time. This allowed Cable to hone his craft on a weekly basis. Demons coach Ern Henfry was also pivotal in enabling Cable to learn his art of roving:

> Ernie was a terrific coach, one that was good for young people because he was a real teacher. I just like the way that he spoke. His knowledge of the game was outstanding and he was one of the people that helped me in the early days. I said to him one day, which was a bad mistake, that I did not like being shifted from the wing to roving. He promptly told me in a nice way that maybe it might be better if I understood that he was the coach and I was the player. I got dropped next week and it was a good lesson for me because it was the only time I spent in the reserves. I put in a heavier pre-season in 1964 and that was my first year as a rover.[83]

This move to the following division for the Demons would reap immediate results as Cable won his first Sandover medal in 1964 and the following year he went on to play in his first state game. From 1966 to 1968, Perth would win three premierships, defeating East Perth on all occasions. Cable would be pivotal to the Demons' success as he picked up the Simpson medal as best afield in all three grand finals and another Sandover in 1968. Cable reflects on this time and the influence that Perth captain-coach Mal Atwell had on him:

> He was a very demanding type person; he was an aggressive player himself and he expected that of all the players he had underneath him. He had a very clear direction of what he wanted to do and he was not very tolerant of those that didn't want to toe the line, and he made that very clear from day one. He asked me to be his vice-captain of the club and I said I'd be really honoured to be vice-captain of the club. He was a very shrewd coach. Mal in his own way brought around a lot of things that happened...He said when [our] guys get the ball and if I was in the right position to handball it out [to me] and with my

kicking skills we could really destroy the opposition. In those days that was the beginning of the running game. They all do it now but they weren't doing it then, and a lot of people don't credit Mal but that is a fact. I used to drop back onto the half-back flank and many times I'd be running past the half-backers and they could give it to me so I could bomb it straight down to our forward line.[84]

By the late-1960s, Barry Cable was becoming a household name, alongside players like Polly Farmer, Bill Walker and Austin Robertson and many eastern states clubs were starting to sniff around the dynamic rover. One such person was recruitment manager Ron Joseph. Joseph was a tireless worker for the North Melbourne Football Club who would go to great lengths to source those players he felt North Melbourne most needed. In Cable, Joseph could see a great many characteristics that would serve North Melbourne well:

Ron Joseph came and had a good chat with me about North Melbourne. I'd had a good run with the Perth footy club and he asked if I'd like to come over there and give them a hand. I had a contract with the Perth Football Club that would allow me to go to Victoria for one year to see what it was like. So I selected 1970. I was turning 28 that year, and I went to North and it was all the things I thought it would be playing Victorian footy. I'd heard so much about it being a tighter game, muddier conditions and bigger crowds. We only won two or three games for the year and the tough thing being the gun recruit and being in the bottom team [was] they just hammered you all day. The thing was to get through the year and even though North didn't do well I had to play well for myself.[85]

Cable did very well despite it being his debut season. He won the Syd Barker medal as North Melbourne's Best and Fairest, and ran fourth in the Brownlow medal. He returned to Perth, satisfied that he could match it with the best in the VFL and set about capitalising on his position in the WAFL so he could play more VFL. Cable played solidly for the next few years, picking up state selection and another Sandover medal in 1973. In a massive recruitment drive by North Melbourne in late 1973, Cable, aged 31, found himself once more back at Arden Street. With quality players like Keith Greig, Barry Davis, David Dench, Wayne Schimmelbusch and Malcolm Blight, the Kangaroos were set for a golden era which in many ways was characterised by the coaching style of Ron Barassi, and the following division of Mick Nolan, Barry Davis, Cable and John Burns:

> Going back to Melbourne was a fantastic thrill because it was towards the end of my career and we were virtually coming from the bottom up. It was quite amazing, four years in a row we played in [grand finals] and a record seventeen finals in a row. We never missed a final. In 1976, I was picked in my first state game for Victoria; at the age of 33 it was a dream come true. [86]

When Cable returned to Perth in 1978 he was set to join East Perth as the captain–coach, unseating Polly Farmer from his coaching role at the Royals and managing to get both a clearance from his old club Perth and poaching ex-Perth champion Ian Miller, who was returning from Fitzroy in the VFL. The Demons would come to rue both of these outcomes as Cable captain–coached East Perth to a 2-point win against his old team in 1978.

Today Barry Cable is able to reflect on the many challenges he has faced: from growing up in country Western Australia, to scaling the heights of his chosen sporting profession, to overcoming horrendous injuries from the tractor accident. He has also had to endure some people's incredulity as to his identity:

> My mother was fair like myself and was born on the Brookton Reserve. My mother could barely read or write. In those days you weren't allowed on the streets after five o'clock if you were an Aboriginal person unless you had a card and able to show you were a good citizen in the town. My mother never used that as an excuse for her not to work hard and be like any other person.[87]

Cable can see how history has impacted upon Indigenous Australians and what needs to be done to address certain issues:

> I think you'll find history tells very clearly that they always found it very hard to get anywhere purely and simply just because they were Aboriginal people. The philosophy in those days amongst a lot of people was they were lazy, they didn't want to work, they're never on time, this and that. In other words, people never necessarily looked at the actual culture and the way that they were as people. Aboriginal people have lived here for 50 or 60,000 years and I suppose one could look at that and say, 'Well, since European settlement what has happened?' One could say the rivers are polluted, there's hardly

any fish in the rivers and seas. Have a look at the introduced fauna for example and the things that have caused the most trouble in this country. They haven't been the animals that have lived in this country and are Indigenous to our country; they're basically goats, pigs, camels, the fox and the cat, they are the species that were introduced.[88]

Cable continues:

I think the biggest problem is that non-Indigenous Australians see Indigenous people as second-class citizens and uneducated. I think young people today need to appreciate that if they [Aboriginal people] are going to continue, we really need some sort of an education where they can actually work because employment gives you that feeling of satisfaction. So therefore they need an education. But you can't forget your culture and where you came from and what it means to your Mum and Dad and your grandparents.[89]

The transition from player to coach was a fairly organic process for Cable and one that would see him go on to coach for several years, both in the WAFL and the VFL. However, this was also the time that his tractor accident injury occurred. Reflecting on that difficult event is something that Cable is now happy to talk about:

There were a lot of things going through my mind. It was real clear that I was trapped and I knew my leg was caught and I realised I wasn't going to get out easily if I ever could get out. I knew it was going to be a hell of a long day. I felt I really needed to survive. So I guess from that point of view and because of my footy background I was fortunate enough to realise it all quickly. I just had to survive no matter what.[90]

Barry Cable, the small boy from Narrogin, has come along way. He is living proof that total dedication to a sport and building up the resilience to become a top-line footballer has the benefits that can pay off in other aspects of life.

MICHAEL 'FLASH' GRAHAM

RECORD

1971–1986

Games: 282
Goals: 455
State: South Australia 11
Premierships: Sturt 1974, 1976
Sturt Team of the Century (half-forward flank)

'Because we were the first Aboriginal family down in Penola and we were a footballing family it opened all the doors. We had no prejudice or nothing. Penola welcomed us with open arms because all my brothers could all play footy. The Penola Football Club became a strength.'

Michael 'Flash' Graham

It had been a long painful week for Michael Graham. For a bloke whose nickname was 'Flash' for his electrifying speed, in the last six days he had felt anything but fast. Graham's hip had been giving him merry hell and he had been getting over an appendix operation and a hernia. But as he sat lacing up his footy boots for a masters game with old mates in Darwin, he marvelled at how he always seemed to come right when he had the chance to play. For two hours his body felt good and he did not have a worry in the world. Graham reached into his bag and brought out a bottle of Goanna Oil. He poured it sparingly onto his knees and rubbed it in, feeling the liniment ease the tightness. It felt good. A team-mate sitting next to him asked, 'All ready for another big one, Flash?' Graham looked at him and winked. 'Yeah I'm ready, willing and not quite disabled,' he replied in his distinctive raspy voice.

Graham got up and headed to the toilet to clean the greasy residue off his hands. He looked into the mirror. His long black locks had given way to a bald head and his handlebar moustache had turned silver. But there was still a twinkle in Flash Graham's eye. As the warm soapy water ran through his hands, his mind drifted. The year was 1976. The year Sturt beat the very strong and much-favoured Port Adelaide for the South Australian National Football League (SANFL) premiership. Closing his eyes, he could hear the roar of the crowd and for a minute he felt like he was there again. 'Hey Flash, have you finished using the tap?' one of his team-mates asked, interrupting his daydream. 'Yeah, yeah…just making sure my hair looks good for all the ladies out there, hey bro.' Graham walked back into the change rooms and noticed it was empty; all his team-mates were out on the ground warming up. Graham walked to the door and stopped. His body felt good. He was young again.

I first met Michael Graham at the well-known Darwin coffee house, Cool Spot, in Fannie Bay. What I noticed about him was how he appeared to be very relaxed and easygoing man who was happy to sit and discuss his life and his football:

> My group is from South Australia. On my mother's side I'm Kaurna and on my father's side I'm Ngarrindjeri, which goes through from the bottom of South Australia, [Port] Augusta way and Port Pirie. I'm the second youngest of fifteen; eleven boys and four girls.[91]

Graham's recollections of his family and home life of growing up in the country are very positive:

> I was born in a place called Wallaroo. Initially Port Pierce mission was where we lived. We shifted from there and were the first Aboriginal family relocated under the old government relocation system at that time. We shifted to Penola which is in the southeast of South Australia and our family went down there and that's where we grew up most of our lives. I was 5 when we first went there and when I left Penola I was 18.[92]

Moving to Penola was a very good choice for the Graham family as they slipped into the community easily. Having older brothers and a father who played football was something that helped Graham's family become part of the Penola community:

> Because we were the first Aboriginal family down in Penola and we were a footballing family it opened all the doors. We had no prejudice or nothing. Penola welcomed us with open arms because all my brothers could all play footy. The Penola Football Club became a strength. It originally started off in the South Eastern Border League and then they went to a stronger league, the Western Border League, which came up against strong sides like Mt Gambier, Millicent, Hamilton and Portland. My brothers and father were champions. They used to tell me about my father, how good he was. They reckon that Dad whenever he took a mark fifty metres out, that the umpires would just run back to the centre, that's how good he was. He was a dead cert.[93]

Graham firmly believes that his success in football and other areas of his life come from having a strong home life; something which gave him a solid sense of right and wrong and helped to engender discipline:

> I would thank my Mum and Dad because they were strict on us. We weren't allowed to do just anything. If we were home late we'd be flogged. Not by Dad but by Mum. Dad never laid a hand on us Mum flogged us. She was only a little woman and even later if I'd go back to Adelaide and go and stay with Mum, I stayed out of her way.[94]

Graham was a natural sportsman and this allowed him to be accepted at school. But it was in football that Graham was to make his biggest mark:

> At school we did athletics; I was high school champion at athletics. I was captain of the basketball side. I was also a prefect at high school. I started playing A-grade at 16 and I remember I came third in the [association] medal when I was 16, third in the medal when I was 17 and I won it when I was 18. The same bloke I was runner-up to for two years, I ending up beating. To me it was a big thing at 18. In the Western Border League, which was very strong, I made the representative side. Everyone said I was quick but I just loved playing footy.[95]

The SANFL clubs in Adelaide began to hear of a super-quick rover from Penola, a stand-out junior. As Graham was a huge Sturt fan, when the Double Blues started to show interest in him there was little chance he would play with anyone else:

> I was a Sturt man from way back and a bloke by the name of Alan Fenn was a recruitment officer for Sturt. He spoke to me, and then after [that] the general manager came down because they'd heard about me. Then Jack Oatey [Sturt coach] turns up. I was always a Sturt man so it didn't take much for them to get me.[96]

Once he had made the decision to play full-time with Sturt it meant that Graham needed to commit to the transition process of going to play football in Adelaide. As with many country recruits, this was not easy:

> I got picked by Sturt and Dad and I went for the start of the year [1969]. They tried to put me into a Christian boarding school which was no good to me. Coming from a big family you miss your family. So

I ended up going back to Penola and that's when I won the association medal. The following year Mum and Dad shifted up to Elizabeth. That wasn't a good thing for me because Elizabeth in Adelaide was way out the other side of town. I had to commute from Elizabeth to Unley Oval to train. I did that for a few years from Elizabeth because I was playing with Sturt. I done a lot of commuting for my football but I didn't mind it at that time, because I would go anywhere to play footy and Sturt was my side.[97]

Graham's arrival at Sturt in 1971 coincided nicely with the club having just been through a very successful period, one which saw them win five premierships in a row. Graham still recalls this time with great enthusiasm:

When I came along we had won the five premierships. I come along in 1971. That was my first year. A bloke called Trevor Clarke he dropped out of the side and I came in on the wing. For a young Aboriginal bloke at 18 years of age it was pretty awesome to think that I'm running around with all my idols playing football with them. To me Sturt were great. They all treated me really well. With Jack Oatey being there he was like a second father to me and he looked after me. Then when I got married I wasn't getting the big bucks but if I needed a fridge or a washing machine for home the club would look after me.[98]

Debuting in 1971 in a fiery match against Torrens, the Double Blues would win by a margin of 41 points and Graham impressed everyone with his speed and skills, especially his pin-point kicking. He would finish the game with 20 possessions. Graham consolidated his position within the team which was trying to rebuild after the success of the 1960s. This was borne out in the 1973 finals series where Sturt showed great promise but were soundly beaten by Glenelg in the first semi-final, and then North Adelaide in the preliminary final. Sturt would take these lessons into 1974.

Graham married a Darwin girl in the early 1970s. Sturt Football Club would come to play a significant part in the big day, and the Darwin connection would also have a lasting impact on Graham:

I got married to a Darwin woman called Debra Hunter and had four kids. We got married down at the Sturt Football Club. I then came up to [Darwin] to play football for St Mary's from Sturt. It was my pre-season training to follow my family up to play with St Mary's. The [Darwin] mob said, 'Why don't you play for Buffaloes?' Because they were the Double Blues and the same colour as Sturt, I just stayed with St Mary's because it was like a big family thing.[99]

For five years in the 1970s, Graham would play the winter months in Adelaide and then head to Darwin to play in the Wet. Playing football all year saw him maintain an excellent fitness level. It also enabled him and his wife to maintain kinship relations with family in South Australia and in the Top End. In playing for St Mary's, Graham would win back-to-back Nichols medals in 1973 and 1974, and be awarded the Best and Fairest player in the Northern Territory Football league. Given the calibre of footballers playing in Darwin at the time this was a considerable effort. It also allowed him to make some lasting friendships with players who would eventually head south to play football, mainly the Long family:

> When I first come up here I played with Jack Long for St Mary's. I reckon it shaped my career coming to St Mary's. Michael [Long] and I have been close from footy and we are like brother boys. Because I played with St Mary's it gave me a bit of a kindred connection, Benny Vigona played with St Mary's, Basil Campbell played with St Mary's, so too Cyril Rioli and Dean Rioli. I've got that connection right through St Mary's footy club, which was from me coming up from South Australia and playing for St Mary's. It gave me a bond with those guys because I played with all those champions before they went down and became champions down south.[100]

In 1974, Graham won the first of two premierships with Sturt against Glenelg. It was a great season for Graham as he gained 60-odd games' experience, and became an astute reader of the play, a reliable goal kicker and was widely considered the quickest man in the SANFL. It was also around this time that Graham had a brief taste of the VFL. The Melbourne Demons were interested in him but, inexplicably, nothing seemed to eventuate after the initial contact:

> I never played AFL but I suppose I could have. I came up here [Darwin] and I was playing in the finals for St Mary's. I got signed up by Melbourne in Adelaide and I thought I was going back to Melbourne to play but no one contacted me back. I wasn't disappointed I didn't go but in hindsight I could have.[101]

Graham remembers racism being present in the SANFL, but he is at pains to say that it did not impact upon him greatly:

There was name-calling, but my Mum and Dad always said, 'Sticks and stones will break your bones, but names will never hurt you.' Names don't hurt you unless you listen to them. It was always the opposition mob and I'd always just point to the score.[102]

He continues:

Some of the guys that played let it [racism] affect them. Robbie Muir is my best mate, him and I used to knock around a lot. When I first left Sturt, I went and played footy up in the country. Me, Robbie and Chris Long, Michael's brother, we were playing on the day and this bloke started up [sledging]. I'm running through the centre and this bloke's called me a black this and black that. Next thing I see the bloke was running for the boundary with Robbie running after him trying to smash him. 'Don't you call my brother that,' Robbie said. I just fronted Robbie and said, 'Get back over here and don't worry about it.' I've never ever worried about that shit in my life. Nicky Winmar said it all, didn't he? He lifted his guernsey up and said, 'I'm black and I'm proud.' He didn't need to say anything.[103]

Graham's crowning glory came with the win in the 1976 SANFL grand final. Sturt's run at the grand final had begun late in the last quarter of the first semi-final against Norwood. Down by 21 points at half-time, it took a great individual effort by Graham to spark the Double Blues. At the 22-minute mark of the last quarter Graham received the ball in the centre of the ground and headed for the goal line. Bouncing the ball at pace and weaving through the opposition backline he straightened up and kicked a goal. It was the impetus Sturt needed to beat Norwood and the ignition for their finals campaign. Sturt then went on to beat Glenelg by 7 points in the qualifying final, only to come up against the very powerful and highly fancied Port Adelaide in the grand final. Many felt that Sturt were too old and slow, but the final result saw the Double Blues win easily by 41 points. Graham would go on to play for Sturt for another nine years, retiring in 1985, having played 282 games and kicked 455 goals.

These days Michael Graham lives in Darwin and has lived and worked across Australia, which has given him a great understanding about what the social and economic ramifications have been for Indigenous Australians:

White people don't understand us and they don't know us. White people should learn to live like Aboriginal people. I've always said I can go anywhere because I'm black. If I go to WA, Queensland or wherever and I see someone of my own colour I'd go and say, 'How you going brother' He'd say, 'Where're you from?' and we could talk. But if you went to a white person in Melbourne that I don't know you from a bar of soap, they would say, 'What the hell are you doing talking to me?' That's the difference. They grow up with their blinkers on and they don't understand the hardship that people are facing. I've read up on what happened to us mob. They came and they shot us, and they just took over and it's [disadvantage] still happening.[104]

Graham is now retired but his life in football and working in the government sector in several states has given him a good understanding of the challenges facing Indigenous people and an honesty about what he thinks Indigenous people and families need to do to improve their situations:

From my point of view, coming from Point Pearce mission to Penola, the main thing that kept us at school was our parents. Parents these days don't give a shit. There's too much TV, too much video games and grog and drugs are available to them. Young kids get to high school, what do they do? They hang with the wrong kids at school and then they have a bit of a smoke then someone says, 'Let's go cut school.' The majority of kids these days have got no respect and to me that is the biggest issue. I was taught respect. My mother did not tolerate swearing in front of her. Parents need to pull their finger out and teach their kids to go to school and try to teach them respect.[105]

He continues, highlighting the complexity of the situation:

If you haven't got good teachers, strong teachers at school, they are going to fail. If you've got a classroom of thirty kids and if they haven't got a teacher's aide with them, it's hard. Half the time they put them at the back where they can't hear or understand what the teacher's saying. And they won't put their hand up and say, 'Excuse me teacher.'[106]

Graham believes that the issues of the classroom are related to bigger questions of history and dispossession and how that legacy still has an impact on Indigenous Australians today:

They'll never be able to erase that [history] from the memories of us mob. We'll never ever forget. The government is worried about things happening overseas. They're not worried about their own backyard and what has happened to us. They [government departments] walk into communities and say, 'Oh yeah, who's doing such and such' and then they leave. They don't follow through and that needs to change.[107]

In reflecting on his career, Graham cites his selection into the Indigenous Team of the Century as his biggest achievement. He recalls the day:

For me it was very important. It was an honour being picked in the side. When they announced it I didn't think I was in at first. When I went down for the function Billy [Dempsey] was at our table. A bloke came along and said to us, 'Bill you're in,' and Billy went up. Then this bloke come up behind me with a camera and sat behind me and my wife. Then the next thing they said: 'Michael Graham — interchange for the Indigenous Team of the Century.' I was the last person up. That Indigenous Team of the Century is the highlight of my career and very, very special.[108]

MAURICE RIOLI

RECORD

1975–1987

Games: 286: South Fremantle 168; Richmond 118
Goals: Total goals not available: Richmond 80
State: Western Australia 13
Premierships: South Fremantle 1980
Norm Smith medal: Richmond 1982
Simpson medal: 1980, 1981, 1983
Club Best and Fairest: Richmond 1982, 1983
All-Australian: 1983, 1986, 1988

'For me my football was my life I guess. Any spare time that I had it was mainly football: during school breaks, at the end of school, after school, weekends, even the off-season. Football was my life and you know, growing up right through my school years there wasn't too many moments when I was doing anything else.'

Maurice Rioli

The year is 1964. The place, a dead-end street in Darwin. It is mid-November and the weather is heavy with tropical heat as the build-up in the Top End starts to kick in. Later in the day the clouds will gather and lightning will crack across the tropical north, but for now the sun bursts out from behind the clouds. Assembled in the street are twelve boys all aged between 7 and 10. Their bodies glisten with sweat. On a closer inspection it can be seen that don't actually have a football, but a homemade spheroid constructed from things they can scavenge: newspaper and tape. The paper has been dampened and made into mâché so it can be moulded into the shape of a football. It has been allowed to dry before the tape was added to hold the ball in shape. At either end of the cul-de-sac are the goals; eight piles of shirts that stand in for the goal and behind posts. No one is wearing shoes and there are no umpires. This is street footy, Darwin-style.

As the ball goes up in the air the two rucks jump from a standing start, like a basketball game. The ball comes to ground and is soccered off the hot tarmac by a quick young fella who follows the ball up on the wing. He has to move deftly because in these confined spaces your opponent will be right on your tail. This is desperate stuff as no one wants to shirk the issue, but neither do they want to get hurt. He gathers the ball and looks up and sees his cousin coming in at him at speed. He baulks and spins blindly. Like a dancer he lands beautifully and keeps running. However, he has not seen the opposition ruckman who has been following his movements. He quickly tries another baulk but this time he slips and crashes to the bitumen, landing on both knees and elbows while the ball spills free. The initial hard jolt of his body quickly gives way to a stinging sensation. He feels sick in his stomach. 'Hey Maurice,' one of the boys calls out, 'Keep your feet bruz, keep your feet!'

Young Maurice Rioli sits up, checks the damage and brushes out the little bits of bitumen and sand from his knees. He gently places his hands on the bleeding knees and removes them. Standing up, he rubs the blood into his palms, making them sticky. Maurice nods to the others that he is okay. He places his hands on his hips, chewing casually on some PK chewing gum. He makes a silent promise to himself that he will never go to ground again. The pain from the bitumen stings like blazes and the goal that he gave to the opposition stings just as badly.

There is one word that describes Maurice Rioli more than any other footballer, and that word is poise. My recollection of watching Rioli in the WAFL in the late-1970s and early 1980s was that his every move was simply panther-like. He was just one of those players who always seemed to know what to do at precisely the right time. He never seemed to make mistakes and he was always balanced. He was regarded as one of the best players in the nation for more than a decade. Coming from the Top End, Rioli's name now has become synonymous with quality football which had been honed on those hot Darwin streets and the Tiwi Islands:

> My early football memories would no doubt be playing in Darwin. My family moved from the Island and we lived in Darwin for a period of time, probably when I was 3 or 4. We moved back when I was 14, 15. So I spent a fair bit of time playing in the school grounds in Darwin, and also in the streets after school where we organised to pick teams on most days and learnt our skills and our balance, because when you're playing on bitumen streets you rip off a fair bit of bark if you fall over. For me my football was my life I guess. Any spare time that I had it was mainly football: during school breaks, at the end of school, after school, weekends, even the off-season. Football was my life and you know, growing up right through my school years there wasn't too many moments when I was doing anything else.[109]

Rioli played other sports and he hunted, something that he claims, as does Michael Long, helped in developing his football:

> We played sports at school. Rugby League. Boxing was another and we played cricket. I spent a lot of my time with family going out hunting for seafood and crabs and fish, turtles and dugong. You've got to have the skill to go out hunting and catch your food and be able to develop those skills. A lot of it comes down to how much time you

spend on [tracking] a kangaroo or wallaby or a carpet snake. It takes a particular type of skill and effort and to make sure you're not wasting too much effort in capturing your next meal.[110]

If the desire to hunt and catch food both directly and indirectly influenced certain aspects of Rioli's football ability, the influence of his family saw him play for three clubs before he went to the VFL:

Football was something that all our family and friends and extended family were involved in. When I came back home [to the Tiwis] my home team at Garden Point were called the Imalu Tigers. Then I went to Darwin and the St Mary's Football Club who were closely affiliated with the Tiwi Island footballers. They helped make up the St Mary's Club. Then the main reason I went to South [Fremantle] was Basil Campbell and my brother Sebastian Rioli were in Perth while I was still at school up here in Darwin. They were the first two to make the long trek down to Perth and I followed behind them.[111]

There was also another reason for Rioli heading down to Perth; something beyond his control:

Cyclone Tracy hit Darwin in 1974 at Christmas. There was a cleaning up period and I was in my last year of school. I had just turned 17 and I decided to go down to Perth as my older brother was there. I stayed with him for a couple of years so I certainly had help settling, he was able to assist me in my preparation [in the WAFL].[112]

In many ways the South Fremantle Football Club was the perfect fit for Rioli as it was a multicultural club with a long history of Italian and Yugoslav players. For Rioli, South Fremantle was a great club which helped steer him in the right direction to become a top-line footballer:

Souths I believe were very professional from day one in handling and managing the Indigenous players in West Australia. When you look at the number of players that have come through South Fremantle and gone onto the VFL and AFL, well I don't think you get a better record than that over the years. They were very professional and made me feel welcome, even though the weather was an issue. But in the end you realise that this is all part and parcel of playing football in the south and you just need to adapt and get on like anyone else. If you wanted it bad enough it's something that you overcame and you take full advantage of the opportunities that are presented for you. It was a big move but I had dreams like most footballers and South gave me that opportunity to at least have a go playing in the big time.[113]

The standard of the WAFL competition allowed Rioli to show off his great skill as a footballer and to compete against other great players:

Some say it was as good as any competition in the land because you had some great names playing in each of the teams. A lot of those players ended up playing in the VFL/AFL at the time. It was a fairly tough competition and a fairly even one.[114]

The other main influence on Rioli was the South Fremantle coach and Western Australian football legend, Mal Brown:

Brownie had his coaching method. [We] were all equal [but] if you can understand [we] were treated differently. Some were given privileges. If he felt they were looking good on the track he took it on himself to make decisions so players could have an early shower. That was the type of person he was.[115]

Another significant influence was the South Fremantle champion ruckman, Stephen Michael:

I'd have to say Stephen Michael is probably the best Indigenous footballer who I've played with and who I've seen. I mean I never saw Polly Farmer at his best other than replays and the TV. But pound for pound there'd probably be no better footballer, even though he never played AFL, than Stephen Michael. I still rate him above any Indigenous footballer I've ever seen.[116]

During the 1970s and 1980s, Rioli established himself as a 'blue-chip' player in the WAFL. He played in several finals campaigns for the Bulldogs and was a regular in Western Australia's state side. He also won back-to-back Simpson medals for best-on-ground performances in the WAFL grand finals in 1980 and 1981. It was simply a matter of time before a VFL club signed him and the move to Melbourne was made. This came in 1982, which saw a significant cohort of Indigenous talent move from the WAFL into the VFL. The Krakouer brothers went to North Melbourne and Rioli was signed to VFL powerhouse,

Richmond. Rioli's signing was significant as he was the first Top End blackfella of note to make the move to Melbourne.[117]

Rioli had a meteoric rise in the VFL in his first season. He played stylish, assured football which saw him win Richmond's Best and Fairest and a Norm Smith medal for best afield in Richmond's losing grand final side. In doing this he became the first Indigenous player, as well as the first player from a losing grand final side, to do so. In 1983, he was the runner up in the Brownlow medal, being beaten by North Melbourne champion Ross Glendinning. Reflecting on the transition to Melbourne and the VFL Rioli is very modest about his skills:

> The [VFL] grounds suited me, they were a lot heavier and I didn't think I was the quickest player but I had enough pace to get myself out of trouble and be able to get to a contest. It was certainly different to Perth where you had the sandy surfaces. In Melbourne at the time you had cricket pitches in the middle of the ground which didn't help at all. When you fell in the mud you probably picked up three or four kilos of mud with you. Going into a new environment I had to re-establish myself as one of the top players. I went over there with a reputation and I guess I put a fair bit of pressure on myself. I hated the cold but there was nothing I could do about it on training nights when you are thinking about how warm it is back in Darwin. It was always something playing on my mind but I basically just had to get on with it.[118]

There was also the verbally expressed pressure Rioli experienced which no doubt came from the fact that he was an extremely dangerous player for Richmond:

> They [opposition players] had a go at me. I tried to use it [to] motivate me. I knew at the time they were using it as tactics to put me off my game. I kept it at the back of my mind and took note of the player [and] when he came near the ball I might have hit him a bit harder. It wasn't easy and certainly you copped it but you couldn't take the law into our own hands. You just did it a bit more subtly when it came to retaliating.[119]

In some ways the greatest pity about Rioli's career was that it was simply too short. As he played only 118 games from 1982 to 1987, it is easy to feel that the VFL career of this great player should have been longer. Interestingly, his career was not cut short by chronic injury or burnout, but by a recruitment wrangle. In 1986, Rioli tried to gain a clearance from Richmond to the Sydney

Swans as the new private owner of the Sydney Swans, Geoffrey Edelsten, had been signing up VFL talent to play in Sydney. Rioli was announced as one of his many high-profile signings. Meanwhile the VFL was trying to reduce wage inflation because some of the weaker clubs were finding it difficult to attract and maintain players with their limited resources. To counter this the VFL instigated a salary cap system. It was the salary cap that derailed Rioli going to Sydney and he eventually returned to the Tigers to start the 1986 season, only to find that his number 17 had been allocated to another player.[120] This seems to have been the beginning of a slow decline of this great player, and by 1987 his VFL career was over. Rioli headed back to South Fremantle as captain. Here he played consistent football and in the summer months headed back to Darwin to captain–coach the Waratahs Football Club during the Wet. In 1988 he won All-Australian honours for a third time following the Bicentennial Carnival.

Rioli later headed back to the Top End and in 1992 was elected as the Australian Labor Party's Member for Arafura in the Northern Territory Legislative Assembly. He held this position until 2001 when he retired from Parliament. Rioli remained involved in football even though his coaching experiences could only be called interesting:

> My claim to fame as a coach of the Muluwurri Team over at Milakapiti was that I came in and coached the team half way during the year. I took over as coach, because the [other] coach wasn't that much interested in coaching the players. I took over and coached them and we just made the final four. [Then] we won the first semi and then we won the preliminary final. We got into the grand final. That week, half an hour before the grand final was about to start, I was sacked as coach. The old coach came into the change rooms and said, 'I'm the bloody coach here! I should be coaching this team!' and I asked the players, 'Well who do you want to coach?' They never said nothing so I walked out. Maybe they were frightened to say anything because the fella was a bit aggressive and angry. I'm not that type of person. I'm a lover not a fighter. I thought, oh well I don't want any more trouble I'll walk away, and they lost the grand final. It's unheard of, there's nowhere on record where a coach has been sacked half an hour before a grand final.[121]

Perhaps it was Rioli's many different life experiences that helped him deal with this situation because he smiled all the way through this anecdote. This story also plays down the very important role football has on the Tiwi Islanders.

Rioli has played a major role as a mentor and assistant coach to the Tiwi Bombers who came into the Darwin competition in 2008. Rioli saw how football could enable many positive things to happen, and he was the very proof of that. Rioli became more serious when I asked him what he felt were the biggest challenges that face Indigenous Australians:

> In most of the places that I've been to most Indigenous people don't believe they're good enough. I guess more or less it's their negative thinking of themselves and that puts us behind the eight ball. We think negatively about our ability and that prevents a lot of Indigenous people from going forward. But if there's a message I can put across to any young Indigenous person it is this: if you have a dream and you believe in the dream whether it's football, whether it's work, whether it's anything in life, dreaming is what motivates you, dreaming is what your goals are, what you want to be, where you want to be. Football was my first love and I always dreamt about playing in the VFL at the time. Playing with the big guys, like the Jesaulenkos, and if you believe it and you work hard enough you'll achieve your dreams.[122]

In a sad twist, Rioli's life was cut short. On Christmas Day 2010, Rioli collapsed and died of a heart attack at a family barbeque in Darwin. He was 53 years old. Because of his contribution to football and politics in the Northern Territory and the Tiwi Islands, Maurice Rioli was given a state funeral, one which recognised his legacy as a great Australian who participated in public life and who lived by his creed of working hard and achieving his dreams.

STEPHEN MICHAEL

RECORD

1975–1985

Games: 243
Goals: 231
State: Western Australia 17
Premierships: South Fremantle 1980
Sandover medal: 1980; 1981
Simpson medal: 1983
Tassie medal: 1983
Captain: All-Australian 1983
Club Best and Fairest: South Fremantle 1977, 1978, 1979, 1981,1983
AFL Hall of Fame Inductee

'I went over to Geelong and looked around but the bloody cold weather frightened hell out of me. We went out to some bloke's farm for a barbeque in the middle of winter and he is trying to convince me to come over to Geelong and it is belting down rain. Geelong were very good to me but my family was my main thing and sport came second. I just thought it would take Mum and Dad four hours to fly to Melbourne and it only takes two to drive from Koji [Kojonup]. It was a lot easier for my Dad to come up to Perth and spend the weekend than to fly to Melbourne.'

Stephen Michael

My most enduring memory of Stephen Michael occurred on 3 October 1981 at Subiaco Oval in Perth. I was 12 and it was the day of the WAFL grand final between South Fremantle and my team, Claremont. For many football followers in Western Australia, the 1981 grand final is remembered as one of the most fiery in living memory. South Fremantle were coached by the wily Mal Brown and they bristled with talent. Claremont also had a good mix of players and were captain–coached by 1977 Brownlow medallist, Graham Moss. South Fremantle were seen as tough and skilful, whereas over many years Claremont had developed a reputation for being 'soft', and they had not won a premiership since 1964. For me there were four players who would have a significant influence on the game: Jim and Phil Krakouer for Claremont, and Maurice Rioli and Stephen Michael for South Fremantle.

From the opening bounce the game was poised on a knife's edge. Claremont's Barry Beecroft won the opening ruck contest against Michael by smashing the ball towards the Claremont half-forward line. Rioli swooped and gathered the ball cleanly but came under immediate pressure from Jim Krakouer, and as he kicked the ball he mistimed it, forcing it high. The ball came down and was marked by Beecroft. As Beecroft turned to go back and take his kick, South Fremantle's fearsome strongman Basil Campbell, a Tiwi Islander, came in and applied a late shirtfront. The Claremont players saw this as an aggressive act and the game erupted into a massive all-in brawl. As Beecroft lay on the ground, Campbell was set upon by several of the nearby Claremont players.

Sprinting and weaving through the bodies, Jim Krakouer made a beeline towards Campbell. But just as Krakouer arrived to meet Campbell the cluster of bodies became tighter and he could not get in a clean punch because of the restricted space. Seeing the danger unfolding, Stephen Michael quickly wedged his big frame between Krakouer and Campbell. This action provided the grand final with its great symbolic moment, with two great Noongar athletes trying to achieve the same thing: protection. For Jim it was his team-mate Beecroft and for Michael it was his countryman, Krakouer. As Michael tucked Jim snugly under his left armpit he acted like a great shield, eventually pushing Krakouer out of Campbell's way. Many still remember this as the start of the wildest grand final in WAFL history as fights began to break out all over the ground — and the game had only just begun.

Stephen Michael was born in 1956 in Wagin, Western Australia, but was raised in Kojonup, Western Australia, 250 km south of Perth. For the local Noongar people, Kojonup is a significant site; the place of the Kodja or stone axe in the heart of Kaniyang country:

> I grew up in Kojonup. My Dad worked on the railways for many years and retired there (Kojonup). Mum and Dad lived all around the Central Great Southern, Kojonup, Beverley, Brookton, Wagin, Boyup Brook. They'd travel to work. So we've got ties with everyone [in] the Noongar community.[123]

Michael remembers sport in general, not just football, was a very important part of his growing up:

> I don't think footy was very important to me but I do think sport was very important. We loved it. Footy was the main thing and your parents would go and support you. It was nothing to have three hundred people at a game on a Sunday, parked around the ground in their cars. It was very important in that way because the community all got together. Basketball was very all-seasons. When footy wasn't there it was basketball. A couple of Aboriginal kids played cricket but not many of us. Cricket is a team sport but it is an individual sport at the same time. It was basically football, basketball and netball. Going roo shooting, we called a sport too, because we loved going out in the bush and running around.[124]

The chance to play sport provided Stephen Michael with a very important pathway which allowed his Noongar community to participate in the broader Kojonup community. However, the issues of sport and politics were never far away and they became very apparent from his early teens:

> We had a very good Aboriginal side in the basketball competition in Kojonup. But unfortunately it got disbanded because no other sides could touch us. So we more or less had to disband the side. We said to the association that it was unfair that they could dictate to us these terms. We were young at the time and it was disappointing because we weren't asked, we was told.[125]

As Michael grew older, football began to make greater inroads into his life:

> I was picked in a junior colts side and went up to play in Perth. We got billeted out with the Perth parents for the weekend and we went and watched East Fremantle and Perth play. I didn't know Cable from a bar of soap. I saw Cable play and from then on I supported Perth [Football Club] because he was this little blond-haired left-footer and a super star. He was my idol. I started playing league football at 15 and showed a bit of ability and it all just started from there.[126]

In late 1974, aged about 18, Michael and another Noongar called Nicky Dyson travelled to Perth to participate in a country footy carnival. Because of the zoning laws of the WAFL, the Central Great Southern area where Michael lived meant that the team would be South Fremantle, if he was to be picked up. Michael saw it as a great chance to see just how far he could take his football:

> Ken Brindley, our President, took Nicky Dyson and me up to Fremantle to play. I can remember him [Dyson] kicking 20 goals one day on a bloke who used to be a policeman in Kojonup. Nicky was a very good full-forward and a very good player [but] Nicky didn't carry on with it. I was very fortunate, I had support from Mum and Dad. For me it was the challenge and a chance to open doors. You can't stay in Mum's home all your life. I think you've got to move on. I think you've got to set your own goals.[127]

The transition to Perth was not an easy one for Michael, as he juggled training and playing commitments with an over-riding feeling of homesickness:

> The first two years were very, very hard. I had no one to communicate with, no one to understand work commitments. You were in a rat race. Not like when you work on the Shire where it's laidback and pretty easy. You have to start fending for yourself. Me and my first wife went up there [and] we had no relations up that way until we got to know a few. It was like jumping out from behind Mum's apron strings into the bloody big blue yonder.[128]

South Fremantle Football Club became a hub to everything for Michael and his wife and the people in it played a very important role in maintaining Michael's wellbeing, both on and off the field:

> The club's a very good club. I think specifically, when you look at Fremantle it was a very multi-racial club and had Italian, Yugoslavs and Indigenous people. It didn't matter who you was. We had very good people who ran the club; you wasn't a number, you was a person. The Hayward brothers really opened the doorway there at South, as did Sibby Rioli, Maurice [Rioli], Benny [Vigona] and Basil [Campbell] who had come down from Darwin. You also had Nicky [Winmar] come from Pingelly plus the Collards, it was good.[129]

Michael's comfort and sense of belonging at South Fremantle seems to have been a large factor for his playing career. Being settled at South Fremantle seemed to translate into good on-field performances and Michael became a regular fixture in the South Fremantle League line-up. In many respects this had to do with the coaches he played under, too:

> Colin Beard came back from Richmond Football Club and he was a great team man. Percy Johnson was the next one and he was a very intelligent coach. Then Malcolm Gregory Brown came along and I'd say Malcolm would be the best coach that I ever had because he was always thinking football and Browny had the knack of getting the best out of players and I think he was a little before his time. At South he had two guys, Benny Vigona and Nicky Winmar, who needed a little bit more. Nicky found it very hard. But he [Brown] did give certain boys a bit of latitude.[130]

Michael had many key attributes. His skills were excellent and he had great pace which saw him play at a consistently high level over many games. As well, he had great strength and a massive spring which saw him able to compete

effectively with opposition ruckmen like Graham Moss and Swan District's
Ron Boucher:

> Graham is a great guy. I admire Graham. I reckon he would be one of
> the hardest guys to play against. He gave 110 per cent all the time and
> I always say Mossy's the best ruckman I played against…Ron Boucher
> [is] a very hard person until you got to know him. Off the footy field
> Ron could be the most pleasant guy you could ever meet. Ron was a
> guy where you never knew what he's going to do but he never ran out
> a full game because he always had a lot of problems with injury.[131]

The year 1977 proved to be a watershed year for Michael as he won the first of
five club Best and Fairests for South Fremantle. He would win again in 1978,
1979, 1981 and 1983. Stephen Michael also made his state debut in 1977 where
he was the number two ruck to Moss, a pattern that continued all year until the
inaugural State of Origin game on 8 October at Subiaco Oval. In this particular
game Michael was overlooked and the state rucking duties were given to Moss
and Ron Alexander. Despite being overlooked again for state selection in
early 1978 and because of a 100-point flogging at the hands of the Victorians,
Michael found his way back into the black-and-gold guernsey and was rarely
seen out of it for several years. By the late 1970s and early 1980s, Stephen
Michael was arguably the best ruckman in the land and in 1980 he led the state
rucking division for the first time. He also saw success at club level in 1980
when he won his first Sandover medal and a premiership for South Fremantle.
In the following year he won another Sandover, but the grand final was lost
to Claremont. In 1983, Michael won the Tassie medal and was awarded the
captaincy of the All-Australian side, the first time that an Indigenous captain
had been given this honour.

In late 1983, Michael's career was put in jeopardy due to a shooting mishap
where he sustained leg injuries. Kangaroo hunting was seen by Noongar people
as both a sport and a way to maintain cultural connection to their ancestry
but it nearly led to Michael having a short-lived football career. He recalls the
incident:

> I was very fortunate it happened off-season and there wasn't any
> damage. Browny rings me up and asked if I had been shot and I said,
> 'Yeah.' The media wanted to get onboard but I didn't want to make
> a mountain out of a molehill. It [the wound] was only superficial.
> There's still two pellets left in my leg and if it had of damaged my

ligaments or my hamstring or anything it might have been a different story.[132]

With his considerable success at WAFL and state level and his profile as one of the best rucks in the land, the VFL clubs were very keen to lure Michael's services east. Geelong were the frontrunners in this regard. Michael recalls:

Geelong were very, very close. I went over to Geelong and looked around but the bloody cold weather frightened hell out of me. We went out to some bloke's farm for a barbeque in the middle of winter and he is trying to convince me to come over to Geelong and it is belting down rain. Geelong were very good to me but my family was my main thing and sport came second. I just thought it would take Mum and Dad four hours to fly to Melbourne and it only takes two to drive from Koji [Kojonup]. It was a lot easier for my Dad to come up to Perth and spend the weekend than to fly to Melbourne.[133]

With his shooting injury having an impact on his running, Michael played out his career until 1985 when he retired from WAFL football. Ironically, having resisted the big contracts to head east during his career, Michael headed to the West Australian goldfields to help provide an income for his family. Having worked with Hindle's trucking company when he began playing with South Fremantle in 1975, Michael continued driving for Hindle's in the goldfields until 1989 when he and his family moved to Collie to work in the state's southwest. It was in the country leagues that the issue of racism in football first presented itself to the great champion:

I think my size helped. I copped very little in the WAFL but after I finished playing with Souths I went and played for Boulder in the Kalgoorlie competition. One guy ran out and said, 'Michael you black so-and-so, how about going back to Perth to earn your money.' I said to him, 'Did you catch some black so-and-so with your wife, mate?' I always maintain what's said on the footy field stays on there. It stays in the circle, you walk off and have a cup of tea with an opposition club. But I think a lot of it does go on.[134]

Stephen Michael's memories of sport, and his participation in it, have provided him with positive experiences and opened many doors that would not have otherwise been opened. Remembering the ceremony at Crown Casino, Michael is very honest about what it meant to be named in the Indigenous Team of the

Century. It goes some way to explaining how he sees many things generally, and his concern for others:

> It was an honour to achieve an award like that there. But I thought there was a lot of players that missed out. To see some of these players missing out was really heartbreaking but it's part and parcel of footy.[135]

These days Stephen Michael works for Premier Coal, just outside Collie in southwestern Western Australia. Here he drives heavy machinery, D11s, 793 dump trucks, dozers, excavators and loaders. He is the first person to admit that his standing as a footballer within the community means that his life post-football is assured, with a job that enables him to support his family. However, he is mindful of the challenges that face many Indigenous people and families:

> With sport, if Indigenous kids show a bit of potential generally they can get themselves a job. The biggest problem is the barriers. [If] you don't know the history of the land or history of the people then there will be barriers between the Indigenous and the white people. A lot of white people won't invite Indigenous people into their house. They might work with them or play sport with them, but they won't say 'come in for a cup of tea' or something. These little things go a long way to help.[136]

Michael is very direct about football and the legacy it has created for Indigenous Australians:

> I think it has left a very good taste in people's mouths about Aboriginal people. I think we opened the doorway for a lot of Aboriginal kids to come through and now clubs in Australia include Aboriginal players, which is really good. But people have to remember the culture of the Aboriginal person. It's about the parents, the uncles and aunties, their grandparents and seeing them as one unit. When we have problems or whatever we go back to our people and tell them what's going on. They help nut things out and help get your life back on track.[137]

GLENN JAMES

RECORD

1977–1985

Games: 166
Grand finals: 1982, 1984
OAM 1987

' My first game it was just fantastic. It was Fitzroy and Footscray out at VFL Park in 1977. It was on my daughter's 9th birthday. Dennis Collins picked it up from the middle of the ground and he was on the edge of the square and he handballed it to Bernie Quinlan and Bernie banged it through from about 70 metres out at VFL Park. Running back to the centre I think 27 seconds had gone on the board and I knew straight away that this was a different type of footy, this was a different game. '

Glenn James

In round five of the 1982 VFL season, North Melbourne were set to take on Collingwood at Arden Street, North Melbourne's home ground. Their previous home game against the recently relocated Sydney Swans attracted only 12,885 people through the turnstiles. With the Collingwood army on the march across town, the crowd at Arden Street was nearly double, with 23,405 people turning up to watch. The Kangaroos had been on a roll, winning three of their first four games and were bristling with seasoned talent in David Dench, Gary Dempsey, Keith Greig, Wayne Shimmelbusch and Malcolm Blight. North Melbourne were also set to showcase the electrifying football talents of Jim and Phil Krakouer who were gaining blanket media attention. The question on many people's lips was how would the boys from the west handle the physical intensity of the Collingwood team and the hostility of the Magpie army.

Glenn James was the main umpire for the day. Ironically for him, being a black man dressed in white seemed only to ensure that he would be on the end of some of the most savage verbal barrages in Australian football history. Even the most crotchety football fan would have seen James either as the bravest man in Australia or the most foolhardy.

Early in the first quarter, the ball trickled out of bounds and needed to be thrown in. As Gary Dempsey and Wes Fellows jostled for position awaiting the throw-in, Jim, Phil and James were standing close to each other. As the Magpie and Kangaroos' fans were settling in for the day there was a small lull in the crowd noise. From the silence came the booming voice of a Collingwood supporter, 'Why don't you go and put some socks on James, you scruffy bastard.' As the official uniform of VFL umpires at the time was white shirts, white shorts, white boots and black socks it was anyone's guess how James would handle it. Jim and Phil Krakouer looked at one another and then at James, who immediately started to giggle. The Krakouers started giggling too. In that brief moment a small bond was made between the three. In the blink of an eye the football arced skyward as the boundary umpire threw the ball in and the game was back on.

Glenn James is a proud Aboriginal man with an interesting family history:

> I'm Yorta Yorta man whose mob are located on the Murray and Goulburn Rivers and both on my Mum and Dad's side. Mum is a total Aboriginal but my father is bit of a mixture. My Dad's father was a Mauritian and he came to Australia and married an Aboriginal lady who was my grandmother, Ada Cooper. His name was Thomas Shadrach James. He was training to be a doctor at University of New South Wales but he got the shakes halfway through and that was a no-no. He then went to a place called Barmah in Victoria which is right on the river between Moama and Nathalia. He became the headmaster of the school, the herbalist, the doctor and the minister. He was out of this world in terms of what he did for the community at that time up there. My mother come from a place called Moonaculla which is further up into New South Wales near Deniliquin and Dad grew up on the mission at Barmah across the river at Cummeragunja.[138]

Born in 1946, James was raised in the Shepparton area and has very fond memories of growing up there:

> There is fourteen kids in our family. I grew up in Shepparton and Mooroopna. I can still remember the sight when I was 5 or 6 from the highway. Quite often we'd go and play on the highway and you'd look back and you could see the smoke coming up out of the chimney of each dwelling on the river. It was just a great memory. It was a completely different world to how things are now.[139]

Despite the hardships, James' father worked all his life, something which became the springboard for the children's work ethic later in life. Every member of the fourteen children was engaged in regular employment, which was a reflection of the true inspiration from their Dad's example:

> My Dad was a labourer at the Ardmona cannery which was probably 5 to 6 miles [8 to 9.5 km] away from where we lived and he rode his bike across the highway for twenty-four years. He was the first Aboriginal guy in the Goulburn Valley to work at one place for twenty years. I remember when I was 9 we moved out of the shanty and into a rented house in town on Anzac Avenue.[140]

James remembers sports, especially football, were played eagerly by the local boys, both black and white:

> My earliest memories were we used to play football every Sunday in the local paddock. All the kids would come around, my brothers, and their mates. The rules were that if you weren't picked to play you'd have to go and get a sixpence [5 cents] worth of bikkies from the shop. Biscuits came in tins in those days. Your big brother would give you a clip in the ear if the shopkeeper put the dry biscuits in the tin and not the sweet ones. That was my first memory of playing competitive football in the paddocks and the vacant blocks within and around Anzac Avenue. It was just neighbourhood games. Us black kids we never shunned a white kid from playing with us ever, but there were lots of occasions when those kids' parents wouldn't allow us to their place. I can remember going to people's places after school and they would go in and ask their Mum if we could play and the kid would come out and say, 'Mum's said you've got to go home.' That happened continually.[141]

From these situations James started to understand how racial differences were impacting upon him and others around him:

> As I got a bit older, like towards grade 5 or 6, you started to understand that this was a them-and-us situation. We became quite friendly with all the Italians and the Macedonians and the Greeks and all those sorts who were in the same sort of boat as us. We got on because they were getting treated like we were.[142]

It was with school football that James began to see how sport could help change people's viewpoints:

> I guess that all changed with the next competitive level in football when I was eleven or twelve when footy started to be competitive

for me in my life. In the primary school team we never lost a game of football. We won close games and there was this fantastic bond between the whole lot of us.[143]

From his early teenage years, the discipline his mother and father had instilled in him was to benefit James. This was aided by going to church and listening to Pastor Doug Nicholls, a man who had become an icon to many Indigenous Australians:

> We'd go to church because Pastor Doug Nicholls would come up to the Church of Christ at Mooroopna and to us he was a cult hero. We'd jump on the bus and go over there on the Sunday night. It was just one of those things that we were lucky to have. I remember him having a long and enduring fight for his people. For him to keep standing up after being knocked down was amazing. He saw how people were treated simply because of the colour of their skin and were put into missions and how children were taken from their families. He was fighting for all that to cease but in the end the only consolation and solace he got was from the Aboriginal people themselves. They supported him through all that.[144]

The next phase of James's life would see him face considerable challenges and eventually lead him to the role of football umpiring:

> I played for Lemnos in the Goulburn Valley League. They were a team in Shepparton. It was formed and run by Greeks from Lemnos Island. I played with Lemnos under-17s and then when I was 18, I went and played two years with a team called Wunghnu. Then I got called up in '68 for National Service. I did basic training at Puckapunyal, core training in Sydney, jungle training at Canungra in Queensland and then went to Vietnam for a year and then I came back home in 1970. I come back from Vietnam in June and started playing again and I got my jaw broken in the last home game from a king-hit. By the start of the next season it hadn't mended properly and the doctor said you've got to give it away for a year. I had been umpiring the kids in the morning and playing footy in the afternoon, so I thought I might as well keep umpiring and that's when my umpiring career kicked in.[145]

James found immediate success, despite his recalling of the first time he bounced a ball in match:

In my first game I bounced the ball straight into my forehead. I nearly knocked myself out. I could see stars. The players actually stopped playing to see if I was alright. In my first year I umpired a third's grand final in the Picola footy league and that year I won the best first-year umpire. I won a pair of umpiring boots for it. Then in '72, I umpired a couple of grand finals around the Murray Football League in the seconds. I'd been umpiring a game of footy and a VFL umpiring observer was there to watch another guy in respect to him going into the VFL Seniors. He saw me and said that I was better than the bloke he wanted to see. He said, 'Have you ever thought of umpiring in Melbourne?' The guys who I was working with at the time, some of them decided to become teachers. I thought I might do that too. So I came down to Melbourne and did a course at college and after my two years of teacher training I got placed at Box Hill in Melbourne.[146]

With a focus on becoming a teacher, a senior umpiring role in his sights and a happy-go-lucky attitude, James was well on his way to becoming a success. But James also felt the full weight of the VFL Umpires Board in 1973, which saw him suspended for the first four weeks of the home-and-away round:

I went and had an interview with the VFL Board and the Umpires Board and they said, 'Yeah we'll accept you.' But then I got four weeks' suspension before the season even started. They had a meeting planned at the umpires' offices. I was late because I couldn't find a car park. There was an accident on the way and it was absolutely pouring with rain as it does in Melbourne and I kept driving around. In the end I went home unable to find the meeting venue. The next day at school there was a call from the VFL, Mr Frank Leverett, who was the secretary of the VFL Reserve Grade umpires and in charge of all the local competitions in the metropolitan leagues. He said, 'You've been suspended for the first four weeks of the season.'[147]

Despite this setback James worked hard over the next few years to be promoted to the senior umpires and worked around country competitions, something he revelled in. He proved himself in these competitions and still distinctly remembers his first senior VFL game:

My first game it was just fantastic. It was Fitzroy and Footscray out at VFL Park in 1977. It was on my daughter's 9th birthday. Dennis Collins picked it up from the middle of the ground and he was on the edge of the square and he handballed it to Bernie Quinlan and Bernie banged it through from about seventy metres out at VFL Park. Running back to the centre I think 27 seconds had gone on the board and I knew straight away that this was a different type of footy, this was a different game. It was just at that tempo all day and it stayed there. I performed pretty well in my first game and I stayed in for the rest of the season.[148]

From 1977 on, Glenn James became one of the most popular umpires in the league, despite the fact he was regularly abused based on his identity. Perhaps the reason he was able to handle many of the players was due to a very simple strategy, rapport:

Wherever I went to umpire a game of footy, whether it be Wagga in the South West Footy League or the Diamond Valley League I knew everybody's nickname by quarter time. Whether it was Badger, Springer or Spinner, because if you knew them by their nickname then you had them eating out of your hand.[149]

He continues:

The other things that stood me in really good stead was I understood the frustrations about playing because I played footy at a senior level. Also I had really good hand–eye coordination as do most Indigenous players. I had some fantastic games of footy in the country, everybody just made you so welcome and you had a good time. This was a huge learning curve as sometimes it meant you had to sit in the pub on your lonesome waiting for the taxi to pick you up and the home team were beaten by a point. What better character-building situation could you have? I grew up ever so quickly.[150]

Another time James recalls starting a game late due to a heavyweight title bout:

It was a final in the Hampden League and Joe Frazier was fighting Muhammad Ali and I went in to inspect the boots and here's both teams sitting in there watching the fight before the game. I went in there and both the captains come up and said can we start the game ten or fifteen minutes later? 'No worries as long as you don't take that stuff out on the ground,' I said. So when we started it was at ten to three instead of two-thirty and they just played a fantastic game of footy.[151]

The pinnacle of James's career came in the early 1980s with his first grand final:

> My first grand final was 1982 and it was Carlton and Richmond at the MCG. It was just something special in your life. You get told by the League that you will umpire the game but you get sworn to secrecy. I rang my brother in Shepparton and it was in the Shepparton paper first thing next morning. I remember going to school the next morning and the principal said we've got a special assembly Friday morning and that was to announce that I had the grand final. It was the result of a lot of hard work by lots of people, my kids and wife and I wanted to make it just a normal day but then I went to the game, it kicks in big time then.[152]

He recalls the match:

> I can remember the whole game virtually. As the game started it was raining at one end and the sun was shining at the other. Carlton kicked three goals in a couple of minutes. Jimmy Jess knocked Ken Hunter out. The grand final, like all the finals are played at a different level so you just have to be on your mettle and we performed fantastically in that grand final I thought.[153]

Having umpired from 1977 to 1985 and controlling 166 games of football, Glenn James is in a unique position to talk about those issues that impacted upon him as well as the Indigenous players who played in that era. James's experiences of umpiring have enabled him to develop many friendships over time and it has been through football that he has seen barriers break down:

> I just like talking to people. It basically just tells them that you are the same sort of person that they are. You like a beer, you like a bet, you like to talk with girls, you like to be friendly and it just breaks down so many barriers. I mean as Aboriginal people I think we have a uniqueness about us that non-Indigenous [people] don't have. That is we can go from one end of this country to another and see another Aboriginal person and we can start talking to them immediately as if we have known them all our life.[154]

It is this sense of camaraderie that James recalls from the Indigenous Team of the Century ceremony:

It was just so fantastic to be recognised with all those great sportsman over such a long period of time. I felt really proud because there was a lot of the people who played and were in it [the VFL] a long time that didn't get any recognition. I was able to enjoy the respect that they should have been given. I thought that was just a fantastic day. The people who made that team, they didn't just make the team, those blokes were paving the way and everybody embraced that and they respected that and understood it.[155]

James believes there is still much to be done in trying to raise the issues that Indigenous people face in the broader society, and football is just one area that is trying to do this. He admits that more needs to be done by other sports:

I think there's totally a lack of understanding and ignorance when it comes to Indigenous issues in Australia. People generalise about Aboriginal people too much. I believe these guys [Indigenous Australians] are our living treasures. I want to see Aboriginal people doing more things and in more cases promoting our country for things other than the Olympic Games or big events. I want more Indigenous people to be recognised. We have some terrific and talented people who play in all sorts of sports. The only sports that we really haven't got anyone in, is swimming, cricket and tennis apart from Evonne Goolagong [Cawley]. But you look at all the other sports that Aboriginals take part in and they are good at it. They just want to be part of it.[156]

James continues:

I guess politicians have got to take some of the blame. I mean we should have better administered funds and grants so we can set up a thing so we can teach people to be accountants and lawyers and doctors. I think that politicians need to get off their hands and make sure that these things can happen. I just want to see things becoming better for our people. They're just basic civil rights. Times have been tough but we as proud Indigenous Australians have been tough as well and we can do.[157]

Recalling his life, James is very grateful to the opportunities that football has has afforded him and how he has been able to follow a pathway that is not readily linked with Indigenous achievement:

Football was an outlet for us, a springboard for our lives really. When I was umpiring, [abuse] came and went. But I was conditioned to all that stuff from the time I was born…but I gave as good as I got. I would talk to players behind the play and try to have a laugh sometimes to take the pressure off. I didn't understand that so many Aboriginal people in the community were so proud of me. I do now.[158]

JIM KRAKOUER

RECORD

1977–1991

Games: 244: Claremont 88; North Melbourne 143; St Kilda 13
Goals: 450: Claremont 214; North Melbourne 229; St Kilda 7
State: Western Australia 7
Premierships: Claremont 1981
Simpson medal: 1981
Club Best and Fairest: North Melbourne 1986
Club Leading Goalkicker: North Melbourne 1983, 1986, 1988
All-Australian: 1987
North Melbourne Team of the Century (interchange)

'There'd be a footy around most times because we used to have a lot of relations and that in town and if we didn't have a footy we went to their place and they'd have one. Either we'd kick around home or we would go to the reserve and just get out in the paddocks and put your shirts for the goals [at] each end and have a good little rough-and-tumble game.'

Jim Krakouer

On 13 October 1958, Jim Krakouer and Janie Pickles were born in the Mount Barker, Western Australia, regional hospital, a few minutes apart. The common bond of a birthday would see them remain friends for life. For Janie and Jim, however, these common threads were in contrast to the different circumstances that both their families came from. Pickles was from an established farming family and a prefect in primary school. Her father was a prominent member of the Mount Barker community, President of the primary school's Parents' and Citizens' Association and on the board of the Mount Barker Co-op. Jim Krakouer, on the other hand, had spent his formative childhood days growing up on a reserve a few miles out of town, next to the railway line and adjacent to the stockyards. For the families who lived there, there was no running water or electricity and the Krakouer family home consisted of kerosene tins that had been flattened and made into a shelter. Krakouer's father, Eric, was a shearer and his mother Phoebe would raise thirteen children.

One day at primary school Janie and Jim found themselves sitting together outside their classroom on the jarrah bench. Both had been sent outside for mucking around during class. For Jim this was a regular occurrence, one that would see him sent up to the main office where the principal would punish him with the cane. Janie had never been sent outside before and was fearful of how she would broach the issue with her parents. She was on the verge of tears. Janie turned to Jim; he was composed and relaxed as he stared out at the schoolyard. The principal, Mr McGuiness, walked up to them. He stopped and stood in front of the two students. Janie was about to break down when McGuiness spoke, 'Well, well, well, if it isn't Master Krakouer again. What have we done this time?' he asked rhetorically. 'It's okay Janie, you can go inside now. Come with me, Krakouer. I would have thought that by now you could at least be by yourself without having a minder.' As Mr McGuiness grabbed Jim by the upper arm and escorted him towards his office, Jim turned back towards Pickles and winked. It was a knowing wink and Janie knew that Jim, the boy with whom she shared so much, would not lag on her and would take the punishment for both of them.

For many people in the football world, the name Krakouer epitomises much of what is celebrated and marvelled about with Indigenous footballers. Seamless play, timing, skill, speed and what has become known as the x-factor. Jim and Phillip Krakouer's arrival at the WAFL in the late 1970s and the VFL in the early 1980s was significant because it changed the way people saw the game being played. While there had been Indigenous players in the WAFL before, none had played in a way that was so complementary or so devastating. Their recruitment into the VFL saw this became even more pronounced as it was the first time that two Indigenous players had been recruited as a package to play in the same team. They exploded onto the football scene in Melbourne in 1982. Today it is not so incredible to see a cohort of Indigenous players on an AFL list, but prior to 1982 such a simultaneous recruitment had never been seen. Jim Krakouer's story starts in the late 1950s in the deep south of Western Australia:

> I'm a Noongar, which is in the southwest of Western Australia at a place called Mount Barker near Albany.[159]

Jim remembers Mount Barker was a great place to grow up:

> Life was pretty simple down there. [I] had a lot of brothers and sister and cousins to play with. Life was real simple. It did not seem hard at all. We'd go looking for fruit, apples mainly, catch gilgies [small freshwater crayfish] and all that type of stuff. I remember Dad just as a hard worker and Mum just looking after a pretty large family.[160]

Despite the difficulties of life on a reserve, the Krakouer family was a happy one with Eric and Phoebe providing a stable family environment. Eric's time was broken between Mount Barker and Narrogin, in the wheatbelt, where he had a shearing run. This would sometimes see the young Krakouer family spend a few months of each year in the heart of the wheatbelt. Jim remembers Eric going shearing 'but sometimes Mum and all us used to go up to school in Narrogin, and when the shearing season finished we would go back to Mount Barker'.[161]

For Jim and Phillip, a football became a companion that accompanied them everywhere:

> There'd be a footy around most times because we used to have a lot of relations and that in town and if we didn't have a footy we went to their place and they'd have one. Either we'd kick around home or we would go to the reserve and just get out in the paddocks and put your shirts for the goals [at] each end and have a good little rough-and-tumble game.[162]

He continues:

> If we had to go to town and had a footy we'd pick out a target and just practise our kicking like that. We would kick through the gap of two trees and wherever it landed on the other side the other one would take his shot.[163]

Jim recalls his first football memory and his affiliation with the North Mount Barker Football Club:

> Playing nippers for North Mount Barker, Ginger Sounness was our coach. I would have been around 8. Football was just something we did. It was seasonal in that way, cricket in the summer and footy in the winter. It was just something we did for fun. I loved my sports. I loved basketball and cricket but it was 'footy first' for me. I loved footy because I was better at it. North were a good footy club and my Dad was a good player for them. Dad played for North all his footy life and that saw me and Phil head that way.[164]

As Jim and his younger brother Phillip were making a name for themselves as junior footballers in the Great Southern Football League (GSFL), what sticks in Jim's mind was the chance to go to Perth with a family friend to see the 1970 WAFL grand final between South Fremantle and Perth. For the 12-year-old Jim Krakouer it was a chance to watch his idol, Barry Cable, play:

> Yeah it was a good little experience. I'd hardly ever been to Perth before and [I'd] never seen a league game in Perth so it was all new. Big crowds, just the experience to come up and see a game like that was good.[165]

Returning home, Jim set about to be the best footballer he could and, along with his brother Phil, became a stand-out player in the GSFL. Success on the football field was curtailed when problems at school saw Jim come into contact with the authorities and he was sent away to the Mount Lawley Reception Home for 'at risk' youth:

> I'd been in trouble a few times fighting around. I remember we had a faction sports and I had a fight with one kid; I was 13 or 14 and they sent me away for that.[166]

Once released and back home, Jim's reputation as a footballer was nothing short of remarkable. In 1974, at the age of 16, Jim made his league debut for the North Mount Barker Football Club and he kicked five goals. The following year, despite missing a third of the season due to time in jail, he took out all the local awards. In 1976, the coach of WAFL Claremont Club, Mal Brown, was on a recruitment drive and this would prove to be Jim's path out of Mount Barker and an antidote to his trouble. Jim recalls the time:

> I had not a bad year in the country and then Mal Brown from Claremont came down. Brownie was coaching at the time and we had a yarn and decided to come up the next year and have a crack. I didn't know anything about much else and I probably would have stayed down in the country. I didn't know much about Perth football let alone Melbourne footy…It was all a bit far away.[167]

Early in 1977, Jim Krakouer made the move to Perth to try his luck in the WAFL. He found he was dealing with new experiences, where everyday activities were unfamiliar and his family was hundreds of miles away. He recalls:

> It was pretty hard. We used to try and get back as much as we could to [Mount] Barker. I had always been around the family and Perth was a lot different to the country. Everything was new, bigger and busier. There were more people. [I] just had to get used to it.[168]

Despite being a big football name in the GSFL, Krakouer realised quickly that he was new to the club, and the WAFL, and he needed to establish himself as a colts player first and foremost, and then try and work his way into the reserves and league sides:

> I was pretty nervous as I come from the country and I had to try and start a career. Training was a step up. I guess you had to start off down

the bottom. Start off in your age group and then just see what happens from there. I'd have probably been happy enough to play in the colts that year and see what eventuated out of that.[169]

Krakouer's first colts coach was Syd Dufall, a traditional, old-style coach. One day after a game where Krakouer had not played well Dufall singled him out for his lacklustre performance:

> I was nearly going to chuck it. I mustn't have played that good that day. Old Syd Dufall he came out and said that I came up with a big reputation and got stuck into me a bit. I was nearly going to give it away that day. I don't know what made me stay but it's good that I did.[170]

With the Claremont league side struggling, Krakouer was encouraged by the coaching panel to have a good game. This included the 1977 Brownlow medal winner and Claremont captain–coach, Graham Moss. He duly responded and was selected to play league football for Claremont against Subiaco. Krakouer reflects:

> Once I'd been able to play seniors, I just wanted to keep playing for Claremont because of the higher challenge to play against the better players.[171]

The following year, Jim was joined by his younger brother Phillip and they made many people in the football world take notice. Playing in complementary roles, Jim as starting rover and Phil as a wing-cum-half-forward, they were able to capitalise on their intimate knowledge of the way the other played. Media reports began talking about 'Krakouer magic'. For the brothers there was no magic involved, just confidence. Midway through the 1978 season, opposing sides were trying a range of tactics to break the Krakouer playing unit, such was their playing potency. This took various forms of both physical and verbal pressure; on many occasions, both. As Jim bore the brunt of the abuse, he also became a regular at the WAFL tribunal. Jim explains:

> I'm not sure when it started but early on in my career it was pretty bad. It was another step up from the country as no one said those things to me down there. I found it difficult being an adult and having adults saying things. It was pretty hard to take.[172]

He continues:

I guess when people have said anything racist about me I just get
wild straight away and retaliate. Probably because from schooldays
you used to get sick of people calling you names and I'd just get wild
straight away.[173]

If the pressure on the Krakouers to perform came in many guises it did not
seem to curtail the impact they were having. Jim came into contention for state
selection and he was picked in his first game against South Australia in 1979
where he was named in the forward pocket and one of the best players for
Western Australia. As the seasons progressed the Krakouer brothers' profile
increased, making them targets for prospective VFL clubs. The two main clubs
vying for the Krakouers' signatures were Geelong and North Melbourne. When
they signed in 1981, the Krakouers were two of the biggest recruits ever to come
to Melbourne, with the deal estimated in the vicinity of $750,000. The money
was important, but so too was the way the contract was drawn up. The added
bonus was that Krakouer's boyhood idol, Barry Cable, was coaching North
Melbourne:

It was very close. The money was more or less the same but North
Melbourne's was guaranteed and Geelong's was sort of a performance-
based contract. So North Melbourne's was guaranteed and I think
they knew that Cabes was going to take over as coach so that sort of
helped to persuade us too.[174]

Before leaving to go to Melbourne the Krakouers played in the 1981 WAFL
grand final. Both Jim and Phil helped steer Claremont to victory with the Tigers
running out winners over their highly fancied rival, South Fremantle. Jim, who
had kicked 1.1 in the grand final, the same as in his first game for Claremont,
reflected on his time in the WAFL, 'We'd given our best to Claremont and we
sort of had to move on to another challenge.'[175]

In 1982, with the Krakouers' arrival in Melbourne, the North Melbourne
team boasted players from their 1970s glory days, with names like Malcolm
Blight, Arnold Briedis, Gary Dempsey, Ross Glendinning, Keith Greig and
Wayne Schimmelbusch. Jim Krakouer took this all in his stride:

I wasn't really intimidated by the champion players with the big
names. You just hope that you could try to prove yourself and be
amongst them. It was sort of an honour playing alongside the players
with names.[176]

The transition to Melbourne also seemed to mirror a general ease that Jim and Phil made moving into the VFL competition:

> We were pretty lucky really. I think the hardest move was when we left Mount Barker to come to Perth. Then when we went over there [Melbourne] it wasn't as hard and we adjusted pretty well straight away.[177]

With everything set in place, the Krakouers began to show the Victorian football-going public what all the fuss was about. In Jim's first VFL/AFL match against a strong Richmond side, it took no longer than ten seconds for Jim Krakouer to score a goal with his first kick. Finishing the game with 4 goals and Phil kicking 1, the Krakouers were on their way to establishing themselves as a football force in the VFL, a situation that would last a decade.

Throughout the 1980s, North Melbourne's form was erratic and it was the skills of the Krakouers that saw the turnstile at Arden Street ticking over. The Krakouers were consistent contributors in that decade, and they shared North Melbourne's leading goal-kicking award five times. They regularly played state football and Jim won the 1986 Syd Barker award as North Melbourne's Best and Fairest. A news article in *The Herald* surfaced in May 1987 discussing the statistics and the brothers' form. It drew the conclusion that when the Krakouer brothers played together, and were not out due to injury or suspension, North Melbourne won 62 per cent of their games. Such was the impact of their combined abilities, Sydney Swans President Dr Geoffery Edelsten offered North Melbourne $1,000,000 for the brothers. The offer was declined.

Jim's recollections of playing in the VFL and against some quality opposition are positive ones:

> Most of the teams had really good players who were in the resting pocket. Carlton had Wayne Harms and Des English, Hawthorn had Michael Tuck. Shane Kerrison for Collingwood was a champion player. And Geelong had Ian Nankervis and Neville Bruns. With Neville Bruns whenever we played I thought we had a good little duel and just played fair footy with no scragging. With Neville it was just a fair, hard contest.[178]

With senior North Melbourne coach John Kennedy retiring from the position in 1989, and Wayne Shimmelbusch taking over the coaching duties in the newly established AFL in 1990, Jim found himself on the outer. With Phil battling a knee injury, Jim decided to try his luck with St Kilda. The choice of his new club was no random selection; rather it was a measured consideration. He thought that of all the sides in the competition St Kilda was the side that offered the most, and recalls:

> I just thought they had a side that could go places with big Plugger Lockett, Stewie Loewe, Nicky Winmar, Burke and Harvey. I thought they were a good chance to make the finals.[179]

Despite his first game, where he had 36 possessions for the Saints against Footscray, Jim's two seasons at Moorabbin would yield only 13 games and 7 goals in total, as injury and suspension took their toll. The years out of football would see Jim convicted of a serious drug-trafficking offence where he served nearly nine years in jail. Yet despite his transgression, he was recognised in the Indigenous Team of the Century and he is very grateful for having been selected. He recalls the ceremony at Crown Casino:

> It was nice to be recognised for something, for your ability. You'll probably look back later in life and appreciate it more. It makes you feel proud. It's a big achievement to be awarded. It was good to see all those champion players and what they had done.[180]

These days Jim is taking advantage of the mining boom in Western Australia:

> I'm working up at Karratha at the moment. I have been up there for a few years now and things are going well. I was a trade assistant for a few companies and they are involved in the LNG gas plant. The works has been good. The money is good and its good to be involved in the mining industry and get lots of opportunities.[181]

Jim is very mindful of these opportunities given that his education went only to Year 10 and that past policies have also impacted upon his life:

> We weren't recognised as a race until the late '60s [1967 referendum]. I'm a bit saddened by that and a bit angry. It made you feel like you were second class. It was pretty hard growing up in racist towns. I guess I could have done better at it [education]. I used to like maths and I was pretty good at it. I look back on it now and it would have been good to go on to fourth and fifth years and get a better education. I was 15 and in third-year high school and once that finished I left.[182]

The legacy the Krakouer brothers have left is massive. Jim and Phil Krakouer played football from their early childhood and developed a deep understanding of one another's way of playing; football was just part of their everyday activities. But their skills were so enmeshed that their seamless play both confounded and excited people, especially in the early 1980s in the VFL. Football followers in Victoria had never seen this type of phenomenon before. It was a once-in-a-lifetime occurrence and, despite the influx of Indigenous players into the AFL, it has not been seen since.

MICHAEL McLEAN

RECORD

1983–1997

Games: Total games not available: Footscray 95; Brisbane Bears 88

Goals: Total goals not available: Footscray 23; Brisbane Bears 17

State: Northern Territory 5

Captain: Indigenous Allstars (Inaugural) 1994

Coach: Indigenous Allstars 2002, 2005, 2007; Territory Thunder (Inaugural): AFLQ

Club Best and Fairest: Brisbane Bears 1991, 1993

All-Australian: 1988

Brisbane Lions Hall of Fame

AFLNT Legend Hall of Fame

'I recall it was pretty difficult moving. I was only used to going away for a week at a time on footy trips so to go to Melbourne you start to realise that you're actually packing a big suitcase, with everything in it. It wasn't just the team tracksuit and your boots, you were taking the lot.'

Michael McLean

In early 1983 when Michael McLean walked into the weights room at the Western oval. It was around 8 am. He had gone to the gym early because he wanted to miss the other Footscray players who were now his team-mates. Being shy, McLean was way out of his comfort zone. To make matters worse, Melbourne was a very different world to Darwin, and McLean felt unsettled and uncomfortable.

The day before he had meandered around the club trying to take it all in. Walking through the clubrooms, he stepped into the gym, which was three-quarters full of Bulldogs players. Some acknowledged him, others did not. Blokes like Doug Hawkins winked and joked around as they worked in the gym while others concentrated hard on the task of building their bodies. McLean sat down and watched some of the players bench-pressing. McLean had never used weights before. The main football ingredients he had needed in Darwin were speed and skill and McLean had these in spades. McLean would come to understand that in Melbourne speed and skill will only get you so far; strength was the key. Sitting in the gym, McLean watched intently as the players took the bar loaded up with heavy metal plates on either end and eased it down to their chests. They pumped out ten smooth repetitions. 'Nothing to it,' McLean told himself. But here he stood, the following day, at the same bench with the same weights, not really knowing what he was doing.

He sat on the bench and tentatively lay back. He looked up at the stainless steel bar and placed his hands on it, making sure they were in a straight line with his shoulders. McLean took a deep breath and pushed the bar up over the lip of the metal stand. It felt good. He slowly lowered the bar. Just as his elbows started to bend, McLean felt like the room was pressing in on him. His arms gave way and the bar landed on his chest with a jolt. As his body tensed he tried to push the bar up again. He huffed and puffed uncomfortably, feeling as if he was going to be crushed. McLean tried to get up, and in doing so tilted the bar. The metal plates on the right fell off, crashing into the floor. Just as quickly the plates fell off the left side, resulting in more metal crashing onto the concrete.

The Bulldogs' property steward ran in from the adjoining office and saw a red-faced McLean with a embarrassed grin on his face. 'You alright son?' he asked. McLean nodded wearily. 'Best we get the conditioning coach to show you what to do before you drop something on your toes. Not even Teddy Whitten could play on one foot.' McLean nodded shyly. His journey into the tough world of football had only just begun.

Meeting Michael McLean for the first time, it is hard to believe that he was once a scrawny kid who struggled in the weights room. In the Darwin coffee shop, McLean seems to be chiselled out of hardwood from years of gym work. McLean is relaxed and happy to talk about his life in football and his family life growing up in the far north:

> When I grew in Darwin I thought I was a mixture of Thursday Island and Torres Strait Island and Aboriginal. I've only just recently found out that I'm from the Yadhaigana people from far North Queensland. For my family it was never an issue as you had a mixture of everything. Mum's from the Torres Strait, her mother is from Shelburne Bay which is just off the top of the far north [Qld]. Dad's a white man from Homehill, Townsville. My grandmother on my Mum's side is Aboriginal; her husband, my granddad, was Indonesian. He used to travel across by sea and he got caught for smuggling guns back in the day. They had thirteen kids together and one of them, my Mum, her maiden name was Tatipata who are very well renowned up on Thursday Island.[183]

McLean was born and bred in Darwin and during his formative childhood years had plenty of time on his hands. As McLean's father was an avid believer in the benefits of physical activity, some of his earliest memories are of playing sport:

> As far as a family goes we were very sporty. My Dad was heavily into boxing and Rugby League. Mum and Dad weren't into Aussie Rules. Dad was a fisherman, he was out every school holidays and Mum virtually bought us up in town. We spent a fair bit of time playing

different codes and we did a bit of boxing, a bit of athletics, bit of Rugby League and Aussie Rules. It was just to keep the boredom out and to stay out of trouble I guess. Mum just encouraged us to get out there and play and to fill our day up and burn ourselves out. I don't think Mum realised how good we were you know, as far as sporting feats went. It was just to keep us busy.[184]

McLean's earliest memories of football was playing with his mates in Darwin:

I remember playing at primary school level and getting picked up in the back of a ute by our coach, John Hodson. There'd be fifteen of us in the back of a ute; we used to get picked up. Uncle Johnny used to come around and tap on the window and I used to be up with me boots on and ready to go, hair everywhere, and jump in the back with the rest of the guys and go down to the ground.[185]

As McLean grew older, he started to excel in football, Rugby League and boxing and was faced with making a decision about what he would concentrate on:

It was a hard one for me. I don't know why I chose footy. Still to this day I think and I wonder if I would have made it in Rugby League. Dad always wanted me to box because I had ten fights as a young fella and won them all. I represented the Territory in different footy codes and Rugby League was one of my passions as well. I used to be a five-eighth. I had an option of going to the Balmain Tigers. They came up to have a look at me. I had to make a decision. Dad wanted me to go to Rugby League because he was a Queenslander and I ended up saying to him, 'No I'm going to go to the VFL', because I just probably enjoyed it more. I'm not sure why because I won plenty of awards playing Rugby League. That's the path I took and I have no regrets at all.[186]

McLean's pathway through football was set from the junior clubs he played with which were close to his schooling and community:

I grew up at Milner. Did primary school at Milner Primary. Then I played with Waratahs Football Club as a junior. I was twelve years old, playing under-16s at the time and then we moved back to Milner and I went to Nightcliff High. I then played with Nightcliff Tigers as a junior and then played A-grade at fifteen.[187]

From here McLean's football success went to another level as he began to make it into representative sides, and this brought him to the attention of the VFL scouts:

> I had made a couple of representative sides in several of the national carnivals. I was picked for Territory sides for the Teal Cup and state schoolboys. I actually captained the schoolboys' side in 1980 and I got runner-up best in the carnival. I had North Melbourne chasing me. Essendon and Richmond were showing a bit of interest and a heap of South Australian and West Australian clubs. I went down for a possibles/probables game with two or three other guys in the school-holiday period for North Melbourne and they looked after us really well. I met Malcolm Blight and he gave me his jumper. I think they were chasing a few Indigenous guys like the Krakouer brothers. But then they went for Peter Jonas. I ended up going on a Form Four to Footscray.[188]

McLean's relocation to Melbourne was difficult, and probably by today's standards, a little unsophisticated:

> I recall it was pretty difficult moving. I was only used to going away for a week at a time on footy trips so to go to Melbourne you start to realise that you're actually packing a big suitcase, with everything in it. It wasn't just the team tracksuit and your boots, you were taking the lot. I'd just got a girlfriend Linda who is now my wife. I had not met anyone from the Club, just a recruiting person that spotted me playing in the national carnival. I had a few phone calls and then he said that they'd like to sign me up on a Form Four. I got to Melbourne, Tullamarine, and the first guy I met had a Bulldogs t-shirt on. His name was Garry Merrington, he was a football manager at Footscray. I went and stayed at his house and I remember I went into the bedroom, closing the door and just burst into tears.[189]

Settling in was going to prove the hardest thing for McLean. Before he had played one game for the Bulldogs, he needed to work out how he fitted into the club and deal with some of the more unsavoury aspects of club culture:

> When I ventured to Melbourne in '82 at 16, I was touted as a young football star. It was the first time I'd been exposed to racism. It was a bit new to me but I'd copped a fair bit of racism from day one. In

RECORD

1985–1999

Games: 309: South Fremantle 58; St Kilda 230; Western Bulldogs 21
Goals: Total goals not available: St Kilda 283; Western Bulldogs 34
State: Western Australia 8
Club Best and Fairest: St Kilda 1989, 1995
Club Leading Goalkicker: St Kilda 1988, 1991
All-Australian: 1995
St Kilda Team of the Century (wing)

‘We grew up watching our uncles and relatives playing. We idolised our uncles and fathers. I had uncles that were great footballers. My Dad was a shearer and worked on the farms and he wanted something else for me. He trained me and developed me and I just went out there and just worked hard in my training. ’

Nicky Winmar

[When] you played footy everybody wanted to be your friend, everybody loved you, everybody cared for you and when your footy's finished nobody wants to know you.[199]

In the winter of 2008 in the southwest of Western Australia, a unique event took place. At 7:25 am in a shearing shed somewhere near Katanning, it seemed like any other day. As the shearers were loading up their handpieces and oiling their equipment, the wool-presser and his dog were busily pushing sheep into the catching pen for the morning run. The rouseabouts were standing around reading *The West Australian* and having a smoke, trying to stay warm in the chilly May air. The wool-classer, having added up the shearers' tallies from the day before, went over to the shearing shed door and peered out. He looked at his watch. The new rouseabout was cutting it a bit thin, he thought, given the shearers usually dragged their first 'client' out onto the board at 7:30 am on the dot.

The wool-classer went over to the shearing contractor who was sitting on his esky, his head buried in the newspaper. 'When is the new rousey getting here?' The contractor looked up from his paper and shrugged. 'What's his name again?' asked the classer. 'Said his name was Nicky; he sounded pretty quiet, but he was keen as mustard.' The contractor smiled, trying to allay the classer's concerns. The contractor stood up, folded up his newspaper and pushed the esky across the board and out of the way. He walked back slowly to his stand. Just a few more minutes to go before the long day started.

As the sound of the whirring shearing plants drowned out any other noise, the quiet sliding of the shearing shed door was inaudible and the man who stepped through it was not immediately noticed. The man stood near the door and waited. One of the other rouseabouts looked up and nudged the classer. Neil Elvis Winmar slowly walked over to him. 'G'day,' he said. The classer was gobsmacked, 'You're bloody...Nicky bloody Winmar!' he said. Nicky smiled and nodded nervously. 'Sorry I'm a bit late, I took a wrong turn, hey.' Even to the seasoned shearers this was something they would be able to tell their mates down the pub and their grandkids. With that the shearing shed out the back of Katanning ceased being just a normal shed because one of Australian football's most famous figures was on the board and working with them.

Nicky Winmar was born on 25 September 1965 in Kellerberrin, Western Australia. Winmar, more than any Indigenous footballer other than perhaps Michael Long, has come to occupy a distinct place in Australian football and sport by providing us with 'that' moment: the photograph of him holding up his jumper to a hostile Collingwood crowd in round four at Victoria Park in 1993 has come to symbolise Indigenous pride, survival and resistance. The photograph is compelling because it is beautifully composed, but also because it remains a watershed moment where the national discussion about Indigenous involvement in football and racism took root. In a flash it captured an action that spoke of an Indigenous place within the game and it required the public's respect and recognition. For many, it was a reply to the vitriol directed towards Winmar and Gilbert McAdam after St Kilda had won the game. This photograph, and the issues surrounding racial vilification, paved the way for a new dialogue.

I met Nicky Winmar in a hotel at 4 pm on a Thursday afternoon in an eastern working-class suburb of Perth in 2008. He had just finished work with a city council where he was doing a course on how to lay asphalt. His plan was to get his ticket and then head north and cash in on the mining boom, making roads for the big rigs. Despite rumours I had heard over the years, Winmar looked fit and he was happy to talk:

> I am Noongar. I was born in Kellerberrin. Dad's family comes from Quairading and Mum was born in Beverley. Mum and Dad got married in Doodlakine. We moved to Pingelly and grew up as a young kid there. I still remember the days of growing up on the reserve, that was good.[200]

The Pingelly Reserve was designed to house the local Noongar people who had been dispossessed of their land just before the Second World War.[201] Like many Western Australian reserves, Pingelly was located on the fringes of the towns. With strict curfews in place, if you were Aboriginal and in town between 6 pm and 6 am you would be arrested and spend the night in the police lock-up. As an example of the attitude towards Aboriginal people in the late 1960s, one Pingelly magistrate suggested that a horse whip was the best way to deal with the local Noongar population.[202] Despite this ingrained prejudice, young Nicky Winmar and his family found that football provided them with the positive drivers in their life:

> I remember being a young kid just growing up playing footy with the cousins in Pingelly and enjoying childhood life. We used to watch *The Winners* a lot on the ABC. Sometimes we just couldn't wait for the rain to come so we did it ourselves. We used to go out to the backyard and make it all muddy and slippery. [Football] was very important for the young kids. We grew up watching our uncles and relatives playing. We idolised our uncles and fathers. I had uncles that were great footballers. My Dad was a shearer and worked on the farms and he wanted something else for me. He trained me and developed me and I just went out there and just worked hard in my training.[203]

The other sport that really captured Winmar's attention was basketball, even though he did try his hand at other sports:

> I tried a bit of cricket but I was pretty terrified of the cricket ball. Swimming was terrible. Like a rock. I was better at basketball than the other sports. Cricket was too hot during the day. Basketball was played at night when it was cooler. I wanted to play footy and I played with the Pingelly Panthers. When I was fifteen I played seniors and won the Best and Fairest at that age.[204]

With his football on track, it was in the area of education that Nicky seemed to battle, a point he is very honest about:

> I struggled with schooling sometimes as a young kid. I struggled with school and going to school with the mob and hanging around with family and troublemakers. Also as an Aboriginal kid going to mixed [non-Indigenous] schools that was pretty different too.[205]

Nicky's first major football opportunity came in 1982 when Mal Brown, the coach of South Fremantle Football Club at the time and a notorious football figure, came to Pingelly to see if the rumours about Winmar were true. Brown could see that Winmar had all the attributes to make it at WAFL level and offered him the chance to move to Perth and try out with the Bulldogs:

I made the move but found it hard at first, being away from home and the family, but I kept going. I made a lot of mistakes along the way, but I got there. I missed the togetherness and being around people that we grew up with. The lifestyle we lived [in Pingelly] was just a laidback sort of working style more than the sporting style they do in WAFL and AFL. I tried to live by myself first. Found it hard when I was 17. South tried to put you up with other players and that but I don't know, I just sort of found it hard at first. I ended up living with the Collard's in Hamilton Hill [in Perth].[206]

He continues:

Being from a country town you always had family and cars to get you around. In Perth I kept going backwards and forwards between Pingelly and Perth and almost ended up losing my career through travelling back and forth too many times. I almost gave footy away and went back to Pingelly at one stage, but I kept going and played some good games with South [Fremantle].[207]

In four years in the WAFL, Winmar developed into a mercurial player with a cult following. He could run all day but also had explosive power. He was elusive, but had a good defensive side to his game. He could take great high marks and around goals he was lethal. With talk about a national competition in the mid-1980s, it was simply a matter of time before he would make it at VFL level.

With the advent of the West Coast Eagles in 1987, the new side from Perth confidently thought that Winmar would become one of their number.[208] But some very skilful recruitment from St Kilda saw Winmar move to Melbourne in 1987. Moving east brought its own challenges. Not only would Winmar be further away from family, but Melbourne was a very different city to Perth. The VFL/AFL was also a very different prospect to the WAFL:

At first I didn't know what I was doing. I went to Melbourne and I said, 'Oh no! How big is this place?' It was a big move. Sometimes I wish I'd stayed back in Perth and went to the West Coast. But I made a change in life and went to Melbourne, did the training, met a lot of good people and really felt comfortable, but it took a long time, about two or three years. I tried a couple of times to come home but they followed me and wanted me to come back [to Melbourne].[209]

At St Kilda's home ground, Moorabbin, Winmar met some of the future stars of the game, like Tony Lockett. He admitted:

> I didn't even know who Tony Lockett was at the time. St Kilda were always on the bottom [of the ladder]. I was a North Melbourne supporter and all of a sudden this guy comes up and says. 'G'day, I'm Tony Lockett.' That year he won the Brownlow medal.[210]

There would be many things in his first year that would leave Winmar slack-jawed. Like his first night-series game against Essendon and the champions he had watched on TV back in Pingelly:

> The first game I played at Waverley I run out onto the field and here's these guys, Tim Watson, [Paul] Van Der Haar, Bill Duckworth. It was a bit unsettling, what with where I came from.[211]

Winmar proved to be a boon recruit and in his first three years at St Kilda he was the runner-up to the Best and Fairest, and in 1989 he won his first Trevor Barker medal. Winmar was a complete package and revelled in the wet conditions he and his cousins had emulated in the muddy backblocks of the Pingelly Reserve. Winmar reflects on the difficulty in making the choice to pursue his football dreams:

> When I went to Melbourne, I think I had to make the move because as I got older I realised that I had to put myself before my family. They were fantastic, St Kilda, and they really looked after me and helped me out with a lot of things. They really took me in like a family.[212]

In 1990, Nicky's life took significant twists and turns as he turned to religion to help him deal with some of the issues in his life. Then, in the middle of August, he was reported for kicking and eye gouging Hawthorn tough-man Dermott Brereton and was given a ten-week suspension. It was not until Dermott Brereton admitted that he had racially vilified Winmar that the full extent of the situation become apparent. Unfortunately for Winmar, the AFL's anti-vilification laws would not come in until 1995. Sadly, the damage to his reputation would stick for many years. He reflects:

> I found it pretty upsetting and hurting at times. You know you go out there and play against these guys. Guys who you have respect for because they have worked hard through their training to get to where they want to be. You go out on the footy field and all you want to do is

just play and to be racially abused it is the most upsetting and hurtful thing that can ever happen.[213]

The vilification did not ease and nearly three years later, in the International Year of the Indigenous Person, Winmar would point to his skin in the match against Collingwood. He recalls:

> At that time at Victoria Park we went out there and did our job. We played our best. Gilbert was best on ground and I was second best and as we were walking off the field we just got hammered by the Collingwood crowd. At that time I'd just had enough. [I] just wanted to let them know. [I] not only did it for myself but for every Indigenous person.[214]

The week following the game a financial dispute between Winmar and the club saw St Kilda drop him for several weeks. Eventually the matter was reconciled but Winmar's image suffered as a consequence.

The year 1997 saw Winmar experience some of his greatest highs and lows, both on and off the field. Playing consistent football for St Kilda in a forward pocket saw him reach his 200 games, the first Indigenous player to do so. St Kilda then went on to make the grand final to play against Adelaide. Unfortunately, in the days leading up to the game Winmar's father passed away. Winmar decided to play on. In a cruel twist of fate, St Kilda lost, and Winmar had to travel home to Western Australia to bury his father. After another topsy-turvy season in 1998, he parted ways with the Saints and played out his last season in 1999 with the Western Bulldogs. At the Western Oval, Winmar kicked 34 goals from 21 games and helped the Bulldogs get to the finals. He reflects on his time with the Bulldogs:

> I was glad to have the chance to play with Terry Wallace and the Western Bulldogs. At first it was hard because I was at one club for eleven, twelve years. I wished I'd stayed and finished my footy at St Kilda but these things happen.[215]

After his time in the big leagues, Winmar became a gun-for-hire, travelling across Victoria and Australia in search of an income and, in many ways, acceptance. In sitting down with Nicky Winmar in the Perth hotel over a beer, what becomes apparent is that Winmar seems to genuinely love life, despite the challenges he has had to deal with. He knows he has made mistakes and these have cost him dearly. But he has embraced all that life has offered him and is happy to make the most of his future opportunities and not dwell on the past. He explains:

I found it hard after footy, where to go, what to do next. The employment side wasn't very great for me, education side as well. People wanted me to go back to footy and try and help other people come through the juniors but there are so many people out there doing that. Why not let them have a go and just do something else? Footy's not there forever. I just want to do something else in life which is good. I'm not involved in footy. I think being in it for most of your life, for more than thirty years, it's good to do something different. You know I might just go down and watch a local game in the suburbs somewhere. I [have] sort of made a different lifestyle after footy. Just trying to do something to be a normal person.[216]

The transition out of football has not been easy, as the glow of football fame still sees Winmar treated differently:

I just wish that sometimes I could be treated as a normal person. Everybody looks at me as a footy player. It is not a life like when you were young and the only people that ever knew you were your own family. Everybody knows who you are and you have to tread warily and be careful.[217]

What becomes apparent after spending time with Winmar is that he is one of Australian football's true individuals. In many ways the 1993 image of him is powerful because Winmar is a very shy person, but someone who stood up and did what many Indigenous Australians wanted to say, but could not. Although it captures a seemingly simple moment, it is one tied to a complex range of issues that are deeply personal, and bound up in questions of identity, struggle, history and resistance. Perhaps the reason we still talk about what Nicky Winmar did that day is because it cannot be defined or explained simply. It is both a delicately poignant moment and a statement of significant power. It can be seen in two possible ways: it is either Nicky Winmar's most public private moment or his most private public moment. Either way, the action is historic; one which will be remembered as thrilling, brave and significant. It is a comment on the times, and of Nicky Winmar 'the player', and Nicky Winmar the person.

CHRIS LEWIS

RECORD

1986–2002

Games: 268: Claremont 53; West Coast 215
Goals: Total goals not available: West Coast 259
State: Western Australia 5
Premierships: Claremont 1996; West Coast 1992, 1994
Club Best and Fairest: West Coast 1990
All-Australian: 1990
Life membership: West Coast Football Club

'I suppose we were six and seven just playing footy with a lot of my school-mates and mates that lived down the road from Mum's. There was a local footy oval and we used to play three on three on a full ground oval, which was just madness. So you'd just kick it and run.'

Chris Lewis

The first time I heard the name Chris Lewis was when I was fifteen. I was in Year 10. The week previously I had been playing for Northam High School in a final for the CIG Cup when I broke my wrist. Apart from state schoolboys, the CIG was the biggest thing in football for boys who played football in lower high school. Having made the preliminary final, Northam was set to play Christ Church Grammar School. It was a classic case of a very good country football team taking on the strongest private school in the state. I distinctly recall the coach assembling his five best players before the game and saying something like, 'They've got this player. He is very good. We need to stop him. His name is Lewis.' The stakes were high as the prize, should we win, was to play in the curtain-raiser of the Western Australian/Victorian state game the week after in front of 40,000 people. For the boys in our school's football team this was a very big deal.

As I had broken my wrist, I was the goal umpire for the game which was played on a very cold, windswept day at Bassendean Oval, home of WAFL club, Swan Districts. As the teams ran out onto the ground, the captains went to the middle of the ground and flipped the coin, which saw Christ Church kicking to my end in the first quarter. I don't remember anything much of the match except that we lost badly and 'the kid called Lewis' ran amok. He kicked goal after goal and when he was not doing that he was setting goals up and bringing others into the play.

As a consolation prize, the Northam High School football team were given free tickets to the Subiaco Oval to watch Victoria take on Western Australia. All week we ate sour grapes about our total capitulation at the hands of one player. I can't speak for the others, but as we sat there and watched Chris Lewis proceed to do the same as he had in the CIG grand final, I did not feel so bad. The guy was a freak, a champion, and I knew more than anything that he would go on to bigger and better things.

When I conducted the interview for this project, Lewis was working as an assistant coach at the Swan Districts Football Club. As we sat there in the empty upstairs bar overlooking Bassendean Oval, I jogged his memory and asked if he could recall that CIG preliminary final back when he and I were fifteen years old. He smiled and said something like, 'Yeah, Northam High yeah? I had an okay day that day I recall.'

Chris Lewis's story is in many ways one of an urban Indigenous experience. Despite both Lewis' parents coming from the country, the Lewis family were all born and raised in Perth:

> I grew up in the northern suburbs, a place called Nollamara. Mum still lives there but forty years ago it was one of the outer suburbs. I'm a Yamaji. Dad is Yamaji Widi and Mum's a Yamaji Nunda. Dad comes from Morawa and my Mum was born in Galena which is just inland from Kalbarri.[218]

For the young Chris Lewis, football was an ever-present part of his youth:

> I suppose we were six and seven just playing footy with a lot of my school-mates and mates that lived down the road from Mum's. There was a local footy oval and we used to play three on three on a full ground oval, which was just madness. So you'd just kick it and run.[219]

He goes on:

> I was a bit small for my age but I was always playing footy, so I suppose you learn to look after yourself...I just wanted to play for Claremont. I didn't think about it as a job and a career. My brothers were playing for Claremont and my Dad played for Claremont so I just wanted to go there.[220]

Irwin Lewis, Chris's father, played for several seasons with the Claremont Football Club in the WAFL. Irwin was known as a handy, no-nonsense half-back and was a member of the Tigers' 1964 premiership side. Clayton and Cameron Lewis had played league football for the Tigers, thus cementing a strong connection between the Lewis family and the Claremont Football Club.

This came about initially from the Lewis family's connection with Christ Church Grammar. In the 1950s, Irwin Lewis had been lucky enough to receive a Church of England scholarship allowing him to attend Christ Church. Irwin would go on to be the first Indigenous Australian to attend university in Australia and he went on to work in the government sector for many years. The chance to attend Christ Church is something that is not lost on Lewis, who boarded there for much of his high school years:

> Claremont gave us the opportunity to get educated at Christ Church Grammar School. It also gave me the opportunity to experience things that I wouldn't have done at Mirrabooka [local high school]. After the first few weeks when all I wanted to do was go home, I settled down and it turned out to be great.[221]

The private school experience also enabled Lewis to play several sports against highly competitive teams and individuals, helping to push him to another level:

> I played a bit of soccer. Back then it was a bit like the ethnics played that and we played footy but you know as a kid you just got into anything. Cricket was big, basketball was big too. I used to play basketball against [Luc] Longley and [Andrew] Vlahov. But through phys-ed at school you'd be opened up to a whole heap of sports. Except swimming, I didn't like swimming. [222]

The draw of football was the strongest:

> With my brothers' and family influence all I wanted was to play footy. That's still the case these days if you look at it with young players. If you look at footy the gun-play makers and the stars of the game are Indigenous so and I just thought it made an easier sort of career path for Indigenous fellas to play footy. Also it was the only way that Mum could sort of pull me into line was if she banned me from playing footy. It was just something that I wanted to do from such a young age.[223]

It was the next phase of Lewis's footy career that helped to tailor the success he found in later years. In 1985, Western Australia produced one of the strongest Teal Cup sides ever assembled. The Teal Cup was the premier under-age competition which saw the cream of each state's football talent assemble for a national carnival. Even though Lewis was under-age by a year, he was so good that he was able to stake his spot in the team that would become the nucleus of the first West Coast Eagles squad. The side included Guy McKenna, John Worsfold, Chris Waterman, Paul Peos, Allen Jakovich, Peter Sumich and Scott Watters. In the final, Western Australia would beat the Victorians by 40 points. Lewis could have played another year but declined:

> When you're in the Teal Cup you're in there to make yourself known. It's a springboard to the future...I could have played a third year and been the first player to do that but I declined because I didn't see any point. I didn't see how it was going to improve me.[224]

The following year, Lewis would make his WAFL league debut with Claremont, against West Perth. It was in the same year that the first tentative discussions were being had about Lewis's transition into the VFL. Michael Malthouse, the senior coach at Footscray, identified Lewis as potential talent and the Bulldogs decided to fly Lewis and his parents over to Melbourne for discussions:

> I went over with Mum and Dad for a chat with Footscray and we thought it was great...They looked after us well, but looking back on it I think they tried to railroad Mum and Dad a bit...It wasn't until we were buckled into our seatbelts that Mum told me what had gone on...Greg Simpson, my colts manager at Claremont, had told me: 'Whatever you do, don't pick the pen up. Always come home and think about it.'...Graham Moss who was the league coach at Claremont had the job of cranking up the Eagles' list. I was about the twentieth player signed up.[225]

Perhaps a sense of a football destiny did not really dawn on Lewis at this stage; it was just another exciting stage in his football journey:

> It was all razzle dazzle. It was like Hollywood and they wanted immediate success...It was like putting a state team together overnight. It was pretty big just to meet Ross Glendinning...[He] was a home-grown superstar...It was bloody great![226]

By any standard, Lewis had a stellar first season with the Eagles. An inaugural Eagle, and the youngest to debut until Ben Cousins played in 1996, he was selected in the VFL team-of-the-year and would kick 29 goals from nineteen games. However, despite the 'razzle dazzle', and due to his age and identity, Lewis seemed to attract verbal and physical attention. He has mixed feeling about this:

I never really experienced that stuff until I played AFL. It probably started in the first year I played in '87. So it was a bit of an eye-opener and I really did struggle with it early. Where I grew up people came from a lower class and they had a little bit of an understanding about Aboriginal people. I've come to realise that it was a bit of a compliment because of the player I was and obviously opposition sides if they could put me off my game they probably got a bit of tick from their coach. It was something that really made me a bit more passionate about my game and a bit more fiery about my heritage because I just wanted to prove to those non–Indigenous people that I was a good footballer and I was better than them because we really didn't have the vilification laws that are available today.[227]

The early 1990s brought mixed outcomes for Lewis. In 1990, under coach John Todd, he won his first club champion award, played state and was selected in the All-Australian side. In the following year he was again selected to play state but experienced great disappointment as the Eagles were beaten by Hawthorn in the grand final. Lewis also started to come under serious scrutiny from the media. This was highlighted when he was suspended for biting Todd Viney's finger. He received three weeks and his reputation suffered.

The next few years would go some way to redressing the bad reputation as the Eagles won the premierships in 1992 and 1994. Lewis's jubilation at the premiership win was enhanced because he was able to share it with several team-mates; men he had played with for a long time. In 1994 Lewis was awarded life membership to the Eagles.

In the following years Lewis's form seemed to ebb and flow in equal measure. He was picked in some state games but then lost form in 1996. He was dropped back to play WAFL with his old club Claremont where he became a valuable player when the Tigers secured a premiership. It was in the 1998 season that Lewis passed a significant milestone. He became only the second Indigenous player to play 200 AFL games, second only behind Nicky Winmar. In 1999, Lewis did not play because of a foot injury and in the following year, having played just three games, he announced his retirement.

Since retiring from football Lewis has turned his vast football experience to coaching in several states and territories:

In the last five years I've been coaching. I did two years in Darwin, coaching the Buffaloes and we had blokes like Richard Tambling and Tom Logan who plays for Port Adelaide so we had a couple of players that have gone on to become good footballers. Then I ended up moving to Ballarat and coached Sebastapol and did a couple of years coaching over there. That was a great thing for me because I got involved with the Indigenous Radio, National Radio Service, and called a bit of footy. I called two grand finals. Then my partner and me had a baby so we moved back to Perth and I'm involved with Swan Districts and the Indigenous side of things. As it turned out the coach last year [2008] Steve Turner stepped down from the senior coaching role so I ended up coaching the side for the last sixteen games. Which was a good experience but also a bad one. It was a bit like eating someone else's breakfast.[228]

Lewis continues:

Basically what I originally got involved with at the Swans was to run a football program called Kicking Goals which sponsors kids in Port Hedland and Newman. That involves going along to the school and teaching the kids about all aspects of footy. Not all of them are going to play footy but if we can keep them involved in terms of becoming qualified coaches and doing medical courses and teaching the young fellas how to umpire and how to strap it's good. Because in country towns there's a lot of people and they may be short of resources so if we can give them skills then this can alleviate some of those problems. In remote areas we emphasise the underlying values of teamwork and being able to work in a group and trying to influence younger people in terms of making better decisions for their life and that sort of stuff. It's a great gig and I get to get away from Perth once a fortnight, go out the bush and kick the footy around.[229]

Working with Indigenous communities is very rewarding for Lewis, but something that presents challenges:

Basically I'm still involved with footy but more on a development side of it where I try to give advice to the young Aboriginal kids coming through. I'm at the stage where I enjoy working with Aboriginal kids and young footballers but if they don't want to help themselves and they don't want to come half way and their family don't want to support them then it's very hard for me to be able to help them. I try to find kids that want to help themselves and want to do the best they can and I try to concentrate on those kids more than people who probably don't want to put in a 120 per cent. I try to maximise my time with trying to get them to where they want to go.[230]

The issues that many Indigenous kids face today have not been alleviated since Lewis's time in football:

The problems we face at Swans in getting the kids up from Bunbury or getting them down from the Pilbara is trying to find places for them to live, what with all the rents. Then there is the price of food and other things. When I was growing up you'd find people that always wanted to help the footy club in terms of house parents. A lot of kids they'll come and play one or two games and then they'll give it away. They'll say, 'I've played at Swan Districts and that's enough.' We have had off-field dramas which sort of stem from family quarrels and feuds that have been going on for twenty and thirty years, which is beyond me, and you see kids that potentially could be drafted getting into bloody fights.[231]

Lewis sees the breakdown of family units as the biggest issue confronting young people today:

The biggest thing for me when I was playing footy was my family support and I think that's where a lot of kids fall down, like the Mums and Dads are still feeling the effects of Stolen Generation or their parents grew up not going to school. Unfortunately they've grown up to be adults and they've got kids and they may not have the tools that allow them to push their kid in the right direction. So if you've got a kid that wants to come up and play footy and you don't have that spare twenty or thirty grand to be able to pack up house and move to Perth or Melbourne then those kids can't get the support because of the restraints that are put on them. Some parents may have social issues as well; they might be drug addicts or alcoholics so unfortunately they may not be the best role models for that kid. Then on the other hand you do get some Aboriginal people who try their hardest, which is all you can do.[232]

When Lewis reflects on his time in football it would be easy for him to rest on his laurels and think that he had done enough, but his perspective is best summed up in this quote:

I had my ups and downs along the way but the good thing about footy is that for twenty-five weeks of the year, there is always a chance to redeem yourself…When I was growing up, all I wanted to do was play footy so, basically, it was a bit of a lifeline for me to break the cycle and do something with my life.[233]

MICHAEL LONG

RECORD

1987–2001

Games: 212: West Torrens 22; Essendon 190
Goals: Total number not available: Essendon 143
Premierships: Essendon 1993, 2000
Norm Smith medal: 1993
All-Australian: 1988, 1995
Essendon Team of the Century (wing)
AFLNT Hall of Fame Legend
AFL Hall of Fame

'We all know what happened in the past and stories with Syd [Jackson] and Pastor Doug Nicholls and the unspoken stuff too. To see the legacy that was left that these guys carried, it's like that they're enriching Australia even more. It's a great celebration because sport has been our greatest ally. It's opened the eyes of thousands and changed people's minds. It's made them think about things like 'What if it happened to you? How would you feel?''

Michael Long

*Racism denies people the fundamental human right to be judged
by their character, by what is inside. This is why it is not easy to
experience a lifetime of racial abuse, be constantly reminded of
it and yet be expected to ignore it.*[234]

If Michael Long had been born in America his story would have been
turned into a film by now. It probably says something about Australia,
and Australians, that that has not occurred here, nor the significance of
his life and actions more fully understood. In many ways his is a quintessential
Australian story. It begins in the epic north of Australia, in the Tiwi Islands and
Darwin. Here, a skinny boy from a large Indigenous family learns how to hunt
with his father and brothers. He also learns from his father and brothers how
to play a code of football that captures the imagination of the nation. He plays
it so well that he feels that on some days that no one can beat him. As he grows
older he develops an inner strength and conviction that comes from the quiet
discussions he has with someone who is not there, his deceased mother. Her soft
words and strong love help him conjure up the courage and the drive to win.
Agnes Long's boy comes to be known as a big-game player, and in 1993 he wins
a premiership and a Norm Smith medal.

Then, on one of the game's biggest occasions, the first modern-day blockbuster, the 1995 Anzac Day game, that man is vilified for the thing he cannot
change, his skin colour. Unhappy with the way the mediation process went in
the weeks after the game, he sets about the long, slow task of trying to get a
nation to understand how it thinks about matters of racial discrimination. He
becomes a symbol for hope and equality, and is able to travel the country and
have people listen to him, mainly because he could play a style of football that
was simply sublime.

When he retired from the game he took on the role of an ambassador for the
AFL and became a quietly determined spokesperson for Indigenous Australians.
He returned to Darwin to live with his family. Now, every football season the

AFL celebrates its Indigenous round by recognising Indigenous participation in football and the community. All because he dared to say that to vilify him or anyone else based on their ethnicity or religious beliefs was wrong.

To understand Michael Long's story first requires an understanding of his parents' story:

> My parents were taken away as kids and put on a Catholic mission on the Tiwi Islands. They class themselves as Tiwi. My mother's from Daly River [230 km southwest of Darwin] and she is a Maranunggu woman. My father's Aumdjera [Anmatyerre], Ti Tree just north of Alice Springs. My father still lives in the Tiwi Islands today and classes himself as that. He was brought up by the Tiwi people and the old people they taught him how to hunt and fish. Even though he was taken away as a kid he knows where he's from. Mum died at a young age so but we still have a connection with Daly River. So I see myself as three, a Tiwi man, a desert man, as well as from Daly River.[235]

When Long talks, it is clear that his mother's influence on him was immense:

> Mum died of ovarian cancer when I was 14…When you talk about women in football you talk about women like my mother. Her life was football and her children.[236]

Long's earliest football memories contain all of his family:

> My earliest memories I really treasure because they are the early parts of my childhood playing footy. Probably my earliest memories are on Nightcliff school oval in primary school playing footy in the morning. My father was the coach of the school side and Dad always had to leave early because the older boys played footy for St Mary's.[237]

Football occupied a substantial part of the Long family's lives. They played park footy, the unstructured and less regulated game, where Long would be pitted against his older brothers:

> The scratch matches I played with my brothers were some of the toughest I played…It was so competitive that sometimes it was just a case of survival…So I thought, 'If I don't run and use my pace, I'm gonna get hurt.'[238]

Sport was very important to the young Long and he found himself playing footy during the Wet and Rugby League in the Dry. Long even took some time off from these contact sports to play basketball. This was a game that he loved, but his playing was short-lived after a veiled threat from his family suggesting that anyone living in a Long household played one sport: football. As he grew older there was no question, it was football for twelve months of the year:

> I played six football seasons straight, without a break. The Darwin season runs from October to March. In 1987, I played for Saints [St Mary's] and then down in the Alice [Springs]…It meant my skills were at a high level and I had a base to work with when I got to AFL.[239]

The Long family would only play for one side in Darwin: St Mary's. The St Mary's Football Club was established in 1952 to provide an opportunity for Tiwi Islanders who were working in Darwin to play football. The Long family would contribute massively to the Club's success. Between the Long family there is a combined total of 1000 senior games and approximately sixty senior premierships. This figure is approximate because many of the records were lost in 1974 during Cyclone Tracy. Michael Long played some fifty senior games and won two premierships.

Long's fitness and endurance came not just from playing a variety of sports but also from the hunting he and his family did on a regular basis. This helped him to develop not just physically, but it affected many other aspects of his life and his football:

> I grew up hunting magpie geese, a delicacy in Darwin, and we also went crabbing and fishing. Dad taught us to use all our senses: hand-eye coordination, vision, listening, smells, touch…There was an art in making it work. There was a perfection, a precision, about it. Anything less than absolute precision meant absolute failure…Going for the kill was almost like nailing a goal…If you didn't make the kill you didn't eat. My pace came from hunting. We might have to carry ten geese through the swamp back to the car. In terms of strength and core stability that was the best training you could do.[240]

Like many young Indigenous footballers, Long had always secretly harboured an ambition to play AFL football. This would be sparked by the prominence of his countryman, Maurice Rioli, playing for Richmond in the VFL after establishing himself as a superstar with South Fremantle in the WAFL:

We used to watch *The Winners*. Everyone just barracked for Richmond when Maurice was in his heyday. I still remember going around to a good friend, Ted Berry's place, and watching the 1982 grand final there with the family. So everyone followed Maurice because there was that connection. I got my opportunity in 1988 when I played in the Bicentennial Carnival.[241]

The Bicentennial Carnival in Adelaide was really the start of Michael Long's journey to the AFL. Prior to that, football had been a sport Long played with family and friends. It had a modicum of seriousness and was played hard in the Darwin competition, but it was also fun. In Adelaide, the football landscape changed as Long was now representing his family and the Northern Territory at a national level. Consequently he had to see it differently; it was more business-like and dour. In Adelaide he also started to tap into his inner resolve and the memories of his mother as motivation and he took out All-Australian honours in 1988:

In Adelaide I took it a lot more seriously. I was selected in the All-Australian side and was the only person who was only playing local footy in Darwin. I was selected amongst some of the best players going around and [then] I got an opportunity to play with West Torrens. I suppose you looked at your football a bit differently after that. I got a lot of my inspiration from my mother because my mother died at a very young age. She was 42, so I suppose you reflect on some of things that happened in life and the trauma. It is your motivation I suppose and wanting to make it for your family as well.[242]

Having a fantastic 1988 season in the SANFL with West Torrens was helped by the presence of Long's two brothers, Chris and Noel, playing with him. Long ended up winning the Best and Fairest for West Torrens and polled well in the Magarey medal, boosting his confidence. The most fortuitous thing for Long was the help of his coach, Paul Weston, and the links Weston had to Essendon, the club he had played with as a premiership player. In late 1988 Long's fate was sealed and he was drafted to Essendon, debuting with the club the following year. But even with the support of his brother Chris playing in the Essendon reserves, the reality for Michael Long was not whether he could play football, but whether he could tough it out and deal with the loneliness and the cold, wet winters in Melbourne:

Leaving the family for the first ever time and moving away to Adelaide really opened up a new world for me. Then coming to Melbourne, I'd never been here before in my life. It was just another world. I never was prepared [for it]. I knew I could make my football do the talking but I couldn't control anything else because of my lack of education and I was uncomfortable in the mainstream. I felt most comfortable playing on a football field. It was the only thing I could control.[243]

Long continues:

I'd never lived by myself, never had a full-time job, wasn't interested in having an office job, and wasn't used to the hustle and bustle of life in the big city...I didn't understand what I had gotten myself into...I literally had to learn another culture and settle into an environment that was completely foreign to me...I had to catch a tram to work for a 6 am start. It was freezing cold. I hated it...Sometimes I'd sit in the sauna fully clothed, before training, to warm myself up.[244]

With time and patience Long finally came to understand the strange rhythms of Melbourne: its unreliable weather and its football-mad supporters and, once he was comfortable, all he had to concentrate on was the thing he knew best, play football, and that is precisely what he did.

The International Year of the Indigenous Person in 1993 neatly coincided with the AFL finals series. Having amassed 107 possessions over four games in the lead-up to the grand final, Michael Long had come into his own as an elite footballer. In the preliminary final against Adelaide, Essendon came back from being 42 points down at half-time to win and secure a berth in the grand final. The last quarter is now widely regarded as Long's coming-of-age moment as he steered the Bombers to victory. In the following week's grand final, Long went into the game feeling as if he could not be beaten:

I had nothing wrong with my body that day, and my mind was as strong and as sharp as it could have been, and I allowed my emotions to inspire me...The emotions tied up with my family, the hunting skills, the desire, the preparation, the adrenalin.[245]

Essendon won the premiership and Long won the Norm Smith medal for best-on-ground; his name forever etched in the history books. If football gave Michael Long the skills to deal with adversity and the physical and mental resolve of playing at an elite level, he would need to draw on all of his strength for the next phase of his life.

In 1995, the AFL was still grappling with what it meant to be a professional national sporting organisation. The concept of themed rounds began to take shape and the AFL introduced the Anzac Day blockbuster to commemorate the landing at Gallipoli and the myth of the Australian Digger. This game would be played between two powerhouse Victorian clubs: Essendon and Collingwood. Late in the game Long was tackled by Collingwood ruckman, Damian Monkhorst. As the umpire blew the whistle for a 'ball up' Monkhorst turned to Long and said, 'Will someone get this black c**t off me.' Incensed, Long turned to the umpire who apologised, explaining that he could do nothing because there was no law against racial vilification. It was at that moment that Long decided to make a stand against this type of discrimination. The incident with Monkhorst was not the first time Long had experienced vilification either on or off the football field. Instead, it was the confluence of many incidents he had had to deal with regularly over time:

> Going to Adelaide I copped racism on the field. I won't mention his name but it was at Adelaide oval, a very famous name actually just going off at me for no actual reason. I was quite taken back by it. I didn't know how to react, I was still a kid. I'd had a pretty good year that year and no doubt I would have been targeted but nothing verbally like I was that day. None of that shit would have gone down up there [Darwin] because I played with a team in Darwin where I've got a team that's 95 per cent Indigenous and all family. You're speechless and not confident to speak. The other time was down the street where you know someone just walks past you and goes, 'How you going Sambo?' So that was an introduction to Adelaide and my football world and just a taste of what things might be like. There was also letters with no address on the back that, that would come at least once a year. They had stuff like 'You're gonna die in so many days.' I knew the ones that didn't have a return address on the back weren't going to be very nice.[246]

After the very public and drawn-out mediation following that first Anzac Day game, the AFL drafted a set of rules that would become known as the AFL's racial and religious anti-vilification laws, or Rule 30. It states that:

No person subject to these Rules shall act towards or speak to any other person in a manner, or engage in any other conduct which threatens, disparages, vilifies or insults another on the basis of that person's race, religion, colour, descent or national or ethnic origin.[247]

Reflecting on the result, Long is quietly proud of his achievement, but very measured about whether he sees what he has done as special in any way:

I suppose when it first happened you don't actually think what it's going to do to what it is now. I was only really in the moment. I wanted action taken.

I never thought it would have impacted [on] other sports, the workplace and over-the-fence comments of supporters. It changed people's minds, made people think. I think it made players think and realise how much of an impact it had. Someone didn't understand me or my heritage, who I am or where I'm from. I think I'm a bit of a soft person because I generally like people. But that doesn't mean I was soft in terms of my nature. It was a very hard thing to do because I didn't have all the answers or solutions and I didn't get support until later on. For some of the other players I reckon it was a hard thing because they'd be asking 'What's he going on about.' It has benefited all cultures and nationalities that play our great game. Mago [Michael McLean], he was the player I asked to support me and speak up about it. We all know what happened in the past and stories with Syd [Jackson] and Pastor Doug Nicholls and the unspoken stuff too. To see the legacy that was left that these guys carried, it's like that they're enriching Australia even more. It's a great celebration because sport has been our greatest ally. It's opened the eyes of thousands and changed people's minds. It's made them think about things like 'What if it happened to you? How would you feel?'[248]

Long's struggle did not finish with the introduction of Rule 30. In late October 2004, Long had become increasingly upset and demoralised by the social treatment and political indifference being afforded to Indigenous people and issues. Feeling compelled to act, Long made an on-the-spot decision to walk to Canberra to meet Prime Minister John Howard. He loaded up his car as a support vehicle with food and country and western CDs and, with some family members, simply started to walk towards Australia's hub of power. Long's action received massive media attention and Long explained that the reason for his trip was to highlight the gross inequity faced by Indigenous people in a rich and prosperous Australia:

> It's not just an Indigenous problem, it's an Australian problem and it's happening in the year 2004...with Third World conditions in communities. And we have a responsibility, we've got a conscience, we have to be accountable as Indigenous people, but as Australians as well. So we want to be back on the agenda, we want to be part of decision-making in this country as well.[249]

After ten days of walking the back roads to Canberra resulted in physical exhaustion and death threats, Long decided that the risk of harm was too great as he had a duty of care to those in his company. He stopped. At the time he was interviewed on the ABC TV's *7.30 Report:*

> I wrote out my will this morning, you know...there's been [pause] That I will be shot, doing what I believe in. It's the uncertainty, the fear, it's been done before.[250]

In the end John Howard could no longer ignore the thing he did not understand and he was forced to meet Long and discuss his concerns.

Michael Long's legacy is considerable. Even today, in 'retirement', Long spends a great deal of time travelling all over Australia and being the AFL's very public face of coexistence and harmony. He is an AFL ambassador and the head of the Long Walk, the wonderful annual celebration that coincides with the AFL's Indigenous round. The Long Walk highlights the great achievements that have been made in sport and society regarding racial harmony, but Long is still mindful there is a way to go:

> The biggest challenges that are facing young Indigenous people today I think are the drugs and the alcohol. It is the biggest killer. I reckon education is really the key. I'd just mention Cyril [Rioli]. Like he's football was up here and his education was down there. But having finished Year 12 it gave him a better understanding and it gave him more power about how to make better choices in life both on the field and off the field. We use the carrot of football but I truly believe in the power of football and what it can achieve and what opportunities it can bring you in life because it's given me an education. That's the one

thing that he [Cyril] showed, he was just as smart off the field as he was on the field. So if we could improve his schooling to a level where his football was and if he concentrated and focused on it he would succeed. If we focus as much as we do on our sport and translate that to the other side just imagine how powerful that can be and just imagine how many kids out there can be successful in another field as well.[251]

PETER MATERA

RECORD

1990–2002

Games: 253
Goals: 217
State: Western Australia 5
Premierships: West Coast 1992, 1994
Norm Smith medal: 1992
Club Best and Fairest: 1997
All-Australian: 1991, 1993, 1994, 1996, 1997
Italian Team of the Century (wing)
Western Australian Institute of Sport Hall of Champions
WAFL Hall of Fame
AFL Hall of Fame

'When I got to South Fremantle, there was a few other Wagin guys playing in the same squad and then at the end of the year Wally got drafted [to the Eagles]. I thought if Wally can do it I can do it too.'

Peter Matera

As soon as Peter Matera saw the police in the driveway he knew he had some explaining to do. For him, it was a pity that the police had become involved because up until then, he had been having a really good afternoon. After finishing school, he had pushed his motorbike up to the bush block just around the corner from the Matera family home. His mother and father tolerated the motorbike as he had saved up for months to buy it. But there were conditions: no riding on the road and no riding without a helmet.

As Matera ripped around the bush blocks on the southern side of his home town of Wagin, he became more emboldened. He liked the speed and the freedom the bike gave him. The choppy sound of the motorbike also thrilled him as he opened up the throttle and let the wind blow through his hair. Coming around a bend Matera saw some mates from school, propped up against a tree and sharing a cigarette. He stopped, switched off the bike and smiled. 'So boys what do you think of the new machine?' Matera said proudly. 'It's not bad,' one of them said. 'I dare you to ride it up the main drag without your helmet on,' said another. Matera smiled, 'You're on mate.' With that he unbuckled his helmet and dumped it on the ground. He kicked the bike over and it fired up. He revved it a few times and in a flash he left his mates in a spitting trail of dirt and dust.

As he came out onto the sealed road, it was just a few blocks to Tudhoe Street, the main street in Wagin. Matera looked to see if any cars were coming. It was all clear. As he turned the bike into the southern entry point of Tudhoe Street, Matera's confidence grew further. He revved the bike again and felt the adrenalin surge as he rode past familiar faces and drop-jawed locals. They knew young Matera was a bit of a wild boy but this was another level of recklessness.

Arriving at the end of Tudhoe Street, he turned the bike around and went back the way he had come. Reaching the end of the street Matera disappeared back into the bush block on the outskirts of town.

What Peter Matera had not counted on was the speed of the phone calls that were being made to the local police. Delirious with adrenalin and without having thought through the ramifications of his actions, he rode his bike into the driveway and that is where he saw the police paddy wagon. He knew he had some explaining to do, and there would be consequences, but the sensation of having just done something thrilling and dangerous was euphoric. Peter Matera would come to feel that sensation again in the 1992 AFL grand final, but for now he would have to face up to his parents and the police.

The Matera family story does not start in Wagin in the Central Great Southern of Western Australia, but many miles away in Italy, in the town where Matera takes his family name from. Peter Matera's father, Michael would make the journey to Australia in the mid-1930s:

> Mum met Dad when Dad migrated from Italy. He and a few of his mates first come to Australia because they thought there was a lot of work. So he bought a horse and cart and headed down to Katanning. Then he ended up in Wagin. Mum was 13 when they met and they've always been together ever since. He was 17. Mum grew up around the Wagin and Woodanilling area with her brothers and sisters. They just pretty much worked part-time on farms just doing odd jobs here and there and then she eventually went on to the CBH [grain bins]. I was born in Wagin and that's where I grew up down there. It's pretty much a Noongar region and that comes from my mother's side, she's a Collard.[252]

Growing up in a family of seven, Matera has vivid recollections of Wagin:

> In the country I remember all me friends and mates we used to walk miles around Wagin. We'd go coonacking [hunting small freshwater crayfish] and rabbit trapping and all that type of stuff. Then on weekends it was like sport, because there wasn't much down there. Sport was the number one thing.[253]

Wagin's small size meant that a range of sports was not readily available, but Matera was able to play soccer, a choice that came with some problems:

At school I played basketball for a few years and I played soccer. Because Dad had played soccer and I used to watch him playing soccer I thought I would try it; he was a goalie. Footy was the main sport and I used to get told off at school about playing soccer. We had a new teacher and he was soccer mad and a few of my mates said, 'Let's put ourselves down and play in the soccer team.' The school football side then started getting beaten and the headmaster said, 'If you don't get into footy and play in the footy side you're going to have a hard time.' I said, 'I don't care.' I didn't really get on well with the headmaster because I got into a few troubles.[254]

Matera continues:

In Wagin there were two sides. All the Indigenous players played for Federals and all the non-Indigenous boys played for Rovers. I won Best and Fairest for D-grade and my brother he won an award also. I got up and I said my speech and he pretty much said exactly the same thing.[255]

In many respects, Matera and his brothers and friends played football as a means to alleviate boredom and to have something to look forward to on the weekend. It was here that family and his football community's support played an important role in nurturing Matera's talent and focus:

I guess there was nothing down there to do. If you walked the streets you were going to get into trouble in some ways. Weekends was football and Mum always made sure that we went to training and trained because that was the future for us. If I wasn't going to go Mum would get on the phone and said to the coach, 'He is here, come and get him to play because I can't get him there.' We had talent and everyone said you know if you wanted to go to the next level you've got to train hard and do all the hard stuff. So the local people and local families always used to make sure we'd make game days if we had to go and play at Narrogin or Williams. They made sure that we were part of a side. A few of my friends are still playing and a couple of me best mates could have made it but they went the other way.[256]

It seems that Matera was lucky that he too did not go the 'other way'. Young and cavalier, he was up for fun and he took risks:

I bought an old bomb car without Mum and Dad knowing. I bought it out of my own pocket money just through working part-time here and there. I bought it for about 200 bucks I think. It was an old HG Kingswood stationwagon. I used to park it a couple of streets away in the back of a guy's yard. I'd just go bush-bashing in it with all my mates and we'd go around at night siphoning off fuel. I used to get older guys buying drink for me. They'd buy us a bottle of ouzo and we'd buy coke from the deli. We used to jump the fence at the drive-ins and things like that. I could have easy kept on doing it if I didn't have the right people looking after me.[257]

Reflecting on the motorbike story, he says:

I've just pulled in the yard and Mum and Dad just looked at me and said, 'The sergeant wants to talk to you.' He said, 'We know you've been driving on a main road and I've heard you've been doing it for the last few weeks. It's time to come down the police station and have a chat.' So he put me into the back of a paddy wagon. I absolutely shit myself and I've started crying and called out for Mum and Dad. So the cop took me around the block and came back and he opened the thing up. He goes, 'Are you going to do it again?' I said, 'No.' I might have kept on doing those types of things if I never had footy.[258]

Peter Matera began at South Fremantle in 1986. His brother Wally, an inaugural Eagle, was playing with the Bulldogs, which provided something of a spur for Peter, as did the advice from his mother and brother Michael:

Because Wally was up playing footy I thought I'd have a crack. I went up to Perth and started playing colts and ressies for South but I didn't really like it so I went back home. Mum and my older brother Mick, who was pretty well my biggest mentor in my early footy days, said, 'Look if you don't stop doing what you're doing and take footy up seriously you won't go nowhere.' So he said, 'Come up to Perth and live with me and I'll try and get you a job.' That was pretty much the making of me staying in Perth. Wally and Mike put me on the right track to start playing WAFL.[259]

After talks with South Fremantle recruitment managers, Brian Ciccotosto and Santo Pasquale, Matera decide to head back to Perth to play football for South

Fremantle where the coach was Stan Magro. Peter Matera's football worlds started to align when he went to a club he followed as a kid and where many of his idols had played:

> I guess growing up in the country and watching South Fremantle play, Maurice Rioli and Stephen Michael were my idols. Stephen Michael's aunty used to live across the road [in Wagin] and when I was a little bloke he used to come and visit and I used to go across and just stand out on the porch there and look at him standing there all nice and groomed. It was just awesome.[260]

He continues:

> When I got to South Fremantle, there was a few other Wagin guys playing in the same squad and then at the end of the year Wally got drafted [to the Eagles]. I thought if Wally can do it I can do it too. It was a shock to me seeing me brother there and seeing all the fame that he got. It just inspired me more or less. So when I got to South Fremantle I got to see how it all operates. It scared me a bit but then I met up with my relatives the Collard brothers. Brad, Cliff and Derek and I stayed in Perth and got an understanding about how to play WAFL footy. It was just amazing to see how it all operates as I was just a country kid. I was a shy person but to see the Collard boys so respected and then Maurice Rioli walking past was really amazing. To actually be in the change rooms with Stephen [Michael] and Basil Campbell for the first time was great.[261]

Playing for a solid three seasons with South Fremantle in the WAFL, Matera was coming on to the VFL/AFL radar as a quality wing. As his brother Wally had moved from the Eagles to the Fitzroy Lions, there was a distinct possibility that Matera could have gone east:

> I had the Fitzroy President and recruiting blokes ringing me saying they we're going to draft me. Wally said don't talk to anyone else. The Eagles, they were lower on the ladder that year so they got the pick before Fitzroy. I was working down in Freo [Fremantle] as a storeman and I heard it on the radio. The Eagles came around later and presented me with a jumper which was just bizarre because I was thinking that I was going to Fitzroy. I didn't speak to them [West Coast] or anything, they just came around to my house and presented me with a jumper and that was it. I was an Eagle.[262]

In 1990, Matera made his debut for the Eagles in round one against Collingwood at Subiaco Oval. Despite this great start, he struggled with a knee injury and would play only five league games for the year. In the following season, he decided to move from south of the river to closer to the Eagles' home ground of Subiaco, to concentrate more on training. In 1991 he became a regular player for the Eagles. It was in this year that the young wingman began to open up more as a player and a person:

> When I first went down to the Eagles there were some big names. Johnnie Worsfold, David Hart, Chris Mainwaring, Craig Turley, Dwayne Lamb and then all of a sudden now I'm their team-mate. So it was a big shock as I was a rookie. I didn't really care about it much I just flaunted it a bit. Those guys pretty much put me back in my place a few times and then I started becoming more professional. I knew I had pace so it was more trying to fit in playing in a professional team that had team goals and team structures. I needed to know the players that I played against and what their weaknesses and strengths were.[263]

This also fed back into his understanding of the Eagles:

> We pretty much had to gel with everything we did. Outside of footy we did things as a group. At South Fremantle when you'd finished a game and away you'd go. You didn't hang around, you didn't do things during the week. At the Eagles we used to go to restaurants and dinners and lunches and so it became so close that you just knew everyone. You knew everything about each other, that was the biggest thing you had to really get your head around.[264]

This type of commitment and level of professionalism paid serious dividends as the Eagles set the standards for other football clubs to follow in the 1990s. This bore fruit in 1992 and 1994 when they won premierships against Geelong and in 1992 Matera won a Norm Smith medal in the biggest game of the year. Despite the Eagles on-field success, Matera and other Indigenous team-mates did experience other difficulties, namely racism. Matera reflects:

> Once people knew that I had an Italian Dad and an Aboriginal Mum I used to get it. They would say, 'You're not Aboriginal. You think you're Aboriginal but you're not. You're not black. If your mother's black how come you aren't?' All this type of stuff. Lewie [Chris Lewis] and me we're pretty close and he used to get it all. You couldn't really do much, you couldn't over-react. It was just part of footy until they

changed the rules. I thought it was good when they did [bring the rule in] because I remember I used to be close with Nicky Winmar and you'd sit down and have a beer with him after the game and you'd listen to the stories. Before they brought the rule in it was just really bad. I'm not as dark-skinned as those boys but Lewie and Troy Ugle and Phil Narkle used to get hammered all the time.[265]

Identity issues were put to rest with Matera's selection into the Indigenous Team of the Century. He explains:

For all the speculation that I had when I was growing up and that I had to deal with at school and right through about my identity knowing that I was Aboriginal was a great thing. I knew I was. I didn't have to go out there and prove anything. On that night to see the players that I played with and the greats that I watched and to be in the side on my own wing was awesome. With Maurice and Nicky on the other side you can't get any better.[266]

Matera understands the challenges young Indigenous people face today and so the role he provides is an important one in directing them along the right path, similar to what his family had done for him when he was living back in Wagin:

I think the biggest thing for young blackfellas is trying to further their careers as individuals. Realising that yes they're black but they're also Australian. They need to realise that they're not dumb and they are not part of a different society. I think the biggest challenge is for them to realise that you need a job and security because without a job you are going to be just doing the same thing day in, day out. So the challenges for us is to make sure that things are put in place otherwise you're just going to see the same thing happening all the time.[267]

He continues:

The biggest challenge that we've got is that we need to understand how much the parents need to be involved in their kids growing up. Strong families, mentors, anyone that can offer advice is the only way these kids are going to learn anything. It's sad to see some of these kids mucking up because you know inside they're a better person. So if you can touch that inside them and guide them to make the right choices I think that would change things. We go up to communities and there's kids that don't get fed and they've got nothing. The support that they need is huge. As Australians we brought many of the bad things in so somehow Australians have got to help them to fix it because they [Indigenous people] didn't have that shit 100 years ago.[268]

These days working alongside his old West Coast team-mate Chris Lewis are very satisfying, because Matera can identify with many of the challenges young people face in their communities should they choose to relocate to Perth to pursue football:

I'm a full-time development officer at Swan Districts Football Club. I'm an assistant to the league side and I do programs up in our recruiting zone, which is the Pilbara area and also down in Bunbury. Myself and Chris travel and he looks after Newman and I look after Port Hedland. We go out to remote communities to the schools and do coaching, umpiring and medical programs. It's not all about footy because even if they've got no talent we still want them to be involved. With some of the Indigenous boys we bring them down to play and we've got Swan House which the club purchased for the process of getting talented kids up from our zones and trying to help them transition into the AFL. Lewie and I mentor all these Indigenous boys. It's great.[269]

GAVIN WANGANEEN

RECORD

1991–2006

Games: 300: Essendon 127; Port Adelaide 173

Goals: 202: Essendon 64; Port Adelaide 138

State: South Australia 8

Premierships: Essendon 1993; Port Adelaide 2004

Brownlow medal: 1993

Captain: Port Adelaide 1997–2000

Club Best and Fairest: Port Adelaide 2003

All-Australian: 1992, 1993, 1995, 2001, 2003

Essendon Team of the Century (back pocket)

AFL Hall of Fame Inductee 2010

'I remember watching my Uncle Alwyn, or 'Gunny' [father of Alwyn and Aaron Davey] playing in Darwin when I was 6 or 7. That's my earliest memory of football. I thought: 'That's what I'd love to do one day.'

Gavin Wanganeen

As Gavin Wanganeen entered the room where the Brownlow count was to be held in 1993, he would have no idea how the night would unfold. Some of the Brownlow favourites included Carlton's Greg Williams, Hawthorn's Jason Dunstall, North Melbourne's Wayne Carey, Geelong's Gary Ablett Snr and Nathan Buckley from the lowly Brisbane Bears. Wanganeen saw himself, at best, as a second-tier favourite. As it was only his second time at the ceremony, Wanganeen wanted to enjoy himself as he mentally prepared for a grand final, just few days away. By the middle of the count, Carey, Williams, Buckley and Richmond's Matthew Knights were all in equal second place on nine votes, while the bolter was Carey's team-mate, Wayne Schwass on fourteen. Wanganeen had made a slow start and was on five votes, equal with Geelong's Garry Hocking.

As the second half of the count got underway, more votes were polled by Carey, Williams and Dunstall. As people from all around Australia were glued to their TV sets it would take a brave punter to suggest that Wanganeen had any chance. But then a remarkable thing happened. From round sixteen to nineteen, Wanganeen was best-on-ground in three of four games and sat on eighteen votes. At this stage of the count he led Hocking and Williams by two. By round twenty-two, the last game of the home-and-away fixture, the Brownlow was poised on a knife's edge as both Williams and Hocking needed two votes to win. The last round for Hocking was not fruitful. Ross Oakley, the AFL's CEO, read out the votes: 'Carlton versus Sydney. Greg Williams 1 vote.' The Essendon table erupted and Wanganeen sat there stunned. As he made his way to the dais, he seemed to be in slow motion. As he climbed the stairs he felt embarrassed. He looked out across the room. Growing up watching his idol Gary Ablett Snr on television was the thing that made him want to become a footballer.

He saw Ablett on his feet and applauding him. Now this young man from the outer suburbs of northern Adelaide was standing there for the world to see, and somewhere in Adelaide his mother and uncles cheered loudly and the celebrations began.

In many ways, Gavin Wanganeen makes up the holy trinity of Indigenous football in Australia. The other two are Michael Long and Nicky Winmar. The reason Wanganeen's place in Australian football is so important is because he became the first Indigenous player to win a Brownlow medal. This is even more remarkable given that he did so not from the traditional 'winning' roles in the midfield or forward line, but the back pocket. With his courage, balance and ability to read the play, Wanganeen has carved a very special place in AFL history.

This remarkable story begins in a very unremarkable way, on the far eastern side of the Great Australian Bight, which is where Wanganeen's family comes from:

> On my Mum's side her tribe come from the west coast of South Australia. Kokatha, that's the mob. My great grandfather Dick Davey played with the mission at Ceduna. He played for the Koonibba Footy Club in the 1920s and then the family started moving to Port Lincoln and then to Adelaide. I moved from Port Lincoln to Adelaide at the age of five.[270]

Wanganeen has several strong football memories from his time growing up:

> I remember watching my Uncle Alwyn, or 'Gunny' [father of Alwyn and Aaron Davey] playing in Darwin when I was 6 or 7. That's my earliest memory of football. I thought: 'That's what I'd love to do one day.'[271]

He also recalls playing football at about the same age:

> One early football memory was a game I played at Croydon Primary [School]. We got flogged. I don't think we even got a point. The game was against Ridley Grove. They were pretty strong. I had a snap shot in the goal square thinking, 'Yes we'll score here' and someone smothered it. I didn't score. I would have been 7 years old.[272]

Growing up, Wanganeen's was a fairly typical upbringing where football seemed to dominate his thoughts and his time:

> I grew up with my cousins, Troy and Shane Bond…It was great having that day-to-day contact with two other kids who were just as determined as I was to play league footy…It [footy] was pretty much the first thing I thought about when I woke up and the last thing I thought about before I went to sleep.[273]

He continues:

> From a very early age a lot of Aboriginal families just had footies and that's all we did. [Footy] was all we knew, it was what we [the family] did on weekends. We'd have sleepovers and be back and forth over the weekend, even on week nights there was always a footy around here in Adelaide in the northern suburbs. We'd have kicks in the backyard and try and take the big specky to see who could be the biggest hero. I played a little bit of cricket at school but nothing too serious. It was pretty much just footy.[274]

Wanganeen's mother, cousins and uncles played a solid role in nurturing and supporting his interest in football:

> I think with football it was something about being able to run around. The competitive nature of it and the speed and how you can run anywhere and in all different directions, I can't describe it. My Mum's brothers played footy over in the west coast [of South Australia] and were champions and maybe that had something to do with it. Once I started playing I just couldn't get enough of it. My Mum had an influence in taking me to training. She would drop me off at training and go to most of my matches even in the early days. I had other cousins who were playing footy as well and we kept each other interested.[275]

As Wanganeen grew older he became affiliated with the Salisbury North Football Club:

> I played juniors with the Salisbury North Footy Club. The Bond brothers and Michael O'Loughlin played there as well. It was because I lived out in that area and it was the closest club. From there I went to the Port Magpies. I got invited to go and train in their under-17s because that was the Port Adelaide zoning.[276]

He continues:

> It was a shock to the system because I went from training with Salisbury
> North under-14s, which wasn't too hard to doing a full pre-season of
> running, which was unheard of for a 14 year old. But I was keen as
> mustard. I wasn't afraid of stepping up an age group, either. I wanted
> to go as high as I could, as quickly as I could.[277]

If expediency is what Wanganeen wanted for his football career, he got what
he wished for. In 1989, he was drafted to Essendon as a first-round pick at
number twelve but he decided to wait an extra year for his body to mature.
At the time he was 15 and playing reserves in the South Australian National
Football League and playing in the Teal Cup side for South Australia. His first
taste of seniors' football was in 1990 at a pre-season scratch match against
Geelong, playing against his idol Gary Ablett Snr. It was an important year
for Wanganeen as he played in all the home-and-away fixtures and played in a
winning premiership side for the Magpies.

Arriving at Essendon's home ground Windy Hill in 1991, Wanganeen found
the football to his liking and his assured confident play belied his young years.
He also found the transition to Melbourne was good and that Essendon, as a
club, was a good fit for him:

> I went to Melbourne when I was 17. Essendon were excellent. They
> were pretty hands on. They were going out of their way to make
> sure you were okay and nothing was ever too much for them. They
> basically waited on you hand and foot until you got settled. It was
> obviously hard the first year trying to settle in and battle homesickness
> but after you get rid of that and get that first year out of the way you
> sort of get used to it and it all just flowed from there. Being in Adelaide
> and around your family and friends and being comfortable you soon
> realise [with moving] that you need to adapt.[278]

Wanganeen debuted for Essendon in 1991 in round two against Richmond and
quickly began to adjust to the stringent demands that Essendon Football Club
demanded of its players. Being a quality player who was dangerous around
goals, Wanganeen would generally attract a close-tagging player that would
at times see his influence nullified. It was in a game against Geelong at the
MCG that Essendon's long-standing coach, Kevin Sheedy, changed the role of
Wanganeen forever:

> Moving to the back pocket was the key to my career...and I owe an awful lot to Kevin Sheedy for having the vision that I could become a defender. I'd been playing at half-forward with occasional runs on the ball, but I was copping some close checking and Sheeds wanted to free me up...I clearly recall that run down to the backline. It was a major turning point in my career...I enjoyed the freedom and the fact no one was on my hammer all the time. I was the hunter rather than the hunted.[279]

The dividends of this strategy for both Wanganeen and Essendon were immediate. With Wanganeen playing only half a season in defence he was named as one of the All-Australian back pockets in 1992. His fearless approach, which at times bordered on the reckless, became a distinct feature of his game. He would throw himself into packs, leap at the ball in seemingly impossible positions and run full tilt out of the Essendon defence, dodging and weaving as he went. It was thrilling. In 1993 he won the Brownlow medal, becoming the first Indigenous player to do so. He reflects:

> I still get goosebumps thinking about some of the things I attempted in my Brownlow year. I get great pleasure from watching old highlights... Usually it's just the result of doing the basics well — running hard at the ball and keeping your eyes on it.[280]

Despite his courage and immense skill, Wanganeen felt the barbs of racism when he was at the height of his powers:

> In '92 and '93 I got called a couple of names here and there from opposition players. I was a bit surprised. I'm a light-coloured Aboriginal man but they obviously knew I was Aboriginal and they called me some names. I was a bit shocked but I think I just ignored it. I might have sworn back at him and called him a 'hero'. I was hurt by it because it was said in the first place and who had said it. They were older-type players. You expected it more so from a younger player.[281]

After a successful five years at Windy Hill, Wanganeen made the tough decision to return to South Australia where he became the inaugural captain of the Port Adelaide Power who entered the AFL in 1997. It appears that the decision to leave Melbourne was not an easy one:

Leaving Essendon was one of the hardest things I've done in my life. It wasn't always the plan to return to Port Adelaide. It was just a flip-of-the-coin decision. The opportunity to go back home to Adelaide, soak up the more laidback lifestyle, be close to family and friends, and play with my old club had a lot of appeal to it…Whenever we played Essendon, especially in my first three years at Port, I found it very difficult emotionally. It was very hard to come to terms with.[282]

If moving back to Adelaide was a chance to be closer to family and friends, the demands of being a high-profile sportsman at one of Australia's oldest and proudest football clubs presented the young Port Adelaide captain with another set of challenges:

I was an immature 23-year-old when I became captain of Port Adelaide. Suddenly, I had all this responsibility thrust on me that I'd never had before, and maybe I wasn't ready for it. I got suspended a couple of times in that first season, which was out of character… Maybe it was just the strong feeling of responsibility I had for the group.[283]

After four years as Port captain, Wanganeen decided to step down as he felt frustrated by the toll that injuries had taken on his body, which meant he was spending more time watching from the sideline than actually playing. By refocusing his energies on getting fit without the added pressure of the captaincy, Wanganeen entered a new productive stage of his career. This paid dividends in 2003 when Wanganeen played his most consistent injury-free season and won Port Adelaide's Best and Fairest, the John Cahill medal. In the following season, Port Adelaide became one of the AFL's serious finals contenders, making the grand final against the Brisbane Lions. In the grand final, aged 31, Wanganeen played a pivotal role in securing Port Adelaide's first premiership, booting four goals. He reflects upon this achievement:

Not taking anything away from the '93 flag, but I appreciated the Port Adelaide flag more. With Essendon, I was young and didn't know how to appreciate it, but I fully understood what the Port flag meant because of all the hardships we went though to get there. It was a huge relief.[284]

Wanganeen went on to play another couple of seasons with Port Adelaide and played his 300th game in the first round of 2006 against North Melbourne. It would be his last game, and in doing so, he became the first Indigenous player to reach that milestone. He retired at the end of the 2006 season.

Wanganeen's selection in the AFL's Indigenous Team of the Century was a very personal moment and one that recognised the massive contribution that he has made to the code:

> For me it was a really big deal. Being an Indigenous player who has played many years and had a successful career I wanted to be part of it. It was very important for me that I represent my clan from Ceduna. It was great that the AFL embraced it that way and it was very special for all the Indigenous guys selected. To get up there and being named in the team made me feel very proud.[285]

Other personal honours for Wanganeen include being named in Essendon's Team of the Century, being inducted into the AFL's Hall of Fame in 2010 and the announcement of the Gavin Wanganeen medal for the best under-21 Port Power player — these are all testament to a man who has left a considerable legacy to Australian football.

Currently Wanganeen is setting up a gym franchise, Anytime Fitness, in Adelaide. He remains active and knows the benefits of physical exercise and healthy life choices. This follows on from his previous work for the South Australian government as a youth ambassador where he promoted healthy lifestyles and education as a means to helping school children set goals and achieve them:

> My role is a pretty broad role but I go to a few of the high schools and encourage the kids to stay at school. I try to say to them, don't let anyone say you can't do whatever want to do. Look at my story. I was a kid that grew up in Salisbury who went on to to play 300 AFL games. It was the goal I set myself and I put the hard work in and believed in myself and there were people along the way who might have doubted you but I went out and achieved more than what I expected. They too can do that in their own life and it doesn't matter what path they go down.[286]

Wanganeen sees the difficulty of dealing with Indigenous teenagers and children means dealing with the impact that history has had on Indigenous people more generally:

Probably the biggest issue is how we have lost important bits of our culture. I'm talking about going back to my great grandfather. They had to go from the Aboriginal way of life to a white man's way of life and that was something they found very hard to get used to. What happens then when they lost that bit of their culture, it flowed down into their families once they started having kids. Having to deal with racism on a regular basis would have been tough. So with all of those things a lot of them turned to alcohol because they didn't know how to handle these situations. A lot of the kids didn't get the right guidance and support and it became a bit of a cycle. A lot of them turned into alcoholics.[287]

Wanganeen continues:

My Mum and her two sisters were taken away and her younger brother was moved from the guardianship of their father when she was young. She was adopted out to a white family where her and her three sisters had lived. In the end they actually kept in contact and had great respect for that white family. But there have been a lot of challenges over the years that they're Aboriginal people that they have had to face just fitting into society.[288]

Wanganeen reflects on his own situation:

A lot of Aboriginal families are close and will hang out a fair bit. I mean when I was a kid we were close and I probably didn't focus as much on school as I should have. I remember hanging out with cousins on the weekends and maybe not going to school on Mondays and stuff like that. But then if you haven't got a good education you can't go on to employment or further education and so lots of barriers there. Luckily I had footy to fall back on.[289]

He sees the process is a two-way street, and the issues of Indigenous education and the teaching of Indigenous history are important to enabling a greater understanding and acceptance:

I think Aboriginal history needs to be compulsory in the school curriculum. I think that will go a long way toward educating this next

generation because a lot of the parents, white parents, who don't edu-
cate their kids about Aboriginal history I feel. When I was at school I
was forced to do French history. It would have been great to do
Australian history that looked at Indigenous stuff. It would help
break a lot of barriers I think so non-Aboriginal people can get an
understanding of why a lot of Indigenous people keep to themselves
and are not quite as confident in getting out there to find work
and education. They find it hard to fit into the system. They [non-
Indigenous Australians] might understand that a bit more.[290]

Wanganeen then goes on to talk about Indigenous responsibility:

On the other side of the coin, I think Aboriginal people need to get
out there and use opportunities for them to make a better life for
themselves. They can't just sit around and loaf and mope around and
feel sorry for themselves forever. They need to make a change for
themselves so then their kids can see that they've made a change and
they're hard workers, and it will flow down to the next generation and
hopefully the cycle will be broken.[291]

RECORD

1992–2005

Games: 268
Goals: 165
State: Allies 4
Premierships: Brisbane Lions 2001, 2002, 2003
Captain: Indigenous Allstars 2005
AFL Goal of the Year 1992

‘You know it was things like going to funerals and 21sts and birthdays. We miss all that stuff. I missed that for 15 years and I mean some really good friends have passed in that time. Some funerals you get to and some you can't. It's hard like that, life goes on and you end up feeling sorry for the one that's passed away. You mourn for them.’

Darryl White

As a die-hard North Melbourne supporter, it was hard enough for Darryl White to be drafted to the Brisbane Bears and play football in a non-AFL state. But arriving at an early pre-season session in his first year with the Brisbane Bears in 1992, Darryl White had serious cause for concern. It was not so much the training but the specific task itself that had him shaking his head. As coach Robert Walls addressed the players, White reminded himself that things in the AFL would be different, but this was not what he had signed up for. Walls had organised a 120 km bike ride around the Gold Coast hinterland. White knew that this would be no joyride but mile after mile of sheer misery. The players were required to wear helmets, which added insult to potential injury. Some players bought their own bikes whereas others, like White, who did not own a bike, had the club organise one for them. 'This is bullshit,' White muttered underneath his breath as he straddled the mountain bike and prepared for the long ride.

White had not ridden a bike for some time, and that had been his trusty old BMX around the streets of Alice Springs with his mates. Pushing off, the first thing White noticed was that the angle of the seat was not right and he could not get a good rhythm going. He also felt uncomfortable because the height of the seat made him feel as if he was perched like a bird. The brakes were too grippy, the tyres too thin and the glare of the sun bouncing off the road caused him to sweat. It was going to be a long day for Darryl White. As the hours ticked by White became more frustrated and the road just seemed to go on and on. 'This is bullshit,' he said again in a louder voice. White decided to change tack and tried to concentrate on getting his pedalling technique even. As he focused, the heat and humidity closed in on him, but it seemed to work and he felt better.

Just as he was starting to get into a rhythm he looked up to see the road rising. Walls had planned it so the ride ended with a final 8 km mountain climb. It was a strategy to sort the boys from the men. Initially the ascent was alright, but as the incline became steeper, the effort required from already-exhausted bodies was superhuman. If White felt it could not get any worse, suddenly it did. The tension caused by the hill climb saw the chain on his bike start to slip, causing White to lose his balance as well as his momentum. When White noticed a team-mate ride past him, then another, White became angrier.

By the time he reached the summit he noticed some of his spent team-mates cooling off with cold drinks and wet towels. Some were joking and messing around and others were bent over and on the brink of vomiting. White then noticed Robert Walls standing next to some of the trainers and assistant coaches, keeping a hawk-like eye on the riders as they came in. White looked around to see if there was a lookout point that tourists might use to take in the magnificent view. He saw one, rode his bike over to it, got off and in one mighty motion hurled the bike from the platform. He then took his helmet off and threw it into the abyss. As the sweat poured down his face he made his way over to Robert Walls. 'This is bullshit. I came to this club to play football not ride bikes.' He then stormed off to find some water and a towel to cool off. Robert Walls stood there for a moment nonplussed. Then a small smile came to his face. In White he could see that he did indeed have a footballer, but just how good he would be only time would tell.

Heading to Darryl White's place in Brisbane in late 2008 was a great thrill for me. I had often marvelled at White's ability to do something mercurial or freakish when he was playing for the Bears/Lions. I think the reason I liked watching him play so much was because he was a rangy, seemingly languid player whose gait seemed to belie a truly wonderful player and a very intelligent footballer. White was a fluid player who seemed to be able to play anywhere on a footy oval; he could play a variety of roles during a game, or play on any type of player. It seemed to me as if he could do anything. When I got to White's house, he was busy getting the house sorted out as he was babysitting his three youngest children. It was my hunch that White could do anything right as he made me a cup of tea, changed nappies and finished the vacuuming. He eventually sat down in his lounge room and talked about his life and his football:

On my Mum's side I'm Eastern Arrernte. We are from the eastern side
of Alice Springs, so all that eastern side mainly from Sixteen Mile to
Harts Range most of our family are from there. The Aboriginal name
for Sixteen Mile is Iibalintja.[292]

From a young age White played a lot of football:

I started [football] in primary school in Alice [Springs]. I would have
liked to have started a bit earlier but there was not any competition
there. So I just started out having a kick in the backyard with my
cousins and then went to the footy and watched my old uncles play
and that. We'd have a kick after games and then in grade 5 we were
allowed to play for our school. I would have been 10. Then I started
really getting into it.[293]

The importance of football for White stemmed from the connections his family
had with it:

In Alice [Springs] football was pretty important in a sense because
all your uncles played and they went down to the SANFL or had
stints in the WAFL. So following in their footsteps was a little bit of a
pipe-dream. The dream was most probably to play in Alice and then
Adelaide or Darwin and if you were good enough have a crack at the
AFL. My Uncle Lance White and blokes like Uncle Lloydie Bray and
Uncle Les Turner, they all went down to Adelaide to play, but they all
came back. That was expected of me as well I suppose. That was just
the way it was. Uncle Richard Bray was the only one that stayed and
he is a Port Adelaide legend.[294]

White remembers one player standing out because he had managed to stick it
out in the big leagues. His name is Gilbert McAdam:

Gilbert McAdam broke that trend a bit. He actually stayed in the
SANFL and in schooling down there [Adelaide] and he ended up
taking the path to the big time. Maybe that was the track that most of
them [White's uncles] tried but they just didn't stick it out. Gilbert was
awesome because no one had really done it besides him. Not many
Territory blokes anyway.[295]

Football was important to White growing up, but he was able to play other
sports too:

In Alice there was an abundance of sports. I did athletics from a young
age and I continued right through to about 13 or 14. I did mainly
running and jumping events. I'd win everything except discus because
I couldn't really master it. In the track events I was quick but not
overly quick. In Australia at the time I was about fourth in the high
jump and the long jump in the Pacific School Games.[296]

It was football and not athletics that captured White's imagination and he began
playing with the Alice Springs Pioneers before making the move to Western
Australia:

I played in Alice Springs for Pioneers [in the Central Australian Football
League] all my life. In '88 and '89 I went over to Western Australia and
lived with Dad's side of the family. They'd [White's parents] moved
over there, and I played in Carnarvon for a team called Warriors. Then
in 1989, I moved to a club called Gascoigne in the same competition.
Then I did a bit of time in Longmore juvenile detention centre for
about two months. I came out and played for the Kardinya footy club
in Perth in the under-17s under my idol, the great Maurice Rioli. I
always wore the number seventeen because of Maurice. When I came
back from WA in 1990 I was playing for Pioneers when I got picked
and played Teal Cup. That year I played only four or five games with
Pioneers. Uncle Lance was coaching Rovers [in the CAFL] and he was
me idol. We went to Tennant Creek and I ended up staying because
Uncle Lance lured me with $200 a game and as a 16-year-old that was
cool. I could go because I never signed a piece of paper for the Club
[Pioneers]. They [Rovers] offered me an apprenticeship and so I ended
up taking it. I didn't like it in the end because I was playing against all
me mates and family. It was a bit tough and daunting but I'm glad I'd
done it at an early age because I got through it and it sort of got me
ready in a sense with the AFL. I thought, 'This is what it's going to be
like in the big time,' but ten times worse.[297]

It was just a matter of time before White would get to test out his theory about
the AFL. In the interim, and in the 1990 Teal Cup championship, White stood
out and many of the AFL scouts took notice. The thing that impressed the
recruitment staff of the Brisbane Bears was White's clean ball-handling skills,
his leap and his ability to play on players who were taller and seemingly
stronger than him. It has now become part of the Brisbane Lions' folklore that

the day White arrived at his new club he did so wearing a purple LA Lakers basketball singlet, bouncing a basketball. This obviously showed White was an individual, and the first thing White noticed about playing in the AFL was that his individuality ran second to the concerns and dictum of the team. He explains:

> When you're back home you had different influences, your likes and dislikes. When you got to the big time all of that was irrelevant, they didn't care how you felt, what you liked, what you didn't like. You did what fifty other blokes did so it was hard in that regard. Don't get me wrong, there's no stone left unturned for you, they'll do everything in their power to help but sometimes they deny you things that make you happy.[298]

White continues:

> You know it was things like going to funerals and 21sts and birthdays. We miss all that stuff. I missed that for 15 years and I mean some really good friends have passed in that time. Some funerals you get to and some you can't. It's hard like that, life goes on and you end up feeling sorry for the one that's passed away. You mourn for them.[299]

White had to deal with many mental hurdles in coming to the Brisbane Bears, a team who were not successful for some time. If White felt uneasy or uncomfortable in his new surrounds, his football was not showing it. Not only would White become part of an illustrious group who would boot a goal with their first kick in AFL football, but White's first goal would become the 1992 goal of the year. White was also an early leader in the Brownlow medal voting for the 1992 season and after three rounds had two best on-ground performances.

The transition from Alice Springs to Brisbane was perhaps most keenly felt for White because of the size difference between the two cities. His home town was much more intimate and knowable than Brisbane, but Brisbane also offered opportunities that were not available back in Alice:

> In Alice Springs there's thirty thousand people. You can get to any place in town within fifteen, twenty, minutes. There's no real time constraints or anything like that, no peak hour, nothing. Then you get here [Brisbane] and it just really opens up your eyes. The price of living is different. Back in Alice you were paying an arm and a leg for food. Ten dollars for a kilo of bananas when you can get it here [Brisbane]

for three or four bucks. Family and friends would come down and stay with you because they knew it was cheaper shopping, cheaper living and there were cheaper cars. All the cousins would come down and stay for a week, buy a car and drive back. It was always cheaper for them to come here and buy a washing machine and get a holiday out of it at the same time.[300]

Juggling family responsibilities and a professional sporting career was not easy, especially as the Bears struggled to win games. Then, in 1997, the Brisbane Bears merged with Melbourne club, Fitzroy, to become the Brisbane Lions. It would be another two years before highly respected and decorated coach Leigh Matthews would replace the sacked John Northey, thus paving the way for Brisbane to experience some of the most successful years of the modern football era.

Playing with the Brisbane Lions across half-back, White would play in the next three grand finals (2001–03) and win three AFL premierships, playing along some of the best footballers in the land in Michael Voss, Jason Akermanis, Simon Black and Jonathon Brown. White's ability to play in a champion side and hold his own endeared him to many Brisbane fans. He even managed to provide Brisbane fans with his own signature moment by holding the ball aloft for all the crowd to see after he marked it. It was his skill, reliability and timing that saw him gain full-back selection to the Indigenous Team of the Century. He recalls the moment:

I was a little bit shocked. I had the privilege of being one of the first ones up there so I watched everyone else come up which was good. I'm glad I got picked in a sense because we [Lions] went through all those hard years where we only won three games in two years. I talk to people now and they remind me about the three premierships. With those premierships I think that held me in good regard but also I could play just about anywhere and everywhere.[301]

He continues:

It was a funny moment. John Howard was right there and I shook his hand and then right next to me I had one of my favourite players of all time in Chris Johnson and then I had one of the all-time Darwin greats Uncle Bill [Dempsey] on the other side. It was pretty overwhelming just with the cast of people that were there. It was like, 'How good's this?'[302]

The discipline of playing in the AFL was always understood by White, but at the same time he knew the importance of being home, and was prepared to make sacrifices when he did go back to Alice Springs. He reflects:

> You love your time off for the two or three months you've got. I sort of took that bit extra and I sort of played them [Brisbane] a little bit and I shouldn't have. But I also knew that once I got on the plane back to Brisbane I was back and into training. I didn't worry about any homesickness. It was just hard leaving home so I thought I'd sneak a week or two in and I'd cop the fine. I took it on the chin.[303]

These days White is happy to reflect on his career and his considerable achievements. He helps out at several football clubs and community organisations, something he believes is important for him to do. As to the challenges facing Indigenous Australians, White believes there are many things that could be improved:

> A lot of families are aching still. I think they've got to be compensated in some sort of way because it's sort of hereditary. When people become alienated from their great grandmothers and their grandfathers or whatever then the son is going to get alienated from them. He doesn't know why. My Mum, she never saw much of her father and I was in the same boat as I have only met my grandfather twice. I think a lot of that is still going on. But in saying that too we've got to help ourselves, we can't have whitefellas hold our hand all the time but we can't be pushed around either. With all the sorry stuff and with all the water under the bridge the Apology has been good in healing both sides of Australia.[304]

White is also mindful of the situation many young Indigenous Australians find themselves in, and believes issues of identity and history are vital if things are to be improved:

> For the young ones it can be hard with their mindset. They need to know, 'Yes we're black' but not to think we are second-rate citizens. We've got to get that mentality out and just say we're Indigenous Australians. I see the young ones trying to come face to face with a lot of tough things in remote areas, remote communities and all the problems we have inherited. It's hard but I think we can get there.[305]

CHRIS JOHNSON

RECORD

1994–2007

Games: 264: Fitzroy 59; Brisbane 205
Goals: 172: Fitzroy 67; Brisbane 105
Premierships: Brisbane Lions 2001, 2002, 2003
Co-captain: All-Australian 2005
Club Leading Goalkicker: Fitzroy 1995
All-Australian: 2002, 2004

'I sensed it [football] gave me a lot of security. It gave me something that I could relate to other people with because of how I related to it. When I played football I didn't worry about anything else but football. I wouldn't even think about the score. I had no other worries about being black or white or anything. It gave me a new life.'

Chris Johnson

S unday mornings were always tense affairs for young Chris Johnson. As a wiry 15-year-old playing footy at any given opportunity at school and training all week, Sunday mornings were the moment of truth. The issue for Johnson was not so much if he would get a game with Jacana Football Club, but would he make it to the game at all due to his father's capacity to get lost when driving. 'Have you had a look at the Melways, Dad?' Chris asked. Lloyd Johnson looked up from his newspaper. 'Where you playing?' 'Melton South,' came Chris's reply. 'No problem, I know a short cut,' said Lloyd as he went back to the sports pages.

With the game beginning at 12:20 pm, it was a good half hour's drive from Broadmeadows to Melton South. Johnson would then need a further fifteen minutes to get changed and warm-up for the game. At 11.30 am Lloyd Johnson started the car and winked at his son. 'No problem. I will get you there on time. I have been driving around Victorian roads for years.' Chris shook his head. He had heard this story before. At 12:15 pm Chris Johnson looked over to his father. 'You have no idea where we are do you? You do this all the time Dad. We leave at the last moment and now we are lost...again.' 'Relax,' came the calm reply from Lloyd. 'I have been driving around these roads for years....' Chris jumped in, 'Yeah, yeah you know a short-cut. More like a long-cut. "Long-cut Lloyd" I should call you! Or "Pack-a-cut-lunch-and-a-water-bottle-Lloyd."' No sooner had Chris finished giving his father a bake than Lloyd swung the car into Reserve Road and the home ground of the Melton South Football Club. As Jacana were already out on the field warming up the coach looked up to see Chris Johnson walking briskly towards him. 'Dad get lost again, Chrissy? You should buy him a Melways for Christmas.' 'No point,' Johnson replied, 'he'd still take the short-cut' as he disappeared into the change rooms to get into his footy gear.

In many ways, Chris Johnson holds a special place in the Fitzroy/Brisbane Lions story because he was one of the few Fitzroy players who made the cut to go to Brisbane in 1996. By the time Johnson retired in 2007, he had become the last remaining Fitzroy player to play for Brisbane in the AFL.

Despite being a smaller player, Johnson became known as a tough, and at times, extremely aggressive player. His fighting spirit may have come from his Gunditjmara kinship connections; people who have in their ranks the late Lionel Rose, the 1968 world bantam-weight boxing champion:

> My mob are Gunditjmara that come from down Portland and Warrnambool way. I haven't lived there at all. I haven't got too much memory of it but the memories I do have is of the country and the water.[306]

It was his father's choice for the Johnson family to live in Melbourne:

> As I got older we moved out of the areas where all the relatives were and moved out towards Broadmeadows way. Most of my family lived in Preston and Reservoir. We had things, schooling and football and we had our own lives to live and I guess that was that. I have always stayed connected with the family.[307]

Johnson goes on to speak about his father:

> Dad was a truck driver. He worked for Readymix. He worked for the dairy. He still drives trucks to this day. I think he chose the life of working and being stable where others probably didn't. He wanted a good life for his family. I'm not saying that others didn't but he just went about it in a different way. Back then he lived a white life instead of a black life so to speak. But his brothers and sisters never held grudges against him or anything like that.[308]

For young Chris Johnson, growing up in Broadmeadows and Melbourne, sport and particularly football were big community and social events:

> My earliest football memories is watching Dad play for various teams. I remember watching Dad playing in premierships for Vic Eels and the

Fitzroy Stars. That was fantastic because at those games that's the time when we got to see our cousins and to mingle. In the pre-season I recall travelling to various little parts around the countryside in Victoria. Travelling all these distances just to play footy on a Wednesday night. Travelling two or three hours just to play a game of footy. I also recall Dad playing with the Jacana Football Club, the club I grew up playing for.[309]

Johnson played a variety of sports in Melbourne that seemed to complement his football:

There were a lot of other sports when I was a kid especially when we lived in Melbourne. We played cricket, we played golf, we played basketball and volleyball up at the local school. We'd do any sport that was available. I had a lot of sports at my fingertips and I guess playing all those sports really got me connected with football and helped a lot.[310]

He found the excitement of football alluring and the thing he wanted to pursue. It seemed to give him a sense of release from the everyday pressures of growing up. The football oval was the place where he came to be himself:

I guess with football I enjoyed running and bouncing the ball. It was out on the grass, it was out in the open air, it was competitive, it was rough and I sort of liked that aspect of it. I really liked taking marks. When we were just kicking in the yard and stuff I wouldn't worry about kicking, I'd give it to someone else to kick. I'd just jump at anything. The hangers, they were the most important thing to me.[311]

He continues:

I sensed it [football] gave me a lot of security. It gave me something that I could relate to other people with because of how I related to it. When I played football I didn't worry about anything else but football. I wouldn't even think about the score. I had no other worries about being black or white or anything. It gave me a new life. Then about two or three hours after the game then I'd worry about the score and other stuff.[312]

As Johnson grew older he was, in his words, 'guided' into football by his parents and extended family:

As a young fella I was never pushed. Mum and Dad, they focused on footy a fair bit, but never pushed me. There was never tears or anything like that. Things started becoming serious in the under-18 TAC Cup level and there were times where I wanted to cut corners and did not want to go back. But my parents said, 'You'll thank us later on in life,' and I am.[313]

Having played the majority of his junior football with Jacana Football Club in Melbourne's tough Broadmeadows district, Johnson then went on to play with the West Victorian Eels in the state carnival. Much to some of his family's irritation, Johnson was then coaxed to play with a Melbourne sporting institution, the inner-city Fitzroy Stars. Aged 16, it was here that Johnson got his first taste of tough senior football. Johnson was then invited to try out for the Northern Knights in the TAC Cup competition where he was 'a skinny kid running on the wing and half-forward, sneaking through and kicking a couple of goals here and there.'[314]

In 1994, aged 17, Johnson's big break came when he was drafted to the Fitzroy Lions. He made an immediate impact, missing only a few games in his first three seasons. Coming to Fitzroy meant following in the footsteps of other great Indigenous footballers; players like Joe Johnson and Sir Doug Nicholls. He recalls his first time down at the Brunswick Street Oval:

When I got to Fitzroy there was Ross Lyons, Paul Roos, Peter Satori, James Manson, Jason Baldwin and Mark Zanotti. They were the big names there that had played a lot of footy.[315]

Despite the financial and on-field hardships that Fitzroy faced as a club, Johnson found the experience of playing for one of the old inner-city Melbourne clubs a great thrill:

It was pretty difficult at Fitzroy. We weren't winning many games but it was a great place to be around. The supporters were fantastic and really got behind you and gave you everything. As soon as you walked in the door you were a Fitzroy person. I felt very welcome there. The people that worked there were fantastic. I never felt a little bit out of place. To do our weights though we were in this little shoebox. We all had to squeeze into this little room.[316]

Johnson experienced mixed emotions with the merger of the Brisbane Bears with the Fitzroy Lions in 1996. His first thoughts were how he would handle the transition to Brisbane, if he was selected to play for the new team:

Going back to when the merger was first announced, I was approached I think it was about round sixteen. I was contacted by the Brisbane Lions to sign a contract. They had eight players to bring up so I ended up signing. I just tried not to worry about it and thought hopefully the Brisbane Lions could have more wins than losses. I'd already signed up with the Brisbane Lions and there were still guys waiting in the wings not knowing what was happening. It was a bit strange for me in my last couple of games knowing that I had a future and some of my team-mates didn't. I was uncomfortable with it but I was young and I just wanted to cement myself into the team. I didn't want to go into the draft and wait around to be selected and have an unknown future.[317]

Johnson remembers playing in the last games for Fitzroy, as not being easy:

In our last game in Melbourne my memory is of everyone just coming on to the ground when we done our lap of honour against Richmond at the MCG. I remember sitting in the rooms doing the debrief of the game and you could just hear all the Fitzroy supporters singing from outside. They all wanted to get into the rooms. The race was chokkas, everything was chokkas and everyone was just singing the theme song. In our last game when we were coming off the ground the Freo [Fremantle] players made a line letting us walk off the ground. That was fantastic. I vividly remember a photo of us all in the rooms. It wasn't planned. Blokes were standing up, some were sitting down, some kneeling. I was a bit young and didn't sort of understand what was really happening. I really didn't soak enough in. They're the most valuable memories I have of my last two games at Fitzroy.[318]

When the Fitzroy Football Club disbanded in 1996, Johnson experienced what can only be described as a delayed transitional experience. He had already played in the AFL for three years, whereas many players experience the process of moving away from home early in their careers. Johnson explains:

Moving up here [to Brisbane] the transition was very hard. I was all for it initially thinking like sunny weather, a good life, it was totally different. Coming from a football state and coming here you wouldn't see it [football] on the news, you wouldn't read it in the papers. You're training to be a professional athlete in the elite AFL football comp and there's no AFL football anywhere. It was hard work running in the heat, doing gym in the heat, living in shoeboxes with no air con.

You're up at six o'clock in the morning, you're training until eight o'clock at night, not getting the sleep that you needed because you live in a sweat box. My girlfriend at the time, who is my wife now, she'd moved up and she wanted to move back as she didn't like it. That was the first six months and I sort of thought, 'Geez I'm getting out of here straight away.' I did everything in my power to get back to Melbourne.[319]

Johnson's pleas to the football department fell on sympathetic but somewhat deaf ears, and promises to trade him south amounted to nothing. Luckily for the Brisbane Lions Football Club, their members and fans, and for Johnson himself, the Club kept him:

I'm probably grateful that they [Brisbane Lions] did because I'm fourteen years up here now and I got three premierships and four grand finals and made some fantastic friends along the way.[320]

The move to Brisbane was in many ways a blessing in disguise for Chris Johnson as his career lasted longer than many other footballers and he played an important role in one of the truly great AFL sides in history. His standing in the game as one of the AFL's great back pockets is assured. Despite Johnson's longevity in the game, and his status, he did experience the darker side of racism in the AFL:

Many times I was called various names out on the ground especially coming through the ranks and in juniors. When I came in in '94 that's when the Michael Longs, Winmars and the Wangeneens were getting abused and it started getting publicised in the early '90s. When I came in it was there but opponents wouldn't say it out loud or in front of the group. It would be quiet in the back of your ear where there wasn't a third party. I guess they probably thought they're going to believe me over you, that's the way I looked at it. I used to wear an Aboriginal mouth guard. One player said to me, 'What are you doing? Are you looking for sympathy wearing that?' That's racial vilification I thought and that was pretty weak of him. It was part of the old mentality that once you walk over the white line you can do anything. But I think as a society we've moved on and I would say since I started playing at the Brisbane Lions I've never copped any racial stuff.[321]

Vilification spurred Johnson on:

[It] made me go harder, made me want to achieve more, made me want to beat whoever had said that. Then I'd just go back and laugh in his face and say, 'Not bad for a blackfella' or whatever they had labelled me. You'd come back with something smart. You certainly wouldn't say anything about the colour of their skin because you weren't going to lower yourself to that level. You were going to do better than some of those discriminating people and that's probably what they felt threatened about.[322]

When Johnson was nominated for the AFL's Indigenous Team of the Century he felt very humbled:

Going through my career I never saw myself as a leader or a captain or anything, especially before all the premierships. So to even be in the company of some of the people that were named in that side that had being playing for many, long years and had done it a lot tougher than me, I was very humbled, very proud and very privileged to be alongside those greats. Then getting me in one pocket and Whitey [Darryl White] next to me was fantastic. I guess more than anything I was proud of being named in the side and having a legacy amongst other great players. And hopefully in the years to come my kids, my nieces and nephews and their kids can look to strive to achieve their own individual success in their lives. It was certainly one of my highest achievements.[323]

The day itself holds many valuable memories:

I recall walking nervously down from the Holiday Inn. I didn't know what to expect. Walking down there my palms were getting sweaty and then it started to hit me. As we started going up the escalators and actually seeing all the faces and all the big names that were there I started getting nervous and thought, geez this is pretty big.[324]

By the end of the 2007 season Johnson's body had had enough and he decided to retire:

I could have gone one or two more years but in the last two years that I played I only managed to put 14 to 15 games together. I approached the club with a contract and the club hadn't got back to me and it was sort of getting to the end of the season. It was actually the last week, the last game. The club said, 'We can't guarantee you a contract.' So myself and my wife sat back and had a think about it for a couple of days. I didn't want to put my family through the pressure of a whole pre-season over three months not knowing what my future was with a young family. Then after about two or three weeks after I retired I got a call from Leigh [Matthews] and he offered me a development role and I was more than happy to stay at the club. I could have gone again at another club but I wanted to stay a one-club man. I had a good run, three wooden spoons and three premierships. It was very hard, very emotional but I think I feel I made the right call.[325]

His many experiences leave Johnson uniquely positioned to see how football has enabled Indigenous people to overcome and deal with many issues:

I think one big thing Indigenous people face is family. I think family can hold you back from achieving your goals but Indigenous people are known to rely on family a fair bit. To put it simply, I think there's no reason why we can't achieve what someone else has achieved. We've got the same blood running through our veins, we've got two feet, we've got two arms, it's just a matter of who's holding you back. That's a major factor. It's the people that are around you and maybe you need to break away from that and go and achieve something that you're not used to and get out of your comfort zone. I think some Indigenous people may face this because they don't want to leave their family so they if they leave their family they may feel that they're letting their family down.[326]

Johnson sees that the biggest challenges that young Indigenous people face today are belonging and alienation. He explains:

I think being accepted that's the biggest thing. It probably goes back to when Indigenous people face leaving their family and what they're used to, it's hard because they need to know they will be accepted into non-Indigenous society. I feel that the biggest thing for young Indigenous people could benefit from [is] getting out of their comfort zone and working out that they can achieve anything they put their mind to with the support they need.[327]

He sees the biggest challenge that Indigenous and non-Indigenous Australians face today is coexistence:

Basically accepting each other and understanding that society has got to be a two-way street. We can't have Indigenous people thinking that non-Indigenous Australians won't accept them. We've got to have respect for what they do and they've got to accept what we do. That I think is the hardest thing. But I think the Australian general public will be a lot better off in understanding Indigenous culture and Indigenous people.[328]

At the time of this interview in late 2008, Johnson was working with the Brisbane Lions as a development officer. He had also been able to experience assistant coaching roles with the Brisbane Lions and was named as the coach of the Indigenous Allstars side that beat Adelaide in Darwin early in 2009. He then moved back to Melbourne where he has taken up the senior coaching role for the Avondale Heights Football Club in the Essendon Districts Football League. Today he is working for the AFL in a range of roles, mainly in assisting developing young Indigenous players who have been selected in the Flying Boomerangs squad and assistant coaching roles for the Indigenous Allstars side.

RECORD

1995–2009

Games: 303
Goals: 521
State: South Australia 2
Premierships: Sydney Swans 2005
Bob Skilton medal: 1998
Fos Williams medal: 1998
Club Best and Fairest: Sydney 1998
Club Leading Goalkicker: Sydney 2000, 2001
All-Australian: 1997, 2000

'Uncle Wilbur Wilson played at Central Districts and he played close to 200 games. He was one of the first blackfellas that I saw who was doing well for himself. He was the first guy that I saw that was playing on the TV. That really struck me and naturally that's what I wanted to do. For me that really got me thinking that if you're any good you can actually do okay for yourself. Growing up I idolised Gilbert McAdam. To me he was one of the first Aboriginal players who was just a superstar. I just thought he was the best. He was the king to me and he still is one of my favourite players.'

Michael O'Loughlin

fter the AFL season finished, Michael O'Loughlin looked forward to coming home to South Australia each year. It was a time to catch up and see the mob and have a few laughs and relax. It was in stark contrast to the sacrifices he had to make being a professional footballer. He had missed plenty of anniversaries, birthdays, family reunions, weddings and funerals. For O'Loughlin, getting back home for Christmas and the holidays was special. The first couple of years coming back was a heady time. As he cruised through the familiar streets of Adelaide, O'Loughlin met up with a steady stream of aunties, uncles, cousins, nephews, nieces and mates who were delighted to see him and catch-up with 'Micky O — the footy star'. The attention back home was one of the things O'Loughlin had expected as he shook hands, posed for photos and constantly fielded questions about playing on the MCG, playing with Tony Lockett or getting coached by Ron Barassi. He didn't mind it at all.

All the adulation was good but the thing that made 'Micky O' tick was that he was able to provide a better life for his family. He loved nothing more than arriving unannounced at a relative's place and taking them shopping, or paying their bills or getting their cars serviced. O'Loughlin felt a great sense of pride knowing that come dinner time in several households across Adelaide, the fridge and the pantry would be full of food with the power on. It was this feeling that made him strong; it was better than kicking the winning goal in a final. To put smiles on Swans fans faces was great, but to put smiles on the faces of those nearest and dearest was something else. This, Michael O'Loughlin told himself, was what he played football for. This was what football was all about.

I met O'Loughlin at the Sydney Cricket Ground on a steamy December morning in 2008. O'Louglin was recovering from an ankle injury and probably had an inkling that 2009 would be his final season. Despite the impending end of his career, O'Loughlin was amiable and willing to discuss his life with me. He began by telling me about his Indigenous ancestry:

> My Mum is Narrungga, which is the York Peninsula of South Australia from the community of Point Pearce. My father is Ngarrindjeri which is the Coorong, Point McLeay. But I was born and raised in the city so I'm a city slicker but I have strong links back to both communities.[329]

Football was the biggest thing in his life when O'Loughlin was growing up:

> My earliest football memory was being in the backyard kicking the footy with my uncles. Just having a bit of fun. Football was huge just like it is in every Aboriginal community. Growing up you'd be sitting around at night and you'd hear your father or your uncles talking about how good a certain player was at some stage or who played for a certain team. It was just something that everyone identified with. When you got a bit older you'd play in carnivals and then you'd see other relatives you haven't seen for a long time and everyone got involved. It was really important.[330]

But he played sports other than football:

> I think I started playing football when I was about 8 for the under-9s. Then I played a little bit of cricket but it was mainly basketball and footy. Cricket clashed with the basketball bit. So if it wasn't footy it was basketball or it was cricket, there was always a ball in the hand.[331]

Football won out mainly because of the connections that O'Loughlin and his family had with the code:

> There was no pressure to play, it was just something you did back in Adelaide. As a kid you'd always go and watch those older guys play and then you thought when you got older you'd play as well and it was just, it went from there. Watching them on the field you'd think, 'That looks good I wouldn't mind having a crack at that.'[332]

The real spark for his football interest came from O'Loughlin's mother's side in the form of his Uncle Wilbur Wilson and Magarey medallist, Gilbert McAdam, both of whom played for Central Districts in the SANFL:

[Wilbur] played at Central Districts and he played close to 200 games. He was one of the first blackfellas that I saw who was doing well for himself. He was the first guy that I saw that was playing on the TV. That really struck me and naturally that's what I wanted to do. For me that really got me thinking that if you're any good you can actually do okay for yourself. Growing up I idolised Gilbert McAdam. To me he was one of the first Aboriginal players who was just a superstar. I just thought he was the best. He was the king to me and he still is one of my favourite players.[333]

Once O'Louglin's interest had been sparked and he could see a pathway to a better life, he started to knuckle down and concentrate on how he could become a better player. This took commitment from both O'Loughlin and his family because he chose to play for Elizabeth, despite living half an hour away in Salisbury North:

I played at Elizabeth Footy Club because my cousin played there and we grew up together. He goes, 'Come and play with us,' and I went 'Okay.' I only played two years there because the Salisbury North footy club was a minute walk away. One day I got a knock on the door from one of the coaches at Salisbury North asking if I'd come and play with them. It made it a little bit easier on Mum because the club was only around the corner and she didn't really have to take us anywhere. So it all worked out.[334]

O'Loughlin played with Salisbury North Football Club until he was 16. At that point he was given the opportunity to play colts for Central Districts in the SANFL, ironically, back in Elizabeth. It was when he took the step from junior district football to the SANFL colts that O'Loughlin started to question his ability in himself:

When I went to Central Districts as a 16-year-old I think I really struggled. I found it a bit difficult. I was mixing with the guys but I didn't really know any of them. I just think I needed someone to pull me aside and show me how to deal with the next step up. I was just a kid who came from the suburbs to then be playing against the best kids in South Australia. I still went to training even if I had to catch a bus or a train. But it was tough. Then I must have played a couple of okay games and I made the Teal Cup squad and I think I played okay in that and on the strength of that I got drafted I reckon. If I didn't play Teal Cup I don't think anyone would have taken a chance.[335]

The chance to go to the Swans in 1995 was O'Loughlin's big break, and something he still sees as being very fortunate for him:

Ron Barassi was the coach and the recruitment managers were Rob Snowden and Laurie Dwyer. I put it down to the Swans thinking, 'Let's get him up for a year or two and see how he goes.' I wasn't really a stand-out player at all I thought. I was very lucky to get drafted. I got drafted at number 40.[336]

O'Loughlin's AFL career had an inauspicious start in 1995. He played 11 games and kicked 12 goals, averaging 10 disposals a game. His debut year was also the one when the AFL introduced their racial and religious anti-vilification laws. Reflecting on this now, O'Loughlin sees how important these were in helping him to transition comfortably into the AFL:

I'm very fortunate I haven't been racially taunted from another player. I couldn't imagine playing where every week you'd just be copping it left, right and centre. We don't have to worry about all that kind of stuff because these guys have gone before us have laid the groundwork, laid the foundation and stood up and said, 'Look, enough's enough.' When you are a teenager you've got enough problems as it is moving away from home and dealing with everything and then to go out and play footy, something that you love, and cop it. That's why the past Indigenous players have got so much respect from us younger guys, the AFL and the whole of footballing world. It's just about building empathy. People acknowledge the tough times our people have gone through.[337]

While his on-field performances were taking shape, O'Loughlin was trying to come to grips with living in Sydney, away from his family:

I started off thinking it was going to be all sunshine and lollypops but it certainly was a culture shock training everyday against men and competing with them. That was very difficult. For the first two weeks I was okay and then I just wanted to come home. I was on the phone ringing my Mum almost every day. Mum told me to stay in Sydney and stick it out. Basically they threw me in the deep end. Then once the proper training started and the practice games started I started enjoying it but the first couple of months I found it really tough to come up.[338]

O'Loughlin is also mindful that when he was drafted to Sydney two of the club's greatest champions were also drafted in: Paul Roos from Fitzroy and Tony Lockett from St Kilda. This had a two-fold impact on O'Loughlin, namely that he was able to learn from two great footballers and because of their star status, potential media attention was taken off him:

> I was very lucky that the year I came through it was with two superstars in Roosie and Plugger. So I sort of slipped under the radar a bit and those two took care of all the media and all that kind of stuff. I just sort of came to training and did my thing and it was good. So I was lucky in that sense.[339]

In his second season, O'Loughlin had 381 disposals and kicked 21 goals for the year. O'Loughlin's improved strength and stamina also coincided with the Swans making the grand final, only to be beaten by North Melbourne. It was to be 1996 when he would cement his place in the Swans' forward line. He developed a reputation as a player with many aspects to his game, his stand-out abilities being his anticipation and reading of the play, his agility and his goal kicking. He reflects on this:

> I think in the under-18s back in Adelaide you were sort of all thrown in together to see how you were going to go. Whereas here [at the Swans] they really look at you and go through your faults and list all the things you have got to do. They give you some goals to aim for and someone would sort of sit me down and go through them all. It helped a lot.[340]

The support O'Loughlin's team-mates offered him at the time was crucial, allowing him to focus on playing football, a necessity if he was not to dwell on being homesick:

> I lived with Matty Nicks who is a West Adelaide guy and Simon Arnott. Those guys are older than me and they looked after me. They showed me how to cook and clean, all the stuff that my Mum did. I never did that stuff before. They'd keep me busy and say, 'Righto, Micky your turn to cook,' or 'Let's go and do something.' They could see that I was homesick and they were too, I owe a lot to those two guys.[341]

With Lockett's retirement at the end of the 1999 season, it became a reality that O'Loughlin would fill a key forward role. This paid dividends in 2000 when he had a solid season kicking 53 goals and was selected in the All-Australian team. Subsequently, from 2001 to 2002, O'Loughlin struggled with the role, such was the level of expectation. In 2003, he returned to brilliant form after struggling with niggling leg injuries, only to be cruelly struck down in the last home-and-away fixture against Melbourne and so was unable to take part in the Swans' finals campaign. In 2005, O'Loughlin played in tandem with Barry Hall, and provided a potent forward line attack. That year Sydney made the grand final and were victorious against the West Coast Eagles in one of the most thrilling games ever witnessed at the MCG. The following year O'Loughlin also had a solid year and played in another grand final, only to be beaten by the Eagles by 1 point. At the end of the 2009 season O'Loughlin retired, having kicked 521 goals and played 303 games. In doing so, he became just the third Indigenous player to have achieved this milestone.

In 2005, O'Loughlin was selected as the starting full-forward for the Indigenous Team of the Century, an honour that he still is very proud of today. He recalls the day:

> [When] I first got the letter saying I'd been nominated I just went 'Oh God, please let me be lucky enough. I want to get in this side.' I looked down at the names and thought, 'Shit, where's a spot for me?' On the day I was nervous because obviously the greats were there. I was thinking I was Nicky Winmar in the backyard then going up and meeting him and talking to Cuz [Winmar's nickname] was just great. To go up to Sydie Jackson and Polly and finally shake their hand. Then when your name is read out I was speechless. It was just huge.[342]

Since retiring from football at the end of 2009, O'Loughlin has been involved with the AFL's high-performance talent programs, as well as its Indigenous program. In late 2010, O'Loughlin was appointed the AIS–AFL high-performance coach, replacing Jason McCartney. Reflecting on his life, he is mindful of the opportunities football has provided, but he very aware that there is still a great deal of work needing to be done at a community level:

> Growing up for me I saw alcohol as a huge problem, not just my family but the whole community where I grew up. If there was a problem it was alcohol that was usually behind it. I vowed that I wouldn't go down that path when I was a kid. I enjoy a beer and I love having fun

but drinking and violence against women are all tied up to the same thing. It's easy to get down on yourself and it's easy to grab a bottle and drink your problems away. At the time I thought I had to stay in school and get a job because I didn't think about the AFL in terms of work when I was a kid. It wasn't until I was sort of 16 or 17 did I think about playing AFL. So it is about choices. Making the right choices.[343]

O'Loughlin sees tapping into and bolstering young Indigenous people's esteem as being a key to securing a better future for many of them:

Starting out playing I had so many people tell me that I would never play league footy in South Australia. Those people were right. I didn't play league football in South Australia, I played AFL instead! If I'd listened to those people I wouldn't be here. When I was 16, I thought that I could help my Mum out if I got a job. I was lucky enough to play footy and help my family. That was the big driving force for me I reckon. That was my big thing because I didn't want my younger brothers growing up like everyone else. I have always lived by the idea that the harder you work the luckier you get. I'm the eldest of four brothers and one sister so I wanted them to have things. I decided earlier on that if I get a job I can help out and that is what I did.[344]

Having been involved with the National Aboriginal Sporting Chance Academy (NASCA) for some time, and always working hard, O'Loughlin is living proof that people can change if they take up the opportunities in life that await them:

I have worked with NASCA for over ten years. It's something that I got into when I was 19 and it is close to my heart. It is from here and the principles I learnt from football and working with organisations like NASCA that other chances came about. But there's a million things I want to do but the path laying a solid foundation down is important for it to be good. But I know the future is good.[345]

Following his retirement from the AFL, having become the Sydney Swans' game record holder and playing for sixteen seasons, the man known as Micky O had this to say:

For me, some guys [play] to be recognised and some play for money but I came with the opportunity that the Swans gave me, to help my family live a better life and hopefully I have done that.[346]

ANDREW McLEOD

RECORD

1995–2010

Games: 340

Goals: 275

State: Dream Team 1

Premierships: Adelaide Crows 1997, 1998

Norm Smith medal: 1997, 1998

Captain: All-Australian 2007

All-Australian: 1998, 2000, 2001, 2006

Club Best and Fairest: Adelaide Crows 1997, 2001, 2007

AFLPA MVP Leigh Matthews Trophy: 2001

'Trying to adjust and fit into the organisation took me a while. Adjusting to everything from training which then was maybe three days a week in the SANFL, to training pretty much every day was tough. You had to change everything, your lifestyle gets thrown out the window and the worst thing is you live in a fishbowl. You become public property. Everyone wants to speak to you. Everyone wants a piece of you.'

Andrew McLeod

I've been lucky on my journey. Not only have I been able to play the game I love on the biggest stages, but I've also gone on a journey, finding myself as a person, while also being a role model for young Indigenous boys and girls...That has been the biggest thrill — to know you have done something to help other people.[347]

In the lead-up to the 1997 grand final, there was much drama, both on and off the field, for the two teams that would eventually play off in the last Saturday in September. St Kilda had not won a premiership since 1966, so the 1997 grand final was the culmination of a big year. They had finished on top of the AFL ladder and won their previous 7 games on the trot. Having blown away the Brisbane Lions and North Melbourne in the finals series, the Saints were heavy favourites to win in the grand final. Earlier in the week, St Kilda's champion Robert Harvey won the Brownlow medal. The count finished in spectacular fashion as the Western Bulldogs forward, Chris Grant, polled the highest number of votes but was ineligible due to suspension. The night before the grand final, Nicky Winmar's father passed away, but Winmar decided to play on and return home to Western Australia after the grand final for the funeral.

Adelaide had made the finals for only the second time since joining the AFL in 1993. Finishing fourth that year, their finals' campaign was one that got more intense the longer it went. In the qualifying final, they beat the West Coast Eagles by 33 points. Then they beat Geelong by 8 points in the second semi-final, progressing through to the preliminary final against the Western Bulldogs. In this game the Crows would come from behind to beat the Bulldogs by 2 points but lost their full-forward Tony Modra with a knee injury.

The grand final was itself a tense affair and provided many highlights. St Kilda's Austin Jones would kick one of the greatest goals in grand final history, running nearly the full length of the ground and kicking from deep in the pocket and on the boundary line. Darren Jarman would kick 6 goals for the game, with 5 in the last quarter. With the Saints up by 13 points at half-time, it would be

Jarman's effort that saw the Crows get up to win the game by 31 points. But it was Andrew McLeod's individual performance that saw him take out the coveted Norm Smith medal.

The off-field drama and game-day tension of this grand final was perhaps best summed up in the few fleeting moments between Winmar and McLeod at the end of the game. As the final siren sounded and the MCG erupted, McLeod spotted Winmar and walked over to him. Winmar, having played on pure emotion all day, was spent. The two men met on the hallowed turf and embraced. The power of the moment was palpable. At one level it was simply two men recognising that they have shared a great moment in Australian sporting history. One was the winner, the other had lost. On a deeper level it was the respect of a young player for an elder who has faced massive personal odds to play on football's biggest day. At its heart, though, I think it is saying much more. It was the moment when the mantle was passed from Winmar, the first Indigenous player to reach 200 AFL games, to McLeod, the hottest rising star in the land who went on to be the AFL's Indigenous record holder. In two more seasons, Winmar would no longer be playing at the elite level and McLeod would be a household name across Australia. One small simple action was imbued with so much. The moment is symbolic of many things but in the blink of an eye it was gone as McLeod rubbed Winmar's head and made his way to his Adelaide team-mates to celebrate his victory.

I first met McLeod in his hometown of Darwin early in February 2009. I had been invited by the AFL Players' Association to present to all the Indigenous players in the AFL for their bi-annual camp. Ironically, this culminated with the Indigenous Allstars side, of which McLeod was the captain, taking on Adelaide. As we sat outside in the humid Darwin air, McLeod told me about his family:

> I'm Wardaman and Wargamaygan. Wardaman's from a bit southwest of Katherine and Wargamaygan is from the Torres Strait. So my grandmother was an Aboriginal lady and my grandfather was Torres Strait.[348]

McLeod's earliest football memories originate from his grandmother's country:

> My earliest football memories are when I grew up in Katherine 300 km south of Darwin. From the age of about 2 until I was about 9 I was just playing a bit of footy but watching a lot of footy in Katherine with

my old man. Then coming up here [Darwin] at different stages and watching the Buffaloes playing. All my family played for Buffaloes. My grandfather played for the Buffaloes and my great grandfather was one of the first registered Aboriginal footballers in Darwin. His name was 'Put' Ahmat and those gates at Marrara are named after him. So it was inevitable I was going to play footy at some stage so I ended up playing for Buffaloes.[349]

Moving to Darwin, provided McLeod with a wide variety of other sports he could play all-year round:

I was pretty lucky as I got to play different sports from an early age. There was soccer and both union and league. I did some boxing. My Mum's brother he was a boxer so I spent a bit of time doing that. Back then football wasn't my biggest love. Back in those days I was just about playing union and footy in the Wet season and league and soccer was in the Dry. I'd throw a bit of athletics in also. It was all about what are you doing in different seasons and playing for me was about getting outside and doing things and being part of that. As kids in the territory we were out doing something all day like going hunting with our uncles.[350]

Despite football not being McLeod's number one sporting interest as a child, his family's influence in fostering his talents was important:

My old man played a lot of footy and because he's originally from Victoria and he's a bit of a football nut. He played a lot of footy here for Buffaloes and so there was a bit of an influence from him. In Katherine I'd just follow my brother around. So for me my brother who was older he was like my hero he played footy and whatever my brother did I wanted to do.[351]

The move to Adelaide in 1994 initially took McLeod by surprise:

My old man tricked me into coming down to Adelaide. I was only 17 and thought I'd only be here a couple of weeks. Little did I know I'd be here for good.[352]

He continues:

I did not have any relocation issues really. I hated the winter and stuff, I still hate the winter now, but relocating was fairly easy. When I left

Darwin I only had one bag and that was it. What was meant to be three weeks turned into fifteen years.[353]

McLeod's father could obviously see something special in his son and he implored him to stick at his football. Despite being angry at his father at first, McLeod settled down to play football with the Port Adelaide Magpies. It took him only just over a month to get an opportunity to play in his first senior game with Port Adelaide in 1994:

> I played with the Port Adelaide Magpies in the SANFL. I played 14 games with the Magpies and managed to play in a grand final; I won a premiership and then came back here to Darwin.[354]

McLeod's ability as a footballer meant the recruits sat up and took notice. Fremantle were about to enter the competition as the new side; they would have the first chance to speak to McLeod. In the following weeks, McLeod and his father travelled to Perth for the preliminary meetings. It is now draft folklore that the Dockers passed up one of the game's greatest players. McLeod recalls:

> I put my name in the draft and Fremantle picked me up as a pre-concession. They could pick two players from South Australia and they picked myself and Darryl Wakelin. I went down and had a meeting with them and things didn't go too well so they traded me to Adelaide. At that stage I was happy to stay in Adelaide because I was playing in Adelaide. I was quite happy and it turned out pretty well in the end.[355]

McLeod admits to being 'pretty relaxed', so the biggest adjustment he would need to make would be to commit as a professional footballer:

> Trying to adjust and fit into the organisation took me a while. Adjusting to everything from training which then was maybe three days a week in the SANFL, to training pretty much every day was tough. You had to change everything, your lifestyle gets thrown out the window and the worst thing is you live in a fishbowl. You become public property. Everyone wants to speak to you. Everyone wants a piece of you. Everyone wants to know about you and everyone wants to poke and prod you. A lot of times in the early part of my career I didn't feel like I fitted in. Coming from a small town it was hard to fathom what was going on. I was different because of my upbringing and who I was. A lot of those blokes, all their life was about the club. They'd sorted out

where they wanted to be. Football was number one for them whereas for me, and still to this day, football is number two.[356]

Perhaps the reason for the increasing demand for McLeod was because of the way he played. Many Indigenous players are stereotyped as having silky skills and being quick. McLeod seemed to have these things in spades, but he also had an x-factor, an effortless coolness which was bound up in his ability to seemingly glide across an oval. While some players played if they were playing their last game, McLeod never looked in danger of being run down and tackled. He was also dynamic around goals which he proved to great effect against Hawthorn:

> In my debut against Melbourne I spent a lot of time on the bench and hardly got a touch. I was dropped to play with Port [Adelaide], played alright, and got another game for the Crows against Hawthorn at home. I got some good touches [15 and 2 goals] and it doesn't get much better than kicking the winning goal from a tight angle in front of 45,000 people in your second game.[357]

This was McLeod's welcome to the AFL elite and was as pressure-filled a moment as any young rookie had experienced. The Crows had clawed their way back from a 34-point deficit at half-time and in the dying moments of the game McLeod was being hotly pursued by experienced Hawk half-back, Ray Jencke. Swooping on a loose ball and kicking the goal McLeod reflects upon his bush-hunting skills to explain:

> Clean hands are crucial, especially at ground level. You have to keep practising running flat out and taking the ball one grab. It's a bit like chasing geese in the bush: either you grab them by the neck one grab or they bite you.[358]

Two years later, in the 1997 grand final, and having cemented himself as Adelaide's half-back sweeper, McLeod would hear the roar of nearly 100,000 people as he won the Norm Smith medal for the first time. McLeod also won the Best and Fairest for the Crows in the same year. In 1998, McLeod won his second Norm Smith medal as the Crows won back-to-back premierships. In doing this McLeod stamped himself as one of the AFL's marquee players.

One of the big moments in McLeod's football life was the introduction of Rule 30, the AFL's racial and religious anti-vilification laws. Despite McLeod's standing in the AFL, he was still subject to racism from the crowd and he battled to understand the reasons:

> It was a big moment for me. It was my first year of AFL footy and it [Rule 30] helped my career. I knew about it because of talking to Majo [Michael McLean] and Longie [Michael Long] and the shit that they've been through. So I was in a privileged position because of those blokes who pioneered it. For me, having those guys stand up and pave the way for myself and these younger players has been great. I copped it a lot, not from players but from the crowds. I've been called every name you can think of. When it originally happened my first reaction was, 'I'd love to jump the fence and smack them in the head.' It was hard. I talked to my Dad and my brother about it a lot because when it happened it was hard for me to go and talk to other people in my footy club about it because they didn't understand. So talking to people that understood it and were able to break it down for me helped a bit. I used to get so fired up and it spurred me on more than anything.[359]

For nearly fifteen years, McLeod came to epitomise the success of the Crows. However, despite perhaps his best season in 2001 when he averaged 25 possessions a game and picking up just about every media and peer award in the AFL, he would be runner-up to Jason Akermanis for that year's Brownlow medal. Not even his 37 possessions in the final round against Fremantle would see the umpires give a single vote to McLeod, thus depriving him of the AFL's highest individual award. In some ways this was alleviated by numerous All-Australian selections, and selection in the AFL's Indigenous Team of the Century:

> It was one of the proudest moments in my football career. What it represented was the honouring of the past and the present. It was a bit surreal. I remember standing up there next to bloody Barry Cable and Stephen Michael and all these players that I held in such high regard. You sort of question yourself and whether or not you belong there. I was very proud and it was definitely one of the greatest highlights of my career.[360]

He continues:

> It's not often you get to see that much talent in one room. I was pumped and I always will remember Ernie Dingo running around he was that excited. I've never seen someone so excited; he was just

loving it. He came up to me as he'd just come back from overseas and he had the McLeod tartan which is the same colour as the Aboriginal flag. He's bought it over and gave it to me and it's one of the things that I remember about that, he was so proud to bring it back and to give it to me. It sort of summed up the day.[361]

Aged 34, and despite all of his achievements and milestones, McLeod succumbed to the demands of football and with an ageing body he hung up the boots with the Adelaide Crows at the end of the 2010 season. McLeod understands better than most the importance football has both historically and socially for Indigenous Australians today:

I suppose footy for my family in the early days was a place where people could express themselves. Football was seen as a place where they could be seen on a level playing field. In the early days, society wasn't the way it is now so footy was a place where they could be themselves.[362]

Andrew McLeod believes the history of Indigenous Australians has been a difficult one for many non-Indigenous people to come to terms with, and for Indigenous Australians to overcome:

What happened from the early days from being pushed off and driven away from our land turned a lot of Aboriginal people into beggars. That's probably the biggest thing that we've faced and that stands out to me as us being segregated.[363]

He continues:

I think the biggest thing for us at the moment is education and health. So to turn that around and fix it, that's something we as footballers can promote because of who we are and what we stand for, healthy young men forging a career. Breaking down stereotypes is important. I think we need to stand up and say, 'We're still here, we're survivors, we're still going. We're the oldest living culture in the world and we can adapt.' Changing the mind-set of people out there is important. Education to me is about non-Indigenous people learning about the history of Aboriginal people and having some input and having that awareness. People need to understand our issues and that way we can all move forward. Until the day that we get it [Aboriginal history] into the education system I can't see people understanding it.[364]

McLeod believes that in some ways, this started with the federal Apology to the Stolen Generations:

I remember sitting there and I cried for a while. I thought about my grandmother and what it would have meant to her and all the people that were part of that Stolen Generation. I thought what it would feel like if I was in their shoes. For us as people to move forward and stand up it probably gave me a bit of a spur on and I thought, 'Here's my opportunity to lead and show the way as well for the next generation.' I've already tried to do that with my footy.[365]

Now that football has finished McLeod does not want to rest on his laurels. Instead, he wants to really capitalise on the next phase of his life:

For me I would want to make a difference. Being hands-on and getting out and helping my people in some way shape or form would be great. If I can work closely with the AFL maybe through some programs, that's probably something I'd like to do and try to get the best out of our people.[366]

BYRON PICKETT

RECORD

1997–2007

Games: 204: North Melbourne 120; Port Adelaide 55; Melbourne 29
Goals: 177: North Melbourne 81; Port Adelaide 80; Melbourne 16
State: South Australia 2
Premierships: North Melbourne 1999; Port Adelaide 2004
Pre-season Premierships: 1998
Norm Smith medal: 2004
Norwich Rising Star award: 1998
All-Australian: 1999

'Where I got my confidence and belief in myself was looking up to older people. My great grandmother, who has passed away, she lived until 107. Her name was Clara George...I think that's where I got my confidence and belief in myself and she's probably the main one I always look up to. I just wanted to make my grandmother and my family proud. '

Byron Pickett

S itting on his mate's couch in Adelaide watching the 1996 AFL draft on TV, Byron Pickett reached what could be called a moment of truth. It had been a long journey to get to this point. He had travelled many kilometres and played a lot of football and now his future was staring at him via a 48-inch Samsung. Pickett had made many personal sacrifices to pursue his dream of playing with football's elite and now was the time of reckoning. Sitting alone, watching Wayne Jackson doing the formal part of the draft ceremony in a methodical, clinical tone, belied the tension he felt inside. Pickett sat there chewing on his fingernails, his eyes glued to the set. His senses attuned to every movement and sound the television produced. It had all come down to this.

The main emotion he felt was a stilted kind of hope. He was not as confident as many of the other boys who were nominated for the draft that year. He had spoken to some clubs but not as many as he had hoped for. Did this mean he was not good enough? Did they not think he could cut it? Questions kept rolling through his head on an endless loop until he dared not think about the outcome. Pickett got up, went to the kitchen to get a glass of water, came back to the TV and sat down again.

The number one draft called in 1996 was Michael Gardiner for West Coast. This was followed by Chris Heffernan from Geelong, who went to Essendon. Then Nathan Brown at pick ten went to the Western Bulldogs. Tough Oakleigh Chargers utility, Heath Black, went to Fremantle at number twelve. At fifteen, Max Hudghton went to the Saints. And so it went. Each number read out the small lounge room seemed to push in on him. It was like being in a submarine. The picks went into the twenties, then the thirties, then the forties. Pickett started to pace the room, stopping only to hear each club announce their picks. When his name was not called he let out a heavy sigh: a weird mix of relief and frustration. 'Pick 56. Cameron Mooney,' said North Melbourne's coach Denis Pagan in a monotone. Pickett needed some sort of release from the strange tension he felt. He dropped chest first onto the floor and pumped out twenty quick push-ups. He jumped up ready for the next pick. He felt his chest and arm muscles tingle. It felt good. He loosened his neck muscles like a prize-fighter before a bout. Agonisingly, it kept going. Kevin Sheedy announced, 'Pick 65. Paul Hills.' It was North Melbourne's turn again. There was a brief discussion amongst the North Melbourne coaching staff. Then Dennis Pagan announced, 'Pick 66. Byron Pickett.'

Wide-eyed, Pickett stood as still as a statue. Then he erupted and punched the air while doing a little dance. Pickett looked around and took stock. He picked up the phone and tried to ring his mate who was at work. It rang out. He quickly changed and raced down to the bus stop. He was going to head into town to see his friend and celebrate. As Byron Pickett sat on the bus on the way into Adelaide's CBD, the smile on his face was huge. He reflected on things. His family, his friends and all the games of footy he had played. It had all been worth it because now Byron Pickett was on his way. Byron Pickett was a Kangaroo.

I met Byron Pickett for the first time at the Ceduna Foreshore Hotel and it was no easy task. Two flights, many phone calls and one long walk from my hotel to the Foreshore on a 42-degree day would see me arrive an hour earlier than our designated interview time of 4 pm. As I rehydrated in the air-conditioned splendour of the Foreshore, I reflected on the status that Byron Pickett held in football circles, and strangely, I became concerned. Pickett seemed like a no-nonsense kind of player, a kind of Clubber Lang character of the AFL. Straightforward, hard-hitting, a no-beg-pardons type. What if he took one look at me and did not want to talk? That's what no-nonsense types do, don't they?

As I went back over my questions for the umpteenth time I looked to my left and out onto the bay that sparkled with the hot afternoon sun. No sooner had I mentally drifted off than someone sidled up beside me. It was Pickett. He was smaller than I expected and he looked fit. He smiled and shook my hand. I bought him a beer and we got down to business. He began by explaining his Aboriginal ancestry:

> I've got two sides; my Dad's a West Australian Noongar, Ballardong.
> My Mum's Yamaji and her blackfella name is Budimaya.[367]

Picket was born in Kellerberrin on 11 August 1977, and he grew up in the smaller neighbouring town of Tammin, home of another famous Noongar family, the Kicketts. From here the family moved to Quairading, spent time in the goldfields, then finally ended up in Geraldton and closer to Pickett's mother's family. At some point it was decided that to make a go of things the Pickett family would need to move interstate:

> Mum and Dad thought it was a good thing to move us. Obviously we love our families and that, but you know when you want to go somewhere and do something in life that's one of the sacrifices you've got to make you know. So we come over to get away from family and start our lives over here. I suppose in a way my parents succeeded in what they wanted to do.[368]

Pickett's family's home would now be in Port Lincoln in South Australia:

> We spent most of our lives at Port Lincoln. We grew up there. We've got a lot of friends there. It's pretty much where I grew into a man so to speak.[369]

Despite his strong South Australian connection, Pickett's first football memories are back in Western Australia:

> My Dad and a couple of uncles played for a club named Bencubbin. I played for them in the under-10s. In my first game I actually remember playing with jeans and footy boots and jumper. I just had no footy shorts at that time so I just thought, 'Bugger it, I might as well just play with jeans on.'[370]

As a child, and growing up and moving around a lot, sport was one of the constants. It let him connect with people from the wider Indigenous community, as well as the non-Indigenous community:

> Probably the other sport other than footy that I used to love playing was basketball. I don't know why but blackfellas just seemed to play it. I never really took to cricket. I didn't really take much notice of it. I mean the only cricket I used to love was on the beach or backyard cricket that was probably the only times I played it. Footy and basketball was probably the main two.[371]

The support of his family was crucial to Pickett's pathway in playing football, as was recognising other Indigenous players he could look up to and aspire to:

> I think growing up watching Derek [Kickett] playing and Dale [Kickett] and Nicky Winmar and Longie, you know all those players that really put us on the map, helped me. Also, because blackfellas are really close, especially with their Mum and Dad, I think that was probably the main boost that I got was from them. But probably where I got my confidence and belief in myself was looking up to older people. My great grandmother, who has passed away, she lived until 107. Her name was Clara George. She got a letter from the Queen. I think that's where I got my confidence and belief in myself and she's probably the main one I always look up to. I just wanted to make my grandmother and my family proud.[372]

When playing colts for the Mallee Park Football Club in Port Lincoln, Pickett was one of the many players invited by South Australian clubs to try their luck in the SANFL in 1994. As the long drive to Adelaide from Port Lincoln and back again each weekend was not feasible, Pickett made the difficult decision to live in Adelaide to play colts for the Port Adelaide Magpies:

> When I started in Adelaide with the under-17s with Maggies, Mum come across every couple of weeks and then went back. She caught the bus and had a couple of weeks with me in Adelaide and then went back to the family.[373]

Despite the hardships of living day-to-day in Adelaide, Pickett was playing good football and was being touted by some as having a chance to make it to the next level. However, Pickett came to the stark realisation that it was possible he was not up to the mark, as only a few months out from the AFL draft, he had heard nothing from any AFL clubs. Doubts crept in that he might not realise his dream in the big leagues. Fearing the worst he turned to his mother for advice:

> At one stage I was just sitting down having tea at home with Mum. I had been there [Adelaide] for about a year and a half and I said to Mum, 'I don't think anything's working out here, I might cruise back to Lincoln in a couple of weeks. I haven't been approached by anyone.' She come out and said, 'Well just stay here for the rest of the year,

don't worry about the next two weeks but stay here for the rest of the year and stick at it, you know something positive might happen.'[374]

Pickett continues:

> Then about three weeks later that's when I got the card underneath the door at my house from an Essendon official. Then they rang me and wanted to have lunch, so I had lunch with him. We had a yarn and he asked me to put my name in the draft. They couldn't make any promises about picking me up, but I just put my name in the draft and ended up sitting at my mate's house by myself on draft day.[375]

The relocation to Melbourne was a fairly seamless affair for Pickett:

> It wasn't really that hard. I think that first move to Adelaide really helped. I never thought I'd live in Melbourne though. I always thought it was too big. When I first went to North Melbourne, we stayed in the clubhouse with some of the other draftees. That was pretty good because you got to know the other draftees. So it wasn't too hard for me but it was always a big step and I reckon it took me a year and a half to settle.[376]

The other factor helping the transition to Melbourne was Pickett's North Melbourne team-mates:

> When I first rocked up at North Melbourne Wayne Carey was probably one of the first ones that came up and shook my hand and said, 'How you going? We're glad to have you.' Then the rest of the leadership group like Anthony Stevens, Glen Archer, Micky Martin, they weren't backward in coming forward. So that really helped me when I first went to the club. When Winnie Abraham came I just came out of my shell completely, because I knew that when he got there it made me feel a lot more comfortable.[377]

Despite debuting in 1997, Pickett would play only one senior game with North Melbourne. The following year, the year Abraham arrived from Fremantle, Pickett won the Norwich Rising Star award. The year following that, Pickett would play in the first of two grand finals and became known as one of the league's toughest players.

As a defender, Pickett developed a reputation for a ruthlessness that bordered on the clinical. His hardness and efficiency in disposing of opponents left many feeling that he was a dirty player, but this in many ways was an unfair appraisal as he did so within the rules of the game at the time. He explains:

> Off the field I'm not really aggressive. I'm not a big guy: I'm only five ten [1.78 m]. I've grown up watching my uncles and Dad play that type of footy. They did all that hard stuff. I just learnt from them. I used to do that stuff when I was playing under-17s at Maggies and at Mallee Park as well. Footy is a tough sport and you can't shirk it, you've got to show some aggression and being a tough player you've got to keep your reputation up. They [the AFL tribunal] wanted to get me for years though.[378]

Pickett returned to Port Adelaide in 2003 after 120 games and 81 goals for North Melbourne. Moving back to his old club and playing alongside the Burgoyne brothers, Che Cockatoo Collins and Port captain, Gavin Wanganeen, must have seemed like a homecoming. Pickett kicked 42 goals for Port in his first year but was hampered with injuries in 2004 which kept him out for ten weeks. At finals time Pickett was fit and ready. Despite a patchy preliminary final, Pickett finished with 3 goals and 20 possessions, earning him the Norm Smith medal. By the end of 2005, Pickett's career was over at Port and the Melbourne Demons decided to take a punt on the 28-year-old warhorse. Over the next two seasons Pickett provided valuable service for Melbourne, playing 29 games and providing a degree of steel to their game-day structures. Despite his age and weight issues, he maintained an aggressive defensive style of play that would see any player on him earn their kicks. By the end of the season in 2007, he announced his retirement from the game.

Byron Pickett's dream of playing elite football was realised at three great clubs. He can rest easy in the knowledge that he was a significant contributor, and in many ways helped to highlight the holistic attributes of Indigenous footballers when specific stereotypes about Indigenous players abounded. Pickett has been fundamental in that shift. His selection in the Indigenous Team of the Century was special, as was playing with and against Gavin Wanganeen, whom he considers to be the best Indigenous player he has seen:

> To tell you the truth I had no idea I was going to make that team. I was stunned at first then over the moon. To be amongst all those fellas and selected in the Team of the Century with them was pretty awesome. I've got that poster up in my house at the moment and it comes very close to the premiership teams. But that was obviously a great memory for the rest of my life.[379]

Pickett says this about Wanganeen:

> I didn't really take much notice of him when he first started, but as
> the years went on and the way he played and his leadership on and off
> the field, I think he is right up there. Playing footy with him and to see
> how he went about his training and his footy he was pretty awesome.
> Watching him play was great.[380]

These days Pickett is happy to see what work and football opportunities come
his way:

> For six months I was working with the TWT [Tjutjunaku Worka
> Tjutaand] in Ceduna, helping out with the Department of Sport and
> Recreation in 2008. I've been getting coaching offers from around
> Australia. I got one or two in West Australia and one in Victoria. Right
> now I'm back in Port Lincoln playing for my old club Mallee Park. In
> two or three years I will probably hang the boots up I think.[381]

But it is not just football issues that keep him focused. The events of recent years
have been very interesting to him, given the Apology to the Stolen Generations
on 13 February 2008:

> I think one of the big things we were waiting for was the Sorry Day
> [Apology]. I reckon that's one of the biggest things that have happened
> in the history of Australia. I've had uncles and family who were part
> of the Stolen Generation. When my Dad was young at a place called
> Badjaling near Quairading they come there, they wanted to grab all
> the kids and my Dad's parents and all the other parents just stood up
> with sticks and said if you come and try and take my kids we're going
> to hurt you. If you sit back and think about things that happened back
> in the day it's unbelievable. There's still a bit of hatred around now
> but it's way better than what it was. I think that's probably one of the
> biggest things that happened for all the blackfellas in Australia and it'll
> be obviously remembered that for a long, long time.[382]

In many respects, the decision his parents made to relocate when he was young
was pivotal in Pickett being able to realise his life's goal of playing football at
the AFL level. It also provided both he and his family with issues they needed to
confront and make decisions about:

I think the biggest challenges for me was getting away from family. I think you can stay with your family too long and then you're just going to eat yourself away. You're just going to drink and smoke too much when you're with all your mates. I think the best thing to do is to get away and learn to live by yourself. And if you can learn to live away from your family anything can happen.[383]

He continues:

For me the sacrifices that I made were tough on those that were closest to me. Getting the right support was really important. My wife, Rebecca Saunders, was a massive help and without her I would not have been able to do what I did. She left her hometown of Ceduna for ten years, she made sacrifices and we had five kids together. My motivation was I just wanted to make them proud.[384]

Pickett is also mindful of the issues that young Indigenous Australians face and believes that education is integral to enabling more life choices:

The main thing for young Indigenous kids is to probably stay at school and go as far as you can go. That's what I've been saying to my oldest girls, 'Stay at school and stay there as long as you can.' Every day we have a little argument here and there with the kids to go to school, but a good education is the most important thing and to try and stay away from drugs and all the heavy shit. I think if you have a chance to grow up strong then hopefully they can follow in other Indigenous people's footsteps that have done something with their lives. If you want a future you have to make an effort and do something positive.[385]

PETER BURGOYNE

RECORD

1997–2009

Games: 240
Goals: 193
State: South Australia 1
Premierships: Port Adelaide 2004
All-Australian: 1999, 2003

'In Port Lincoln there is a big Aboriginal community. They've got their own footy club there called the Mallee Park footy club. My father and my uncles they all played there. My Dad was a coach there for a while. I followed in their footsteps so that was the main factor. I liked playing footy because everyone else around me did it.'

Peter Burgoyne

It was the last quarter in the Burgoyne brothers' 'grand final' being played on the bitumen road in Port Lincoln. Out the front of 16 Tulka Terrace, the Burgoyne brothers knew every centimetre of tarmac and they knew all the strengths and weaknesses in one another's football ability. These were tough contests that would go for hours in baking heat or chilling wind. These were never just games for the Burgoyne boys, but grand finals. As the daylight started to fade and the smell of the roast dinner wafted across the road, the final siren was looming. Peter was 5 points down to his younger brothers Shaun and Phil. Peter needed a goal before full-time or he'd never hear the end of it. He could smell victory just like that roast dinner.

Tulka Terrace is not the widest of roads and to make matters trickier it is on a hill. The only concession Peter made for his younger brothers was that he would kick uphill only because he could kick further. Other than that it was dog-eat-dog football. Peter thought he had about a minute to kick the goal he so desperately needed so that bragging rights would be his. As Peter threw the ball up, he and Shaun contested the ruck. Shaun got his fingertips to the ball and gently tapped the dull plum-coloured football towards his 'goal'. As the ball bounced irregularly both brothers scurried towards the footy, their arms outstretched, every muscle straining. Peter got to the ball just ahead of his two brothers and gathered it cleanly. He sold a dummy to his left and seamlessly arced around to his right. Shaun implicitly knew that he would do this as he had seen his older brother do it so many times before. Shaun slightly trailed his brother and was trying hard not to slip over. He kept his feet and kept his eye on his sibling. As he was still on an angle and moving at speed, Peter tried for a quick snap around his body. Peter tried to concentrate as he could feel the breath of his brother on his neck. 'Boooys, time for dinner,' Burgoyne's mother,

Gabriella, called from the front door just at that moment of kicking. The ball slew off Peter's right foot and flew awkwardly through the early evening air. It was out of bounds on the full. Shaun and Phil had won. The younger brothers jumped with joy, high-fiving all the way into the house. Following them was Peter. He held the ball loosely to his hip like a gunslinger. 'Enjoy it boys,' Peter thought to himself. 'Tomorrow I'm going to kick your arses.'

Burgoyne's family has its legacy in the strong ties between South Australia and the Northern Territory:

> My mob is from the South Australian town of Port Lincoln on the Eyre Peninsula. My Dad's people are Kokatha tribe, inland on the far west coast of South Australia. Dad's told us from a young age who our people are; myself and Shaun are pretty much on the ball with it. My Mum's family comes from Adelaide River. They are Warai.[386]

Having lived in Darwin as a young boy, Burgoyne's first football memories come from the Top End in the Northern Territory:

> My earliest football memories are actually when I was living up in Darwin. My Dad played for the St Mary's footy club up here. He played around a hundred games and also played in a few premierships. That's probably my earliest memory when I was probably six or seven. The main thing I recall was Gardens Oval. I used to go there and just play around on the ovals and run around. Also I remember that St Mary's used to win a lot of premierships and were pretty successful.[387]

Even though he liked football in Darwin, it was not until he moved to South Australia that he caught the football bug:

> I moved down to Port Lincoln when I was about 10. That's when I took a really strong liking to footy. I also played a bit of cricket, basketball and athletics. I sort of done all three in the off-season but footy was the main one for me.[388]

The role Burgoyne's family played in guiding him into football was pivotal:

> In Port Lincoln there is a big Aboriginal community. They've got their own footy club there called the Mallee Park footy club. My father and my uncles they all played there. My Dad was a coach there for a while.

I followed in their footsteps so that was the main factor. I liked playing footy because everyone else around me did it.[389]

He continues:

The Mallee Park footy club is pretty famous around Australia. Port Lincoln is a small fishing town of 15,000 and the Aboriginal population is about 3000. But the amount of AFL players that they [Mallee Park] have produced is huge. Graham Johncock, Eddie Betts, Shaun Burgoyne, Byron Pickett, Elijah Ware, Daniel Wells, Harry Miller, they've all got those connections through there. Football there is the number one sport and because we are from the same region we all played for the club.[390]

Burgoyne, whose father Peter was a champion rover for the Port Adelaide Magpies in the SANFL, seemed destined to make it into senior South Australian football ranks. His family upbringing mirrors many Australian families and their engagement with football. He explains:

In our life the father was the one that takes you to footy, it was a father's role to do those things. Mum was the one that cooked the tea and cleaned the house and played that very important role. Our Mum tended to be the one to show a bit more love and was a bit softer. With the old man if you were to play a good game he wouldn't say, 'You played a good game today.' He'd say, 'You could always improve in this area and that area.'[391]

Burgoyne's life was dominated by football, and playing in the Northern Territory and South Australia exposed him to a wide variety of experiences, styles and players:

I played at the Mallee Park footy club for about three years and then I went back up to Darwin and did my high schooling up in Darwin. I played for St Mary's up here. But in the school holidays I would go back down and play with Mallee Park footy club again. Playing for those sides comes back to our fathers and our uncles and the respect we had for them. I have heard stories and seen them play and have no doubt that a lot of them probably could have played AFL but they didn't have the opportunities back then to what we have now.[392]

Those two football clubs were the catalyst for Burgoyne playing with Port Adelaide in the SANFL and Port Power in the AFL:

> Mallee Park is aligned to the Port Adelaide Magpies. All the uncles try to guide them [young players] to get them over to Port Adelaide in the SANFL. So they pretty much all go from Port Lincoln to there [Port Adelaide]. But just because you play at Port Adelaide in the SANFL it doesn't mean you play for the Port Adelaide Power in the AFL. You've got to play in the juniors, the reserves or league and then hope you get drafted, so it's like everyone else. Then you've got to pretty much start all over again.[393]

Peter Burgoyne seems fated to have played for Port Power in the AFL. His family connections were the catalyst for his alignment with the club at the age of 17, and so intent was he on playing for the Power he refused to nominate for the 1995 draft fearing that he would end up with another club. Burgoyne's dream came true and he was drafted to the Port Power as an inaugural member of the squad, and played in the Power's first game against the Collingwood Football Club at the MCG in 1997. Burgoyne's years spent moving between Darwin to Adelaide allowed him to settle into his AFL career:

> For me it wasn't that hard. It was hard in one sense but the thing is when I was living in Port Lincoln I then went to do my schooling up in Darwin. I had to actually leave my parents and come back up here [Darwin] and live with my extended family from a young age. So I pretty much got used to it [living away] and adapted to it. As I got older, around 15, I was thinking about what I was going to do. I knew from then that I wanted to play footy. So going between these places and then moving back to Adelaide took me a while to get used to. But the good thing about it was my family and my parents actually made the sacrifice to leave Port Lincoln where they were living, and come over to Adelaide with me for the two years to help me settle in and that made the transition a lot easier.[394]

Burgoyne needed to juggle the pressure of playing football and having social and work commitments:

> For me, when I first went down to Adelaide I did a TAFE course in Aboriginal Studies. I didn't actually quite complete it but it gave me

something to focus on other than just footy. That was hard. I'd never been to a big high school and because I am a pretty shy person I just wouldn't get myself in a situation where I'd have to talk to someone that I didn't know. That made things a lot harder. Going to TAFE was an eye-opener and being in the city and having to catch buses around took me a while to get used to. I had a girlfriend up in Darwin and all my friends were all back there. I loved being at Port Adelaide but in the back of my mind I missed Darwin and my friends and I always wanted to come back. I'd think, 'What are they doing?' but then I'd ring them and I'd speak to my friends and they'd say, 'Play footy and enjoy the opportunity.'[395]

Burgoyne also drew on the people in his life who were important to him; those he had admired as a young boy:

My idol has always been Michael Long. Coming from Darwin and playing for St Mary's footy club, Longie's probably one of the reasons why I wanted to play AFL because seeing someone from the same club and watching them and following them inspires you.[396]

Burgoyne feels that the Port Adelaide Football Club helped him settle:

That was the good thing about the Port Adelaide Magpies. They also chased me to come down and they wanted me to play for them. They supported me a lot and helped me out with my rent and my transport and all those things, which are small things, but really important. I knuckled down because they can pay your rent or they can pay your board but if you don't want to do it there's no point. I really wanted to do it. I thought I'm okay at this, let's see how far we can go.[397]

Peter Burgoyne exploded onto the AFL scene and developed a reputation as a creative and dangerous small forward. As he gained more experience at the elite level for the Port Power, the coaching staff used him more in the midfield where his offensive skills shone. Added to this, Burgoyne was one of Port's best tacklers and he became one of the game's elite players. His efforts paid off in 1999 when he was selected as part of the International Rules series and played for Australia. Burgoyne's best year was also Port's, when they won the 2004 premiership. This silenced many critics who believed Port were not up to the pressures of finals football. Burgoyne was one of the Port players to be criticised for their finals fade-outs, but his game in the 2004 grand final was a key to their winning. Burgoyne's team-mate Byron Pickett instilled a great deal of confidence in him:

> One of the best players that I've probably played with is Byron Pickett. When he's playing in your side the team's instantly a 3, 4, 5-goal better team because he's the only player that I've ever played with that has presence. If someone was giving me a hard time or whatever I'd just say to my opponent, 'Hey mate, have a look over your shoulder. See who's over there?' and I'd point to Byron. Then I'd say, 'Hey Byron,' and he'd just give him [the opponent] a wink. He did it so many times. But people forget that he was one of the most skilful and polished [players]. He had awareness, he had peripheral vision, he had explosive pace and he could pick the ball up off the ground running at speed. He had the whole package. Gavin Wanganeen was also a champion player.[398]

When Burgoyne was selected in the AFL's Indigenous Team of the Century he was thrilled that Pickett was also selected. He vividly recalls the day:

> For myself personally it's up there with playing in a premiership. I was just rapt to be in there and I got goosebumps thinking that I was just in the initial squad. I told the club that I didn't want to go over [to Melbourne]. I thought it was going to be a waste of time because I was not going to get picked. They said that it was important that I go over. So I did. Then at the ceremony I'm sitting on my table with my idols like Matera, Lewis and Winmar, blokes that you watch growing up. I was just like a little kid in like a candy store. We were sitting down and I heard my name get called, it was quite moving, humbling actually. I was quite embarrassed because of the players alongside you that got selected but also because of the players that didn't get picked.[399]

Burgoyne fully understands the legacy of the players that have come before him and how they have created a space so that he could play to the best of his ability:

> I wasn't quite in the system then [in 1995 and the introduction of Rule 30] but I think it had to be done; it had to be done because if Michael Long and Nicky Winmar didn't make a stand it would probably still be going on today and some people said it's part of game but that kind of sledging goes a lot deeper than that. The hardships that Aboriginal people have had and the obstacles that we've had to overcome have

been huge. It's good now because if it was to happen to me now there's procedures in place and I as a player would go down that line. It probably wouldn't bother me now, unlike when I was a teenager. If someone called me a black bastard or black coon I'd want to talk to the bloke and try to get an understanding about the person and where he's coming from. In the past I probably would have resorted to violence but now as you get older and mature you sort of like deal with things in a lot different ways.[400]

Like many Indigenous people, Burgoyne has experienced racism:

I've experienced it and I've pretty much grown up with racism. I'd be lying if I said I didn't get it along the way. I've been in situations where I'd walk into a shop or a crowded place and I would have a feeling that everyone was staring at me because I was black. I found I wouldn't put myself in that situation where I didn't feel comfortable, like walking into a cafe, because of the perception that people had of me and were staring at me. Because of the colour of my skin, I didn't have a lot of confidence around those issues. If there was a cafe and a fish-and-chip shop, I'd walk into a fish-and-chip shop and get what I needed first before I walked into the cafe. I'd never walk into a cafe and have a coffee when I was younger.[401]

Burgoyne sees that Indigenous Australians have many challenges today, but with the Federal Government's Apology to the Stolen Generations in 2008, he believes that important issues are now starting to be recognised:

Kevin Rudd has made massive inroads and I think that things are starting to look up. To the Stolen Generation he's apologised. It actually choked me up. I thought it was massive. Things are changing slowly. They're not going to change overnight and you've still got people that have got different views and the way they see things in life. But I was listening to a Tupac song the other day and he wrote this song about how, people aren't seeing him for the colour of his skin, they're seeing him for the person and the change he can make in the world. Because just like in America there has been great struggle [in Australia] but theirs [American social justice history] is probably more documented than us [in Australia]. We need more of those things taught in schools.[402]

Burgoyne has now retired from the AFL, and he feels that Australian society has come a long way but there are still many things that need to be considered in terms of race relations in Australia:

> I think things are changing in society and we are changing with them.
> I guess it depends on your upbringing, how you were brought up,
> where you're brought up, where you're born. I was born in Darwin
> and I never experienced racism. I never knew what it was until I left
> the Northern Territory. Up in Darwin it's so multicultural and we play
> sport together and the teams are all mixed together so everyone up
> here for some reason all get along. So I guess by just coming together
> through football white Australia is able to understand us a lot more.
> It's also us understanding them too, it goes both ways it can't be all
> a one-way street. That's what understanding somebody else's culture
> and beliefs is about.[403]

ADAM GOODES

RECORD

1999–Current

Games: 270
Goals: 311
State: Victoria 1
Premierships: Sydney Swans 2005
Brownlow medal: 2003, 2006
Co-captain: Sydney 2008, 2009, 2010, 2011
Club Best and Fairest: 2003, 2006
Club Leading Goalkicker: Sydney 2009, 2010
All-Australian: 2009
Norwich Rising Star award: 1999

'Mum was the biggest thing that directed me into AFL. The only reason I swapped to AFL was when I went to play for a local soccer team Merbein up in Mildura, we went down to the local soccer fields. There was no junior teams, [it] was all seniors. So I would have been a 13-year-old Indigenous boy trying to knock around with all these Italian men. Across the field they happened to be playing AFL and Mum just suggested that I give it a go.'

Adam Goodes

I did not have an entirely happy childhood. Alcohol and domestic abuse were part of my upbringing while my step-father was around; when I was 12 and 13, I used to sneak out the back window and call the cops, just praying they could bring some peace and quiet. It's why we kept moving.[404]

In 1997 Adam Goodes was 17. He was playing for Vic Country against Vic Metro in the under-18s AFL championships. It was a chilly Melbourne day at Princes Park. Goodes started at centre half-back with a modest gathering of interested parents, football scouts and footy die-hards. Goodes was on fire and he stood out due to his rangy athleticism, his spring and his reading of the play. He set up Vic Country's attack time and again. The trajectory towards this moment had not been easy for the young Goodes. But if he knew anything, it's that football could provide him with a ticket out, to somewhere, to be someone. He just needed a bit of luck to balance out all the hard work. Then it happened.

The Vic Metro centre half-forward led out to a team-mate who was running directly towards their goal with the ball. Goodes followed his opponent at full tilt. This is a difficult task and Goodes needed to time his run perfectly; to combine two oppositional forces to beat his opponent: precision and force. As the ball flew through the air like a rocket, the Vic Metro centre half-forward player leapt skyward, his arms outstreched. Goodes leapt at the same time, but his lunge was slightly mistimed and his clenched fist drove into the back of the Vic Metro player's head.

Goodes was penalised, but the umpire's whistle reminded him of another sensation shooting through his hand. It was broken. He took no further part in the championships; it was his one and only game at a national carnival. Goodes began to think. How would this impact on his career? Would his hand be okay? In the shower after the game his hand was packed in ice. He lowered his head beneath the steaming water and closed his eyes. As the hot water doused his black hair, he thought about his family, his childhood, the upheaval, the transience, the obstacles. He was not going back to struggle-street for anything.

He is a footballer; football was his ticket and he was going to take the ride, wherever it took him.

The pathway to becoming an elite AFL footballer did not start off 'normally' for Adam Goodes. He did not play local junior football; instead, he chose to play soccer. This would not be such a great revelation except that Goodes has excelled in a code he did not play in his formative childhood years. Today, Goodes is seen as the epitome of what it means to be an AFL player. As a child, however, he lacked connection to the Indigenous communities of South Australia. And without this link, the opportunity to play football did not seem to present itself in a way that it did with Michael O'Loughlin or Byron Pickett. Goodes explains:

> I grew up on soccer. I wasn't really part of an Indigenous community, to know what it was like to be Indigenous, until I moved away from school. All my friends growing up were white. Obviously I was surrounded by cousins everywhere, but all my friends were white. I grew up in that environment so you hear what perception my friends and their families might have of Indigenous people, but you don't see them in that light because you're actually related to them. You did find yourself not being proud of being of that culture.[405]

Goodes was aware of his Aboriginality but he was made to feel that it was not something he should over-emphasise. Similarly, in having white friends and playing soccer, Goodes's identity was something he negotiated throughout his adolescence. One time he was called a 'coconut' by an extended family member. 'I had to ask Mum what it meant. "Black on the outside. White on the inside," she told me.'[406] But Goodes always knew who he was, and dealing with criticism from either Indigenous or non-Indigenous people based on his identity was something he was able to deal with:

> It wasn't that hard because I thought what really set me apart from being Indigenous or not Indigenous growing up was my confidence. My one weapon I had against racism at school, my one 'in' was always that confidence. I was a very proud Indigenous boy.[407]

This confidence was gleaned directly from his immediate nuclear family and from the sports he played and his willingness to apply himself to the different challenges he overcame:

[I had] the support of my family who made sure that I played soccer, cricket, basketball. I just found that team sports were so important for me growing up because I had this raw ability to just play. I had two younger brothers and we were always knocking about with cricket and basketballs everywhere we went. So without my brothers and a bit of a park to play to hone my skills, who knows what would have happened. I was always at training and always at the games and I give a lot of credit to my coaches and to the families of other kids that I played sport with because my Mum didn't have her licence. She didn't have a car.[408]

This is not to say that the code of Australian Rules did not resonate with Goodes, it did, and it took the form of Gilbert McAdam, from within the humble surroundings of a local hot-dog van:

[My] earliest football memories was working in a hot-dog van at Elizabeth Oval with a school-mate and going out after half-time in the seniors and watching Gilbert McAdam run around for Central Districts. A mate of mine and his family ran it and we just went in there for half a day and watched the footy.[409]

That distinctive memory would have been hatched in the late 1980s, or early 1990s, at a time before McAdam had been drafted by St Kilda and was on his way to become the first Indigenous player to win the SANFL's Magarey medal. This memory is also significant because big changes were taking place both for the AFL and for Goodes himself. At the age of 13, Goodes and his family moved from South Australia to Victoria, arriving in Merbein in 1993. It was here he was faced with a decision that would have significant outcomes for his AFL career in later years:

Mum was the biggest thing that directed me into AFL. The only reason I swapped to AFL was when I went to play for a local soccer team Merbein up in Mildura, we went down to the local soccer fields. There was no junior teams, [it] was all seniors. So I would have been a 13-year-old Indigenous boy trying to knock around with all these Italian men. Across the field they happened to be playing AFL and Mum just suggested that I give it a go. There seemed to be a lot of kids running around there and I was a lot taller and bigger than those kids. It just fitted for me.[410]

Despite being the only Indigenous kid at numerous schools and in the football teams of the towns he lived in, things seemed to 'fit' when it came to Goodes and Australian football. Goodes would play for the Merbein Football Club in Mildura, the Sunnyside Junior Football Club in Horsham and in the seniors for the Horsham Demons Football Club. Eventually he played for the North Ballarat Rebels in the TAC cup, and this brought him under the gaze of the AFL scouts. Reflecting on this, Goodes is honest as to how he was able to negotiate through his teenage years:

> I was always the athlete. The tall kid with skills who stood out on the footy field and, at some point as a teenager, that point of difference seemed to overcome my other point of difference.[411]

Someone else who saw this point of difference was one of Goodes' coaches, Shane Sexton. It was through Sexton's help that Goodes was able to begin the process of making himself into one of the AFL's best footballers:

> Victoria's got a pretty good system of recognising talent. The North Ballarat Rebels are a representative team that kids from all over western Victoria would be selected from to play for this team. Shane Sexton was our recruitment officer in Horsham and he would have to drive anywhere between five to eleven players to training and games on weekends. I think he really put a lot of time and effort into me growing up. He was the one that would always pick me up for training, always drop me off home and put in extra work at training, extra work midweek to work on those deficiencies in my game because I hadn't been playing the game AFL very long. Coming from a soccer background I just felt Shane Sexton put a lot of time and effort into me becoming the person and the footballer I am today.[412]

Despite breaking his hand in the under-18 championships, Goodes recovered well and had a great game in the TAC grand final where he was best afield. In the 1997 national draft, he was picked up by the Sydney Swans at pick forty-three:

> The day of the draft I got a call from Micko [Michael O'Loughlin] and he gave me a welcome to Sydney. He said, 'Did you know that we are cousins?' So I already had Mick O'Loughlin at the football club, plus Troy Cook, Robbie Ahmat and Freddie Campbell. I was just thought of as the next chapter.[413]

The Swans felt that Goodes had potential but really needed to build his body and stamina in the second-tier competition and he spent 1998 in the reserves. In 1999, Goodes got his chance when he filled in for the injured Swans ruck, Greg Stafford. This was the big break Goodes needed, and in his debut year he burst onto the AFL scene, winning the Norwich Rising Star award given to the best first-year player in the AFL. This makes it appear that the transition for Goodes was easy, but this was not the case:

> It was hard living away from home that first year and being away from family and friends but every second week was down to Melbourne playing. I'd travel back to Horsham as much as I possibly could to see them all. But it wasn't until the next year that I really understood what it was or what it was to be an AFL footballer and how much training and that that you have to put into it. Relocation was an easy part for me as I'd just finished Year 12 exams. I've always been travelling to play football so it was a natural progression for me.[414]

He goes on:

> I was super-talented and I relied heavily on my talents. When I wanted to, I could train really well and same with games but I would be very inconsistent. One week I'd be a really good player, the next week I could be the worst player on the team. So the transition for me was hard but at the same time I was able to adjust to it on the big stage and it just made me feel very calm that I could still play really good in big games. To have that ability gave me a lot of confidence that I was up to the same level that most of these other boys were at.[415]

After 1999, Goodes' versatility, height and reliability saw him establish himself as one of the Swan's top players, but for some, a question mark remained over his ability for leadership.[416] With the resignation of coach Rodney Eade, assistant coach Paul Roos stepped into the head coaching position in 2002. Goodes seemed to thrive playing in the ruck and in 2003 he became part of the AFL's elite by winning his first Brownlow in a three-way tie with Adelaide's Mark Ricciuto and Collingwood's Nathan Buckley. This was followed by a Best and Fairest for the Swans and All-Australian selection for the first time. Despite his increasing profile as a marquee footballer and the AFL's anti-vilification laws being in place, Goodes was not exempt from experiencing racial intolerance. In 2002, Goodes was vilified by being called a 'fucking monkey-looking c**t'[417] on the Sydney Cricket Ground (SCG). He reflected on the times that he had been racially abused back in the under-18 competition and compared that with the 2002 incident:

> [Initially] I was just shocked. I felt dirty and felt really like I didn't belong there. This guy thought I didn't belong out there. I didn't even know what it was to be this colour when the first time I was racially vilified which made it pretty easy to get over it, but the next time it happened at senior level really cut me deep and for people to run around on the football field to have that view of an Indigenous person or someone who might be of a different ethnicity. It really hurt me and I made sure that that person knew how much it did hurt me and if that person was to vilify someone else ever again that they'd know what that person felt like.[418]

In 2004, Goodes felt the pressure of being the reigning Brownlow medallist as well as being dogged by niggling injuries. But his 2005 season was fantastic as he played most of his football in the midfield. Freed up from his rucking and backline responsibilities, Goodes could use his agility and pace to produce some truly inspiring football. Helping the Swans to get to the grand final to take on arch rival West Coast, Goodes had a solid game which saw the Swans run out premiers by four points for the first time since 1933.

In 2005, Goodes was inducted into the Indigenous Team of the Century at Crown Casino. This is what he recalls of it:

> I was 23 and to be announced as centre half-back was just a fantastic honour. Especially when I'd only been playing football for maybe eight or nine years. It was definitely up there in winning a premiership medallion. Just being part of such an elite team of pure raw athletes that all had different journeys on how they became AFL footballers. Meeting all the great past players and to be in the same room with so many fantastic footballers of Indigenous background was just sensational. I was sitting on the same table as Mick O'Loughlin and we were just in awe of just how freakish some of those players were.[419]

Early in the 2006 season, Goodes played his 150th consecutive match which, considering the disruptions to his 2004 season, was a considerable achievement. It was testament to his physical and mental fitness and it paid off again as he won his second Brownlow medal: the first Indigenous Australian to do so. When Michael O'Loughlin retired at the end of 2009, it signalled the end of a great era of the Swans as both he and Goodes have been, in many ways, the

AFL's great ambassadors in Sydney. But that does not mean that their off-field or ambassadorial roles will cease:

> Between the AFL and the Sydney Swans Football Club I don't feel like I owe them anything but I do, I do feel like once my football career's over that I'll have a role with the AFL and NSW or the Sydney Swans Football Club in developing younger players or junior talents or having some sort of Academy where myself or Michael [O'Loughlin] will help co-run it and develop Indigenous and non-Indigenous young football talent in NSW.[420]

Taking it on board to do extra study on Indigenous history, Adam Goodes is uniquely placed to begin the next phase of his life as he understands the bigger issues that have impacted upon Indigenous people:

> I think the biggest challenges for any Indigenous person is working out who they are if they have no culture. Without their culture they have no language, they may have no land and some don't even know exactly where they come from so they don't belong. I have no language, I have no culture. My Mum's family was taken to a mission and they were put into foster care. But we are still here, we've adapted and that's the strength of our people, we adapt and we deal with hardships.[421]

Working with young Indigenous Australians seems like the perfect fit for Goodes when he reaches his post-football career. As a role model who has overcome a great deal, it is his achievements and his empathy that will see him achieve great outcomes in whatever field he chooses. For Goodes, the challenges are two-fold and deal with both Indigenous and non-Indigenous Australians:

> I think the biggest challenges for young Indigenous people is just to be part of mainstream Australia. We have a lot of Indigenous people out there, a lot of my cousins, that don't really socialise much with whites or any other part of the community other than blackfellas. To be honest if you want to be part of mainstream Australia you can't live your life like that. It is a shame because these kids aren't part of mainstream, they're just in their own little communities doing whatever they're doing. To improve things you're going to have to deal with non-Indigenous people at some stage in your life.[422]

He continues:

> I'd just say ignorance is the biggest challenge because if non-Indigenous people were more educated to the plight of Indigenous people over the last two hundred years there'd be a lot more understanding. I think if non-Indigenous people had a lot more understanding with Indigenous people and why we are the way we are I think that our relationship could be a lot better than what it is.[423]

DAVID KANTILLA

RECORD

1961–1966

Games: Total games not available: South Adelaide 113, plus 12 seasons St Mary's

Goals: Total goals not available: South Adelaide 106

State: South Australia 4

Premierships: South Adelaide 1964

Club Best and Fairest: South Adelaide 1961, 1962

South Adelaide Hall of Fame

He began his football career with St Mary's in Darwin in the late 1950s, and was recruited to play in the SANFL with South Adelaide in 1961. Being 6'4" (1.93m) highly skilled with an amazing leap, Kantilla debuted against Glenelg in the true full-forward position. His impact with the Panthers was instant.

David Kantilla

Born on Bathurst Island (Tiwi Islands), in the township of Nguiu in 1938, David Kantilla's ancestral name is Amparralamtua. He is recognised as the first Indigenous Australian from a traditional background to play in a southern league, the SANFL. He began his football career with St Mary's in Darwin in the late 1950s, and was recruited to play in the SANFL with South Adelaide in 1961. Being 6'4" [1.93 m], highly skilled with an amazing leap, Kantilla debuted against Glenelg in the true full-forward position. His impact with the Panthers was instant. He kicked 6 goals and, despite his success in the full-forward position, he was moved after only a few games to the ruck. Kantilla's impact as a ruck for South Adelaide was even more significant and over the next two years he would go on to win their Best and Fairest, the Knuckey cup.

As Kantilla battled with the cold temperatures in his adopted hometown of Adelaide, he also had to contend with difficulties faced by his wife, who was profoundly deaf. The lure back to the Tiwis and family was very strong. By focusing on football, Kantilla and coach Neil Kerley led South Adelaide to the SANFL grand final in 1964, where the Panthers ran out winners against Port Adelaide by 27 points. Kantilla played state football for South Australia twice in 1964, an effort that he repeated the following year. At the conclusion of the 1966 season, Kantilla had notched up 113 league games and had kicked 106 goals for the Panthers. As a playing record, this may not appear significant, but the fact that it was the first move by a player from the Tiwi Islands in a less enlightened era says much about Kantilla.

Returning to the Northern Territory soon after the 1966 SANFL season ended, Kantilla became the captain–coach of his old club St Mary's. In 1978 Kantilla was killed in a car accident on Bathurst Island. He is a member of the South Adelaide Football Club Hall of Fame and the main function room at TIO Stadium in Darwin is named 'Kantillas' in his honour.[424]

RECORD

1947–1953

Games: 128
Goals: 3
State: Victoria 2
Premierships: Essendon 1949, 1950
Club Best and Fairest: Essendon 1951

His form in subsequent finals campaigns against Carlton the following year, and North Melbourne in 1950, saw McDonald become one of Essendon's great players. This was exemplified by his winning Essendon's Best and Fairest in 1951 in a team that boasted the likes of club champions John Coleman and Dick Reynolds.

Norm McDonald

Norm McDonald was born in the inner-city Melbourne suburb of Richmond in 1925, just before the Great Depression. A Gunditjmara man, he was gifted with great football ability and was lightning fast. After serving in the Royal Australian Air Force, McDonald began his VFL football career with Essendon in 1947. His debut year saw him take out the Bombers' best first-year player award where he earned a reputation as an inventive and reliable half-back flanker. One of McDonald's signature moves, and an indication of how he was before his time, was that he liked to play off his opponent and to use his pace and reading of the play to create attacking football from the half-back line. This made him a dangerous player and one hard to combat. In 1948, McDonald became a big-game performer as he starred in Essendon's finals series, which saw the Bombers beaten by Melbourne in a rare grand-final replay. His form in subsequent finals campaigns against Carlton the following year, and North Melbourne in 1950, saw McDonald become one of Essendon's great players. This was exemplified by his winning Essendon's Best and Fairest in 1951 in a team that boasted the likes of club champions John Coleman and Dick Reynolds.

In 1952, he was one of the few Indigenous players to win Victorian selection, cementing the claim as a true Indigenous pioneer of the game. McDonald's skill and prowess on a half-back flank were a vital link in Essendon's finals campaigns as well as successive grand finals, where he played in a total of six. In the off-season McDonald kept fit by entering semi-professional sprint meets throughout country Victoria. In 1948, he was the runner-up in the famous Stawell Gift. After retiring from football in 1953, having played 128 league games, McDonald led a quiet life until his death on 28 November 2002 at the age of 76. His legacy is his skill as a great footballer and that he was Essendon's first Indigenous player who played in some of that club's finest teams. He is considered as one of the best half-back flankers the game has seen.[425]

Michael O'Loughlin presents Adam Goodes with the Marn Grook Trophy, AFL round eleven, March 2010.

NOTES

INTRODUCTION

1. M Long, interview with the author, 19 May 2009.
2. C Tatz & P Tatz, *Black Gold: the Aboriginal and Islander Sports Hall of Fame*, Aboriginal Studies Press, Canberra, 2000, p. 8.
3. Australian Football League, *One game for all Australians: how Australian football has acted to counteract racial and religious abuse*, viewed 10 October 2008, <http://www.afl.com.au/Portals/0/afl_docs/afl_hq/Policies/RacialReligious_lr.pdf>.
4. C Tatz, 'The dark side of Australian sport', in D Headon (ed), *The best ever Australian sports writing: a 200 year collection*, Black Inc, Melbourne, 2001, p. 554.
5. S Jackson, interview with the author, 25 September 2008.
6. T Ruddell, 'Albert "Pompey" Austin: the first Aborigine to play senior football', in P Burke & J Senyard (eds), *Behind the play: football in Australia*, Maribyrnong Press, Melbourne, 2008, pp. 89–106.

GRAHAM 'POLLY' FARMER

7. G Farmer, interview with the author, 2 July 2008.
8. For further discussion of Sister Kate's see S Hawke, *Polly Farmer: a biography*, Fremantle Arts Centre Press, Fremantle, 1994, pp. 11–12.
9. G Farmer, interview with the author, 2 July 2008.
10. Hawke, p. 16.
11. *Rabbit-Proof Fence*, motion picture, Australian Film Commission, Woolloomooloo, 2002.
12. G Farmer, interview with the author, 2 July 2008.
13. Hawke, p. 24.
14. G Farmer, interview with the author, 2 July 2008.
15. Ibid.
16. *WAFL Football Legends*, DVD recording, interview of Graham Farmer, Access 31, Perth, n.d.
17. Ibid.
18. G Farmer, interview with the author, 28 February 2002.
19. Hawke, p. 144.
20. Hawke, p. 147.
21. Hawke, p. 157.
22. G Farmer, interview with the author, 28 February 2002.
23. Ibid.
24. Ibid.
25. Ibid.

TED 'SQUARE' KILMURRAY

26. T Kilmurray, interview with the author, 1 July 2008.
27. Ibid.
28. Ibid.
29. Ibid.
30. Ibid.
31. Ibid.
32. Hawke, pp. 24–35.
33. T Kilmurray, interview with the author, 1 July 2008.
34. Ibid.
35. Ibid.
36. Ibid.
37. Ibid.
38. Ibid.
39. Ibid.
40. Ibid.
41. Ibid.

BILL DEMPSEY

42. B Dempsey, interview with the author, 1 July 2008.
43. Ibid.
44. Ibid.
45. Ibid.
46. Ibid.
47. Ibid.
48. Ibid.
49. *WAFL Football Legends*, DVD recording, interview of Bill Dempsey, Access 31, Perth, n.d.
50. Ibid.
51. Ibid.
52. B Dempsey, interview with the author, 1 July 2008.
53. Ibid.
54. *WAFL Football Legends*, DVD recording, interview of Bill Dempsey, Access 31, Perth, n.d.

55. B Dempsey, interview with the author, 1 July 2008.
56. *WAFL Football Legends*, DVD recording, interview of Bill Dempsey, Access 31, Perth, n.d.
57. Ibid.
58. Ibid.
59. B Dempsey, interview with the author, 1 July 2008.
60. Ibid.

SYD JACKSON

61. S Jackson, speech given at Perth NAIDOC Ball, 11 July 2008.
62. B Judd, *On the boundary line: colonial identity in football*, Australian Scholarly Publishing, North Melbourne, 2008.
63. For further references on Syd Jackson's life refer to Judd, pp. 152–225.
64. S Jackson, interview with the author, 25 September 2008.
65. S Jackson, speech given at Perth NAIDOC Ball, 11 July 2008.
66. S Jackson, interview with the author, 25 September 2008.
67. Ibid.
68. Ibid.
69. Hawke, p. 266.
70. S Jackson, interview with the author, 25 September 2008.
71. *AFL Record*, Round 9, May 25–27, 2007, p. 18.
72. Judd, p. 155.
73. S Jackson, speech given at Perth NAIDOC Ball, 11 July 2008.
74. S Jackson, interview with the author, 25 September 2008.
75. S Jackson, speech given at Perth NAIDOC Ball, 11 July 2008.
76. S Jackson, interview with the author, 25 September 2008.

BARRY CABLE

77. R Holmesby & J Main, *The Encyclopedia of AFL footballers: every AFL/VFL player since 1897*, 8th edn, BAS Publishing, Seaford, 2009, p. 116.
78. B Cable, interview with the author, 8 July 2008.
79. Ibid.
80. Ibid.
81. Ibid.
82. Ibid.
83. *WAFL Football Legends*, DVD recording, interview of Barry Cable, Access 31, Perth, n.d.
84. Ibid.
85. B Cable, interview with the author, 8 July 2008.
86. *WAFL Football Legends*, DVD recording, interview of Barry Cable, Access 31, Perth, n.d.
87. B Cable, interview with the author, 8 July 2008.
88. Ibid.
89. Ibid.
90. B Cable, interview with the author, 9 April 2008.

MICHAEL 'FLASH' GRAHAM

91. M Graham, interview with the author, 14 July 2008.
92. Ibid.
93. Ibid.
94. Ibid.
95. Ibid.
96. Ibid.
97. Ibid.
98. Ibid.
99. Ibid.
100. Ibid.
101. Ibid.
102. Ibid.
103. Ibid.
104. Ibid.
105. Ibid.
106. Ibid.
107. Ibid.
108. Ibid.

MAURICE RIOLI

109. M Rioli, interview with the author, 16 July 2008.
110. Ibid.
111. Ibid.
112. Ibid.
113. Ibid.
114. Ibid.
115. Ibid.
116. Ibid.
117. Rueben Cooper from Darwin is listed as playing two games with South Melbourne in 1969 (Holmesby & Main, p. 169).
118. M Rioli, interview with the author, 12 November 2002.
119. Ibid.
120. Holmesby & Main, p. 707.

121. M Rioli, interview with the author, 16 July 2008.
122. Ibid.

STEPHEN MICHAEL

123. S Michael, interview with the author, 3 July 2008.
124. S Michael, interview with the author, 11 April 2002.
125. S Michael, interview with the author, 3 July 2008.
126. S Michael, interview with the author, 11 April 2002.
127. S Michael, interview with the author, 3 July 2008.
128. Ibid.
129. Ibid.
130. Ibid.
131. S Michael, interview with the author, 11 April 2002.
132. Ibid.
133. Ibid.
134. S Michael, interview with the author, 3 July 2008.
135. Ibid.
136. Ibid.
137. Ibid.

GLENN JAMES

138. G James, interview with the author, 16 September 2009.
139. Ibid.
140. Ibid.
141. Ibid.
142. Ibid.
143. Ibid.
144. Ibid.
145. Ibid.
146. Ibid.
147. Ibid.
148. Ibid.
149. Ibid.
150. Ibid.
151. Ibid.
152. Ibid.
153. Ibid.
154. Ibid.
155. Ibid.
156. Ibid.
157. Ibid.
158. *AFL Record*, 'Indigenous round record: celebrating the contribution of Indigenous players', Round 9, May 25–27, 2007, p. 79.

JIM KRAKOUER

159. J Krakouer, interview with the author, 22 November 2010.
160. J Krakouer, interview with the author, 18 April 2002.
161. Ibid.
162. Ibid.
163. Ibid.
164. J Krakouer, interview with the author, 22 November 2010.
165. J Krakouer, interview with the author, 20 July 2001.
166. J Krakouer, interview with the author, 18 April 2002.
167. Ibid.
168. J Krakouer, interview with the author, 18 April 2002.
169. Ibid.
170. Ibid.
171. Ibid.
172. J Krakouer, interview with the author, 22 November 2010.
173. J Krakouer, interview with the author, 18 April 2002.
174. J Krakouer, interview with the author, 10 October 2002.
175. J Krakouer, interview with the author, 18 April 2002.
176. J Krakouer, interview with the author, 17 January 2003.
177. Ibid.
178. J Krakouer, interview with the author, 22 November 2010.
179. J Krakouer, interview with the author, 29 May 2003.
180. J Krakouer, interview with the author, 22 November 2010.
181. Ibid.
182. J Krakouer, interview with the author, 17 January 2003.

MICHAEL McLEAN

183. M McLean, interview with the author, 11 July 2008.
184. Ibid.
185. Ibid.
186. Ibid.
187. Ibid.
188. Ibid.
189. Ibid.
190. Ibid.
191. Ibid.
192. Ibid.
193. Ibid.

194. Ibid.
195. Ibid.
196. Ibid.
197. Ibid.
198. Ibid.

NICKY WINMAR

199. N Winmar, interview with the author, 19 September 2002.
200. N Winmar, interview with the author, 9 July 2008.
201. Q Beresford, *Rob Riley: an Aboriginal leader's quest for justice*, Aboriginal Studies Press, Canberra, 2006, p. 59.
202. Ibid., p. 61.
203. N Winmar, interview with the author, 9 July 2008.
204. Ibid.
205. Ibid.
206. Ibid.
207. N Winmar, interview with the author, 19 September 2002.
208. See AJ Barker, *Behind the play: a history of football in Western Australia from 1868*, Western Australian Football Commission, 2004, p. 209.
209. N Winmar, interview with the author, 9 July 2008.
210. N Winmar, interview with the author, 19 September 2002.
211. Ibid.
212. Ibid.
213. Ibid.
214. Ibid.
215. Ibid.
216. N Winmar, interview with the author, 9 July 2008.
217. N Winmar, interview with the author, 19 September 2002.

CHRIS LEWIS

218. C Lewis, interview with the author, 4 July 2009.
219. Ibid.
220. G Stocks & A East, *Lewie, Lewie: Chris Lewis an Aboriginal champion*, Specialist Sports Management, Perth, 2000, pp. 19–20.
221. Ibid., p. 21.
222. C Lewis, interview with the author, 4 July 2009.
223. Ibid.
224. Stocks & East, p. 25.
225. Stocks & East, p. 31.

226. Stocks & East, p. 32.
227. C Lewis, interview with the author, 4 July 2009.
228. Ibid.
229. Ibid.
230. Ibid.
231. Ibid.
232. Ibid.
233. *AFL Record*, 'Indigenous round record: celebrating the contribution of Indigenous players', Round 9, May 25–27, 2007, p. 23.

MICHAL LONG

234. *The Age*, 23 April 1997, p. 16.
235. M Long, interview with the author, 19 May 2009.
236. B Collins, *Champions: conversations with great players & coaches of Australian football*, Slattery Media Group, Melbourne, 2006, p. 139.
237. M Long, interview with the author, 19 May 2009.
238. Collins, p. 140.
239. Ibid.
240. Ibid.
241. M Long, interview with the author, 19 May 2009.
242. Ibid.
243. Ibid.
244. Collins, p. 143.
245. Ibid., p. 144.
246. M Long, interview with the author, 19 May 2009.
247. Australian Football League, loc. cit.
248. M Long, interview with the author, 19 May 2009.
249. *The 7.30 Report*, television program, Australian Broadcasting Commission, Sydney, 30 November 2004.
250. Ibid.
251. M Long, interview with the author, 19 May 2009.

PETER MATERA

252. P Matera, interview with the author, 23 July 2009.
253. Ibid.
254. Ibid.
255. Ibid.
256. Ibid.
257. Ibid.
258. Ibid.
259. Ibid.
260. Ibid.

261. Ibid.
262. Ibid.
263. Ibid.
264. Ibid.
265. Ibid.
266. Ibid.
267. Ibid.
268. Ibid.
269. Ibid.

GAVIN WANGANEEN

270. G Wanganeen, interview with the author, 28 February 2009.
271. Collins, p. 214.
272. G Wanganeen, interview with the author, 28 February 2009.
273. Collins, p. 214.
274. G Wanganeen, interview with the author, 28 February 2009.
275. Ibid.
276. Ibid.
277. Collins, p. 216.
278. Ibid.
279. Collins, p. 217.
280. Ibid.
281. G Wanganeen, interview with the author, 28 February 2009.
282. Collins, p. 218.
283. Ibid.
284. Collins, p. 221.
285. G Wanganeen, interview with the author, 28 February 2009.
286. Ibid.
287. Ibid.
288. Ibid.
289. Ibid.
290. Ibid.
291. Ibid.

DARRYL WHITE

292. D White, interview with the author, 12 December 2008.
293. Ibid.
294. Ibid.
295. Ibid.
296. Ibid.
297. Ibid.
298. Ibid.
299. Ibid.
300. Ibid.
301. Ibid.
302. Ibid.
303. Ibid.
304. Ibid.

305. Ibid.

CHRIS JOHNSON

306. C Johnson, interview with the author, 12 December 2008.
307. Ibid.
308. Ibid.
309. Ibid.
310. Ibid.
311. Ibid.
312. Ibid.
313. Ibid.
314. Ibid.
315. Ibid.
316. Ibid.
317. Ibid.
318. Ibid.
319. Ibid.
320. Ibid.
321. Ibid.
322. Ibid.
323. Ibid.
324. Ibid.
325. Ibid.
326. Ibid.
327. Ibid.
328. Ibid.

MICHAEL O'LOUGLIN

329. M O'Loughlin, interview with the author, 2 December 2008.
330. Ibid.
331. Ibid.
332. Ibid.
333. Ibid.
334. Ibid.
335. Ibid.
336. Ibid.
337. Ibid.
338. Ibid.
339. Ibid.
340. Ibid.
341. Ibid.
342. Ibid.
343. Ibid.
344. Ibid.
345. Ibid.
346. videosfrombrenton, online videoclip, 'Michael O' Loughlin Retires from Footy', Youtube, 23 June 2009, viewed on 10 October 2008, <http://www.youtube.com/watch?v=DKA7Hd3SGkA>.

ANDREW McLEOD

347. *AFL Record*, 'Indigenous round record: celebrating the contribution of Indigenous players', Round 9, May 25–27, 2007, p. 68.
348. A McLeod, interview with the author, 6 February 2009.
349. Ibid.
350. Ibid.
351. Ibid.
352. Collins, p. 157.
353. A McLeod, interview with the author, 6 February 2009.
354. Ibid.
355. Ibid.
356. Ibid.
357. Collins, p. 158.
358. Ibid.
359. A McLeod, interview with the author, 6 February 2009.
360. Ibid.
361. Ibid.
362. Ibid.
363. Ibid.
364. Ibid.
365. Ibid.
366. Ibid.

BYRON PICKETT

367. B Pickett, interview with the author, 25 February 2009.
368. Ibid.
369. Ibid.
370. Ibid.
371. Ibid.
372. Ibid.
373. Ibid.
374. Ibid.
375. Ibid.
376. Ibid.
377. Ibid.
378. Ibid.
379. Ibid.
380. Ibid.
381. Ibid.
382. Ibid.
383. Ibid.
384. Ibid.
385. Ibid.

PETER BURGOYNE

386. P Burgoyne, interview with the author, 5 February 2009.
387. Ibid.
388. Ibid.

389. Ibid.
390. Ibid.
391. Ibid.
392. Ibid.
393. Ibid.
394. Ibid.
395. Ibid.
396. Ibid.
397. Ibid.
398. Ibid.
399. Ibid.
400. Ibid.
401. Ibid.
402. Ibid.
403. Ibid.

ADAM GOODES

404. A Goodes, 'The Indigenous game: a matter of choice', in G Slattery (ed), *The Australian game of football since 1858*, Geoff Slattery Publishing Pty Ltd, Melbourne, 2008, p. 175.
405. A Goodes, interview with the author, 9 December 2008.
406. Goodes, p. 175.
407. A Goodes, interview with the author, 9 December 2008.
408. Ibid.
409. Ibid.
410. Ibid.
411. Goodes, p. 175.
412. A Goodes, interview with the author, 9 December 2008.
413. Ibid.
414. Ibid.
415. Ibid.
416. Holmesby & Main, p. 310.
417. Goodes, p. 179.
418. A Goodes, interview with the author, 9 December 2008.
419. Ibid.
420. Ibid.
421. Ibid.
422. Ibid.
423. Ibid.

DAVID KANTILLA

424. For more on David Kantilla, see Tatz & Tatz, p. 125.

NORM McDONALD

425. For more on Norm McDonald, see Tatz & Tatz, p. 134.

INDEX

Aboriginal Football Carnival at Punmu, Pilbara region, Western Australia, 2008.
Photo Colin Murty © Newspix / News Ltd / 3rd Party Managed Reproduction &
Supply Rights.